"Hilmar Pabel's *Empowered by the Spirit* is a first-rate combination of comprehensive research, incisive theological thought, and rich pastoral insight. Pabel invites the Catholic community to move beyond the standard categories regularly applied to the diaconate. Echoing the best practices of *ressourcement* and *aggiornamento*, Pabel reclaims undervalued possibilities for diaconal ministry and identifies their implications for the age of synodality. This is a book that merits and rewards close engagement."

—Richard Lennan, professor of systematic theology, Boston College Clough School of Theology and Ministry

"The Catholic Church is currently grappling with the issue of women's access to the diaconate. This presents a valuable opportunity to reflect on the diaconate in fundamental terms. Looking ahead, Hilmar M. Pabel explores how the Church, empowered by her Spirit, should shape her official diaconal ministry for today. He has addressed this challenge with his theological expertise, thus providing the synodally learning Church with valuable guidance."

—Paul Zulehner, professor emeritus for pastoral theology at the University of Vienna

"Already an accomplished historian of the Early Modern period in Europe, as an ordained Catholic deacon, Hilmar Pabel has provided us with a fresh and refreshing look at the theology of the diaconate as restored after Vatican II. In the process, with great skill and prudence, he shows how deacons not only minister to the marginalized but have themselves been marginalized in theology and in practice. Written with deep historical and theological insight, this book can serve as an antidote to shopworn and unreflective approaches to the diaconate. As Pabel himself puts it so well: "A deacon should neither be a clericalist manager nor a liturgical ornament, nor a priest's helper, 'a boy,' whose sole function is 'to carry out certain tasks.'"

—John F. Baldovin, SJ, professor of historical and liturgical theology, Boston College Clough School of Theology and Ministry

Empowered by the Spirit

Deacons and Ministerial Communion in a Synodal Church

Hilmar M. Pabel

LITURGICAL PRESS
Collegeville, Minnesota

litpress.org

Cover image: Presbyter, bishop, and deacon from the Raganaldus Sacramentary, mid-ninth century: a detail from Autun, Bibliothèque municipale, S 19 (19 bis), f. 1v., courtesy of the Institut de Recherche et d'Histoire des Textes—Centre National de la Recherche Scientifique.

Library of Congress Cataloging-in-Publication Data

Names: Pabel, Hilmar M., 1964- author
Title: Empowered by the Spirit : deacons and ministerial communion in a synodal church / Hilmar M. Pabel.
Description: Collegeville, Minnesota : Liturgical Press, [2026] | Includes bibliographical references. | Summary: "In Empowered by the Spirit, Pabel proposes a robust theology of the diaconate to challenge the conceptual and actual marginalization of deacons in the church. The book emphasizes the Holy Spirit in the sacramentality of the diaconate, in the ministerial communion of deacons with their bishop and priests, and in the role of deacons as servant-leaders in a synodal church"-- Provided by publisher.
Identifiers: LCCN 2026018009 | ISBN 9798400802485 trade paperback | ISBN 9798400802492 epub
Subjects: LCSH: Deacons--Catholic Church | Catholic Church--Doctrines
Classification: LCC BX1912 .P225 2026
LC record available at https://lccn.loc.gov/2026018009

In memory of

Sister Mechtilde O'Mara, CSJ

and for

Sister John Mary Sullivan, FSE

Contents

Abbreviations ix

Preface xi

Introduction: The Re-Creation of the Diaconate 1

Chapter 1: Sacramental Grace 21

Chapter 2: Ordained Ministerial Communion 69

Chapter 3: Service to the People of God 127

Conclusion: The Perturbation of the Diaconate 177

Bibliography 189

Index 209

Abbreviations

AA Second Vatican Council, *Apostolicam Actuositatem*, Decree on the Apostolate of the Laity

AG Second Vatican Council, *Ad Gentes*, Decree on the Missionary Activity of the Church

AS *Acta Synodalia Sacrosancti Concilii Oecumenici Vaticani II*, 6 vols., 31 tomes (Vatican City: Typis Polyglottis Vaticanis, 1970–1991)

Basic Norms/Directory Congregation for Catholic Education, Congregation for the Clergy, *Basic Norms for the Formation of Permanent Deacons; Directory for the Ministry and Life of Permanent Deacons* (Vatican City: Libreria Editrice Vaticana, 1998)

c. / cc. canon / canons (Unless otherwise indicated, all references to and quotations from canon law are to *Code of Canon Law: Latin-English Edition*, fourth printing [Washington, DC: Canon Law Society of America, 2023].)

CCC *Catechism of the Catholic Church*

CCSL *Corpus Christianorum, Series Latina* (Turnhout: Brepols, 1953—)

CD Second Vatican Council, *Christus Dominus*, Decree on the Pastoral Office of Bishops in the Church

DV Second Vatican Council, *Dei Verbum*, Dogmatic Constitution on Divine Revelation

GS Second Vatican Council, *Gaudium et Spes*, Pastoral Constitution on the Church in the Modern World

LG Second Vatican Council, *Lumen Gentium*, Dogmatic Constitution on the Church

PO Second Vatican Council, *Presbyterorum Ordinis*, Decree on the Ministry and Life of Priests

SC Second Vatican Council, *Sacrosanctum Concilium*, Constitution on the Sacred Liturgy

Tanner, *Decrees* Norman P. Tanner, ed. *Decrees of the Ecumenical Councils*, 2 vols. (London: Sheed & Ward; Washington, DC: Georgetown University Press, 1990). All translations from the Latin texts of the Council of Trent and of the Second Vatican Council contained in volume 2 are my own.

UR Second Vatican Council, *Unitatis Redintegratio*, Decree on Ecumenism

Preface

Why should a deacon undertake, at his own behest, formal theological study after ordination and write a book about the Roman Catholic theology of the diaconate? Does theological research and writing distract from diaconal ministry to the marginalized? Sherri Vallee warned: "Deacons who are well-educated in theology may be more inclined to want to use that education in preaching and teaching functions rather than devote their time to AIDS hospices, soup kitchens, or visiting those in prison."[1] Are "deacon" and "theologian" incompatible terms, therefore?

One answer to my questions emerged from a requirement that Pope Paul VI stated in *Sacrum Diaconatus Ordinem* (1967), his first *motu proprio* on the diaconate:

> Deacons should not interrupt their studies, especially of sacred doctrine. They should constantly read the divine books of Scripture. They should so devote themselves to the ecclesiastical disciplines that they could correctly explain Catholic doctrine to others and that they might daily become more qualified in teaching and empowering the minds of the faithful.[2]

Deacons exercise their *munus docendi* or, correctly, by virtue of the sacrament of order, they exercise Christ's office of

[1] Sherri L. Vallee, "The Restoration of the Permanent Diaconate: A Blending of Roles," *Worship* 77, no. 6 (November 2003): 551.

[2] Paul VI, "Sacrum Diaconatus Ordinem," *Acta Apostolicae Sedis* 59 (1976): 703, no. 29.

teaching at the service of those whom they teach. While their continuous engagement with theology benefits everyone in general, it empowers Christians in particular. By "the faithful," Paul VI meant Catholic laypeople. Earlier in the *motu proprio*, he insisted that nobody could be a candidate for the diaconate without enjoying "the esteem of the clergy and faithful" for an exemplary Christian life, moral integrity, and "aptitude for ministry."[3] A correct explanation of Catholic doctrine, however, requires equating Christ's faithful—the *Christifideles*—with all the baptized. I seek to empower the minds and hearts of all members of the church to approach the diaconate with theological gravitas, to locate deacons among the synodal people of God with due theological consideration for their ordained ministry. A deacon should neither be a clericalist manager nor a liturgical ornament, nor a priest's helper, "a boy," whose sole function is "to carry out certain tasks."[4]

The pejorative image of the deacon as a busy *ragazzo* under the direction of a priest, exposed and rejected by Pope Francis in his pastoral visit to Milan in March 2017, leads to a second answer to my questions. To write about the theology of the diaconate constitutes a service to deacons as marginalized ministers. Theology serves the marginalized at the very least by pointing out their situation. Michael Ebertz identified several manifestations of the marginalization of deacons. While *diaconia*, Christian ministry to the poor and marginalized, expressed an essential characteristic of the church, deacons are ostensibly dispensable since not all local churches, namely Catholic dioceses, have instituted the diaconate as a stable order of ministry. *Diaconia* is the responsibility of all ecclesial subjects—bishops, priests, and laypeople—not only that of deacons. Their subordination to bishops and priests in the clerical hierarchy and the

[3] Paul VI, "Sacrum Diaconatus Ordinem," 700, no. 12.

[4] Francis, "In visitatione pastorali in Archidioecesi Mediolanensi. Occursus cum sacerdotibus et viris mulieribusque consecratis in templo Cathedrali," *Acta Apostolicae Sedis* 109, no. 4 (April 2017): 376.

limitations on their sacramental ministry—deacons may not celebrate the sacrament of the anointing of the sick, for example—reinforces the marginal status of deacons in the church, Ebertz added.[5]

At the two sessions on the Synod on Synodality in 2023 and 2024, this marginal status was as astonishing as it was barely noticed outside diaconal circles. Only two deacons attended these sessions. These two synodal delegates, as Dominic Cerrato reported, were not identified as deacons and thus did not represent their order. Cerrato, a deacon, wrote in December 2023: "The absence of deacons as an order from the recent assembly in Rome raises questions about their role and voice within the Church, especially when their perspective is directly relevant to the synod's focus on communion, participation and mission."[6] Did the church forget deacons in plain sight?

Forgetting deacons can happen in a local as well in the universal church. A few years before the Synod, Giuseppe Como, a priest and theologian in the Archdiocese of Milan, commented on the situation in his local church. He reported that deacons ministered in an ecclesial context, "in which the presence of a deacon can be helpful, but his absence is overlooked."[7]

Had he lived to observe the work of the Synod, Stefan Sander might have contended that it had overlooked the diaconate despite mentioning it in its Final Document. A formator of deacons in the German diocese of Osnabrück,

[5] Michael N. Ebertz, "Diakon—ein Marginalberuf? Thesen, Anfragen, Zuspitzungen," in *Ständige Diakone—Stellvertreter der Armen? Projekt Pro Diakonia: Prozess—Positionen—Perspectiven*, ed. Klaus Kießling (Berlin: LIT Verlag, 2006), 129, 130, 132.

[6] Dominic Cerrato, "A Synod Without Deacons," *The Deacon*, December 15, 2023, https://www.the-deacon.com/2023/12/15/a-synod-without-deacons/.

[7] Giuseppe Como, "Der Diakon im Leben der Kirche: Die Erfahrung der Diözese Mailand," in *Der Diakonat: Geschichte und Theologie*, ed. Manfred Hauke and Helmut Hoping (Regensburg: Verlag Friedrich Putest, 2019), 150.

director of the International Diaconate Centre, and editor of the Centre's journal, *Diaconia Christi*, Sander, who died in 2020, entitled his last publication on the diaconate "Die Marginalisierten."[8] In his "sorrowful survey of the development of the diaconate," Sander identified "the marginalized" not with the people to whom deacons minister, but with deacons themselves. In their ministry to the peripheries, they risk marginalization owing to their hierarchical subordination "without any plausible reason." Deacons, Sander complained, had been theologically erased from the common priesthood. They possess a "sacramental office without exclusive sacramental symbolic actions" and lack the power of office among other ministries. They function as "volunteers among officials, non-professionals among professionals."[9] Service as pastoral "stopgaps" and ecclesial "jacks-of-all-trades" undermines, Sander believed, a distinctive ministerial identity for deacons.[10]

If Sander's diagnosis of the ecclesial drift of the diaconate seems too gloomy, the inferiority of deacons operates as an ancient and enduring commonplace in the structure of the church's ministry. Consider the eighteenth canon of the Council of Nicaea (325), whose seventeen-hundredth anniversary Christians marked in 2025, and which belongs to

[8] Verena Wodtke-Werner, "+Dr. Stefan Sander: Ein Go-Betweener," in *Das Gesicht der Kirche im Alltag der Menshcen? Der Ort des Diakonischen Amtes in einer diakonischen Kirche*, ed. Klaus Kießling and Verena Wodtke-Werner (Mainz: Matthias Günewald Verlag, 2023), 7.

[9] Stefan Sander, "Die Marginalisierten: Sorgenvolle Bestandsaufnahme zur Entwicklung des Diakonats," in *Das Gesicht der Kirche im Alltag der Menshcen? Der Ort des Diakonischen Amtes in einer diakonischen Kirche*, ed. Klaus Kießling and Verena Wodtke-Werner (Mainz: Matthias Günewald Verlag, 2023), 195. Sander's article first appeared as "Die Marginalisierten: Sorgenvolle Bestandsaufnahme des Diakonats," *Herder Korrespondenz* 74, no. 9 (September 2020): 32–36.

[10] Sander, "Die Marginalisierten" (2023), 190, 192.

the "broken" story of "legal restraints on deacons."[11] The Council of Nicaea decreed:

> It has come to the attention of this holy and great synod that in some places and cities deacons give communion to presbyters, although neither canon nor custom allows this, namely that those who have no authority to offer should give the body of Christ to those who do offer. Moreover it has become known that some of the deacons now receive the eucharist even before the bishops. All these practices must be suppressed. Deacons must remain within their own limits, knowing that they are the ministers (*hupēretai*) of the bishop and subordinate (*elattous*) to the presbyters. Let them receive the eucharist according to their order after the presbyters from the hands of the bishop or the presbyter. Nor shall permission be given for the deacons to sit among the presbyters, for such an arrangement is contrary to the canon and to rank. If anyone refuses to comply even after these decrees, he is to be suspended from the diaconate.[12]

The conciliar regulation was entirely disciplinary and political without any theological import. *Hupēretai* were not ministers as we think of church ministers today. The Greek word literally means "under-rowers." As *hupēretai*, deacons were the "underlings," the personal attendants or servants of the bishop. The canon, furthermore, directed deacons to consider themselves as *elattous*, as inferior to and less important than presbyters.[13]

[11] John N. Collins, *Deacons and the Church: Making Connections between Old and New* (Leominster, Herefordshire: Gracewing; Harrisburg, PA: Morehouse Publishing, 2002), 3.

[12] I have reproduced the English translation in Tanner, *Decrees*, 1: *14–*15 while inserting the two transliterated words from the original Greek text.

[13] For the meaning of *elattous*, the masculine nominative plural of *elassōn*, and of *hupēretai*, the masculine nominative plural of *hupēretēs*, see Henry

Ancient church orders sustained the ecclesial inferiority of deacons. They represented deacons as servants of bishops and of presbyters.[14] Lacking theological significance, diaconal *ministerium* expressed hierarchical subservience. The article on the diaconate in *Lumen Gentium*, the Second Vatican Council's Dogmatic Constitution on the Church, revived the ancient formula: *non ad sacerdotium, sed ad ministerium*. Deacons were ordained "not for the priesthood, but for ministry" (LG 29).[15] This formula abbreviated the earliest ecclesial positioning of the deacon as ordained into the ministry, that is, into the service, of the bishop. Given ancient precedent, perhaps not surprisingly LG 29 began by locating deacons *in gradu inferiori*: "On a lower step of the hierarchy stand the deacons, upon whom hands are laid 'not for the priesthood, but for ministry.'"[16]

This ministerial placement has caused dismay. In his commentary on LG 29, Herbert Vorgimler sought to undermine a downgraded diaconate by replacing "the emphasis on the 'step' (certainly the lowest in the hierarchy)" with the distinctive nature of a deacon's ministry.[17] Karl Rahner, Vorgrimler's fellow advocate for a renewed diaconate, indicated that the deacon's hierarchical placement required theological exploration. How could deacons stand "on a lower step" when LG 29 also claimed their communion with the bishop and his presbyterate? Deacons could be lower than

---

George Liddel and Robert Scott, *A Greek-English Lexicon*, 8th ed., rev. (New York: American Book Company, 1897), 450, 1621.

[14] See, for example, Paul Bradshaw, ed., *The Canons of Hippolytus*, trans. Carol Bebawi (Piscataway, NJ: Gorgias Press, 2010), 14; Marcel Metzger, ed. and trans., *Les Constitutions Apostoliques*, vol. 2, Sources Chrétiennes, vol. 329 (Paris: Les Éditions du Cerf, 1986), 165.

[15] Tanner, *Decrees*, 2: 874. For a detailed discussion of this formula, see below, pp. 44–58.

[16] Tanner, *Decrees*, 2: 874.

[17] Herbert Vorgrimler, "Kommentar zum III. Kapitel, Artikel 29," *Das Zweite Vatikanische Konzil: Konstitutionen, Dekrete und Erklärungen, Latein und Deutsch—Kommentare*, ed. Herbert Vorgrimler, vol. 1 (Freiburg im Breisgau: Herder, 1966), 257.

priests because, unlike priests, they did not celebrate Mass or grant sacramental absolution. But, according to Rahner, their inferiority could not be absolute since it was not clear how ministry to the poor could constitute a "lower step" and since deacons could have no inferior share with priests in a bishop's care for the poor.[18] Cardinal Karl Lehmann, Rahner's student, wondered how the diaconal "lower step" was consistent with Jesus's teaching that his disciples should be servants of, not masters over, each other (Mark 10:42-44).[19] According to Alain Desjonquères, a deacon and former secretary of France's National Committee of the Diaconate, some French priests, "to enhance the value of their priesthood, tend to belittle deacons" by citing *Lumen Gentium*'s reference to the hierarchical inferiority of deacons. A deacon, furthermore, informed Desjonquères that a priest had harangued him: "You deacons, you have nothing but a fake sacrament."[20]

The downgrading or denial of the sacramentality of the diaconate theologically justifies the ministerial marginalization of deacons. If the diaconate were not a graced ministerial order in the church, its subordination in the sacramental economy to the episcopate and presbyterate could make sense. Deacons would have no communion with bishops and priests in the sacrament of order.

Since ecclesiology is "necessarily an exploratory, critical, dialogical, and constructive discipline" with a brief to

[18] Karl Rahner, "Die Lehre des Zweiten Vatikanischen Konzils über den Diakonat," in Rahner, *Schriften zur Theologie*, vol. 8 (Einsiedeln: Benziger Verlag, 1967), 549–50.

[19] Karl Lehmann, "Die Entwicklung des Ständigen Diakonats. Beobachtungen und Überlegungen aus der Sicht des bischöflichen Amtes," in *Ortsbestimmungen: Der Diakonat als kirchlicher Dienst*, ed. Richard Hartmann, Franz Reger, and Stefan Sander (Frankfurt am Main: Verlag Josef Knecht, 2009), 24.

[20] Alain Desjonquères, *Être diacre permanent, pourquoi?* (Paris: Éditions Salvator, 2019), 114: "Vous les diacres, vous n'avez qu'un ersatz de sacrement."

prescribe as well as to describe,[21] a theology of the diaconate should chart a way out of the conceptual and actual marginalization of deacons in the church. Vorgrimler suggested such a way in 1966, when he proposed the communion of bishop, priests, and deacons in service of the church, asserted by LG 29, as "the best possible correction of the concept of a one-way stepladder within the hierarchy."[22] I encourage the Roman Catholic Church to take this way of communion for its own purification and perfection as the synodal people of God.

The image that appears on the cover of this book could be reimagined to portray a communion of ministers. It is a detail of the verso of the first folio of the Raganaldus Sacramentary from the mid-ninth century, reproduced as figure 1. The illumination presents on the same horizontal plane a presbyter seated on a cushion, an enthroned bishop, and a deacon standing as he holds, presumably, the book of the gospels. The bishop commands the attention of the presbyter and the deacon. With their three different postures, the three clerics could suggest a differentiation in ordained ministers. The deacon stands ready for Christ's and the church's mission of evangelization.

[21] Paul Avis, "Introduction to Ecclesiology," in *The Oxford Handbook of Ecclesiology*, ed. Paul Avis (Oxford: Oxford University Press, 2018), 10 (quotation), 11.

[22] Vorgrimler, "Kommentar zum III. Kapitel, Artikel 29," 258.

Figure 1: The ecclesiastical hierarchy portrayed in the Raganaldus Sacramentary, mid-ninth century, Autun, Bibliothèque municipale, S 19 (19 bis), f. 1v., courtesy of the Institut de Recherche et d'Histoire des Textes—Centre National de la Recherche Scientifique.

Given the historical context, however, this reimagining of a Carolingian perspective on ministry amounts to wishful thinking. Representing the major orders of the ecclesiastical hierarchy, the presbyter, bishop, and deacon occupy its top tier. In accordance with the *Statuta ecclesiae antiquae*, a fifth-century Gallic church order, a deacon may sit in the presence of a presbyter only with the presbyter's leave. Obviously, the deacon in the depicted trio did not receive the necessary permission.[23] He is subordinate to the bishop and presbyter. Below the clerics of the major orders, a porter and a lector on one side, and an acolyte and an exorcist on the other, ascend towards the subdeacon—all representatives of the minor orders. The caption at the top of the page crowns the operative concept of ministry in the sacramentary and for most of the church's history: ministry is a matter of a rank-ordered privilege to retain, not of a service to render. Translated, the caption reads: "It is the prerogative of bishops to confer honors by order, and those who receive them should strive to possess them virtuously."[24]

For the diaconate to thrive in the contemporary church, paradigms of ministry that privilege a vertical chain of dignities must dissolve. The ascent of honors, the *cursus honorum*, still in effect owing to the distinction between a diaconate called "transitional" and "permanent," should yield to a horizontal model of a communion of co-responsible ministers, ordained and instituted, in which deacons are free of the subordinating mentality evinced in the eighteenth canon of the Council of Nicaea and the *cursus honorum*. In unwitting contravention of the Nicene canon, I once

[23] Roger E. Reynolds, "The Portrait of the Ecclesiastical Officers in the Raganaldus Sacramentary and its Liturgico-Canonical Significance," *Speculum* 46, no. 3 (July 1971): 437. In its absolute prohibition against the sitting of deacons in the company of the presbyters to enforce the subordination of former to the latter, the eighteenth canon of the Council of Nicaea was more restrictive than the *Statuta*.

[24] "Pontificum est proprium conferre per ordinem honores. Quos qui suscipiunt studeant servare pudice."

gave Holy Communion to a presbyter on his deathbed. He was a priest who, eight years earlier, had welcomed me after my ordination to the diaconate into the church's ministerial communion. I obviously do not advocate a return to a Nicene or Carolingian diaconate, as much as I acknowledge the teaching, sanctifying, and governing authority of bishops as leaders of their local churches and the sacramental ministry of priests, who prefer pastoral care to cushions. At the same time, with Desjonquères, I aspire to an "ensemble" of ordained ministers "at the service of the mission" of the church and "an authentic collegiality" of ministers that forms "around the bishop."[25] In a synodal church, this collegiality should encompass all the baptized who are ordained and instituted for ministry. The variety of ministries, arising from the charisms bestowed on individual believers by the Holy Spirit and from the needs of a Christian community, necessarily exist in relationship with each other to sustain the communion of the church as well as its apostolic character.[26]

In Rome several months before my ordination, my wife and I went into shops that sold liturgical vestments. One salesperson touted a polyester dalmatic as *economico*—inexpensive and thus ideal for deacons. I did not purchase it. Diaconal ministry does not come on the cheap. Nor does the theology of the diaconate. "Cheap grace" is a contradiction in terms. The costly grace of the diaconate in a synodal church deserves and demands all the rigorous analysis that I can muster as an historian and a theologian with a zest for research and a zealous partiality, wherever possible, towards sources in their original languages. All English translations of passages from these sources are my own, unless otherwise indicated.

[25] Desjonquères, *Être diacre permanent, pourquoi?*, 140, 165.

[26] Charles Wackenheim, "Esquisse d'une théologie des ministères," *Revue des Sciences Religieuses* 47, no. 1 (1973): 12–13, 19.

Unpacking a single claim from LG 29 that, "empowered, in fact, by sacramental grace," deacons "serve the People of God in the *diaconia* of the liturgy, of the word, and of charity in communion with their bishop and his presbyterate"[27] has become a theological odyssey. I am grateful to readers who journey with me, even if they cannot accept some or all of my arguments. My gratitude extends to all who made this journey possible. I think of those whom I cannot name—the staff at the libraries of Boston College, who scanned more articles than I could easily count, and at the library of Simon Fraser University, where I teach history, who filled my book requests through interlibrary loan. Professors Richard Lennan and John Baldovin, SJ, of the Clough School of Theology and Ministry (CSTM) at Boston College supervised my STL thesis and recommended that I publish it. The revision of the thesis has become this book. At Liturgical Press, Hans Christoffersen graciously received the recommendation from Professor Lennan and resolutely supported the book's publication, while Stephanie Lancour and Michael Centore afforded expert editorial guidance and work to ease the book's way into print. I am indebted to Professor Rafael Luciani for references to Víctor Codina and an article by Serena Noceti in *Studia Canonica*. I still hear his admonition to remember the poor in a theology of the diaconate. Not only did my wife, Professor Lynda Robitaille, JCD, provost and dean of graduate studies at St. Mark's College, borrow books for me from St. Mark's and the Vancouver School of Theology; as an accomplished and internationally recognized canon lawyer, she also directed me towards publications in several journals of canon law. Most of all, she steadfastly and lovingly encouraged and supported my study of theology at the CSTM and the transformation of the thesis into a book.

[27] Tanner, *Decrees*, 2: 874.

The book's dedication honors two remarkable women whose wisdom, joy, and friendship have sustained me in formative periods of my life. I first met Sister Mechtilde O'Mara, CSJ, some forty years ago when she taught me, a young undergraduate then, medieval Latin at St. Michael's College in the University of Toronto. An example of the Christian convergence of erudition, spirituality, and ministry in the service of the church, she soon became not only someone I admired as a teacher but also a woman of gentle and solid faith, upon whose wise counsel and support I relied long after I left Toronto. Sister Mechtilde readily agreed to provide a reference for me when in 2011 I applied to be accepted for diaconal formation in the Archdiocese of Vancouver. Her death in 2025 was a great loss for her religious community, St. Michael's College, and the many people who love her, to whom I belong. Sister John Mary Sullivan, FSE, certainly supported my theological studies with her invincible Franciscan cheerfulness. As my supervisor, from 2016 to 2025, in the Ministries and Outreach Office of the Archdiocese of Vancouver, she taught me a valuable and unforgettable lesson at the beginning of my diaconal ministry to outstanding women and men who unfortunately experience marginalization in the church and in society: we suffer with those whom we serve. That lesson belongs to the costly grace of all ministry in the church, and for that lesson I remain profoundly indebted to Sister John Mary.

Introduction: The Re-Creation of the Diaconate

In 1961, the German Lutheran theologian Otto Dilschneider coined a theological term: *Geistvergessenheit*. A forgetting of the Holy Spirit by theologians and theology could explain the christological tension between the Jesus of history and the Christ of faith. It is the Spirit, Dilschneider maintained, who grounds the "unique continuum" between these two christological poles.[1] He extended "the certain timidity" of a christological engagement with "the theme of the Holy Spirit" to "the *Geistvergessenheit* of Protestant theology" in general.[2] Paradoxically, this forgetfulness coexisted with a pneumatology that represented "a richly cultivated field of our theological research."[3] As a component of the third article of the Apostles' Creed, belief in the Holy Spirit ought to develop into a pneumatology that functions as "the point of departure for ecclesiology, soteriology, and eschatology."[4] *Geistvergessenheit*, therefore, implied an isolation of the Spirit from the church's theological discourse and, by extension, from the ecclesial life that theology seeks to sustain, challenge, and renew.

Catholicism too must plead guilty to the oblivion that Dilschneider ascribed to Protestant theology. According to

[1] Otto A. Dilschneider, "Die Geistvergessenheit der Theologie: Epilog zur Diskussion über den historischen Jesus und kerygmatischen Christus," *Theologische Literaturzeitung* 86, no. 4 (April 1961): col. 258.

[2] Dilschneider, "Die Geistvergessenheit der Theologie," col. 259.

[3] Dilschneider, "Die Geistvergessenheit der Theologie," col. 260.

[4] Dilschneider, "Die Geistvergessenheit der Theologie," col. 261.

Víctor Codina, "a forgetfulness of the Spirit" marked the theology of the Latin church in its second millennium, a deficit that the Second Vatican Council reversed.[5] He maintained: "Pneumatological forgetfulness harms the church; its rediscovery, however, renews and revitalizes it."[6] Walter Kasper agreed and went further by claiming: "The Holy Spirit does not play a principal role in the average ecclesiastical or theological consciousness."[7] Not simply a matter of the distant past, *Geistvergessenheit* continued in the postconciliar church. Before the council, it had contributed to a rigidly hierarchical church, and it was in part the product of a Western trinitarian theology that emphasized the divine unity of the three Persons at the expense of the specific role of each Person in the economy of salvation.[8] Kasper believed: "Only by means of pneumatology can the church in a theologically appropriate manner effect a connection to the great problems of the present, and only pneumatologically is a truly spiritual renewal of the church and a greater unity possible."[9]

The renewal of the diaconate by the Second Vatican Council as a stable order of ministry in the church awaits a pneumatological framework. A *Geistvergessenheit* marks the theology and praxis of the modern diaconate. With its christological emphasis on the deacon's sacramental configuration to Jesus Christ the servant, that theology tends to leave little room for the Holy Spirit. Such an emphasis carries two contrasting risks. The diaconate either becomes an order subservient to the episcopate and presbyterate and so ignores that deacons by virtue of ordination receive the

[5] Víctor Codina, *Creo en el Espíritu Santo*: *Pneumatología narrativa* (Santander: Editorial Sal Terrae, 1994), 50.

[6] Codina, *Creo en el Espíritu Santo*, 72.

[7] Walter Kasper, "Kirche als Sakarament des Geistes," in *Kirche—Ort des Geistes*, ed. Walter Kasper and Gerhard Sauter (Freiburg im Breisgau: Herder, 1976), 13.

[8] Kasper, "Kirche als Sakarament des Geistes," 17, 18.

[9] Kasper, "Kirche als Sakarament des Geistes," 25.

charism of office, or it becomes a clericalist ministry, motivated by an exclusive christological credential, and so ignores that all the baptized receive charisms from the Spirit for the church's evangelizing mission.

Of course, as Michael Seewald has warned, theology should not remedy a neglect of the Spirit by neglecting Christ. The Second Vatican Council, he recalled, taught that the Spirit is the Spirit of the Father and of the Son and that by the Spirit Christ lives in human beings and in the church.[10] While distinguishable, the trinitarian missions of the Son and the Spirit are interdependent. Yves Congar affirmed that, in the economy of salvation, the Son and the Spirit are "inseparable," rendering effective "the self-revelation and self-communication of God."[11] Christology and pneumatology require each other, Congar insisted.[12] An ecclesiological renewal in the Holy Spirit, necessarily in concert with Christology, funds an "organic vision of the church" that is synodal, encompassing, as Congar wrote, "communion, conciliarity, collegiality, being and life together in one organism of grace and love."[13]

When Francis Deniau repeatedly called the conciliar renewal of the diaconate the "re-creation" of the diaconate,[14]

[10] Michael Seewald, "Die Einwohnung des Heiligen Geistes. Spekulationen über die Pneumatologie von *Lumen gentium* 4," in *Gott ist Geist: Perspektiven der Pneumatologie*, ed. Michael Seewald (Freiburg im Breisgau: Herder, 2023), 221.

[11] Yves Congar, "Le troisième article du Symbole: L'impact de la pneumatologie dans la vie de l'Église," in *Dieu, Église, Société*, ed. Joseph Doré (Paris: Éditions du Centurion, 1985), 291.

[12] Yves Congar, *La Parole et le Souffle* (Paris: Desclée, 1984), 13: "Pas de christologie sans pneumatologie, *pas de pneumatologie sans christologie*"—"No Christology without pneumatology, *no pneumatology without Christology*." The emphasis appeared in the original.

[13] Congar, "Le troisième article du Symbole," 300.

[14] Francis Deniau, "Le diaconat à la lumière des trois 'fonctions' du Christ et de l'Église, selon Vatican II," in *Diaconat, XXIe siècle: Actes du Colloque de Louvain-la-Neuve (13–15 septembre 1994)*, ed. André Haquin and Philippe Weber (Brussels: Éditions Lumen Vitae, 1997), 108, 110, 115.

he did not explicitly associate a re-created diaconate with the Holy Spirit. Yet in attributing this re-creation in large part to "the sacramental dimension of the diaconate,"[15] Deniau provided an opportunity for pneumatology. The epiclesis of the consecratory prayer in the rite of diaconal ordination represents the form of the sacrament of order. The ordaining bishop prays on behalf of the church to God for the deacon: "Send upon him, we ask, Lord, the Holy Spirit, so that by the gift of your sevenfold grace [the Spirit] may empower him to carry out faithfully the work of ministry."[16] The self-gift of the Spirit, invoked in this ancient petition, enables and empowers a renewal of ministry in the church, a ministry widened beyond the priestly confection of the Eucharist and no longer limited by celibacy. The re-created diaconate is the work of the Creator Spirit, who renews creation (Ps. 104:30).

The Spirit moves in and renews the church, as the Second Vatican Council manifestly demonstrated. In defending the post-conciliar liturgy, Pope Francis maintained that the council represented "the most recent stage" of a dynamic tradition that, according to the conciliar Dogmatic Constitution on Divine Revelation, "progresses in the church under the assistance of the Holy Spirit (DV 8)."[17] To doubt the council, Francis continued, means to doubt the conciliar bishops "who exercised their collegial power in a solemn way with Peter and under Peter in an ecumenical council and, in the final analysis, to doubt the same Holy Spirit who

[15] Deniau, "Le diaconat," 108.

[16] *Pontificale Romanum ex decreto sacrosancti oecumenici Concilii Vaticani II renovatum auctoritate Pauli PP. VI editum Ioannis Pauli PP. II cura recognitum: De ordinatione episcopi, presbyterorum et diaconorum*, 2nd ed. (1990; repr., Vatican City: Libreria Editrice Vaticana, 2011), 138, no. 235.

[17] Francis, "Ad Episcopos orbis terrarum in praesentatione Litterarum Apostolicarum Motu Proprio datarum 'Traditionis custodes' de usu Liturgiae Romanae instaurationem anni MCMLXX antecedentis," *Acta Apostolicae Sedis* 113, no. 8 (August 2021): 805. For the passage in *Dei Verbum* from which Pope Francis quoted, see Tanner, *Decrees*, 2: 974.

guides the church."[18] This statement deserves a positive reformulation: to trust the council is to believe in the Holy Spirit who guides the church. The Spirit guided the church in renewing the diaconate at the council.

In *Lumen Gentium*, the Dogmatic Constitution on the Church, the conciliar bishops stated:

> Upon a lower step of the hierarchy stand the deacons, upon whom hands are laid "not for the priesthood, but for ministry." Empowered (*roborati*), in fact, by sacramental grace, they serve the people of God in the *diaconia* of the liturgy, of the word, and of charity in communion with the bishop and his presbyterate. It is the responsibility of the deacon, inasmuch as it will have been assigned to him by a competent authority, to administer baptism solemnly, to reserve and distribute the Eucharist, to assist at and bless a marriage in the name of the church, to bring Viaticum to the dying, to read Sacred Scripture to the faithful, to teach and encourage the people, to preside over the worship and prayer of the faithful, to administer sacramentals, to conduct funeral and also burial rites. Dedicated to the duties of charity and administration, deacons should remember the counsel of Blessed Polycarp: "merciful, diligent, [and] advancing according to the truth of the Lord, who became the servant of all." (LG 29)[19]

[18] Francis, "Ad Episcopos orbis terrarum," 805.

[19] Tanner, *Decrees*, 2: 874. The quotation from Polycarp's epistle to the Philippians reads awkwardly because *Lumen Gentium* quoted a fragment from the following passage in the Latin translation: "Similarly, deacons should be blameless in the sight of [God's] justice, just as ministers of God and of Christ, not of human beings; they should not be slanderers, or double-tongued, or avaricious, but self-restrained in all things, merciful, diligent, [and] advancing according to the truth of the Lord, who became the servant of all." See the edition that *Lumen Gentium* cited: Franz Xaver Funk, ed., *Patres Apostolici*, vol. 1 (Tübingen: Heinrich Laupp, 1901), 301, 303.

Ministerial function preceded a brief christological reference to Christ the servant in what Alphonse Borras repeatedly characterized as the council's "makeshift theology" of the diaconate.[20] Most of the ministries that LG 29 attributed to deacons had previously been the preserve of priests. Consequently, Hervé Legrand held that an objective reading of LG 29 led to the inevitable conclusion that "deacons are only the minor auxiliaries of priests."[21]

Yet, for all its emphasis on function, LG 29 represented a significant development from the schema *De Ecclesia* of 1963. The latter document recognized deacons only as "extraordinary ministers of solemn baptism and of holy communion,"[22] whereas LG 29 implied that baptism and the administration of Communion belonged to the ordinary ministerial competence of deacons. The schema's short section on the diaconate began: "At a lower step in the hierarchical ministry, deacons attend to (*adsistunt*) the bishop and presbyters."[23] LG 29, however, explicitly redirected diaconal service to the church, the people of God, a service undertaken "in communion with the bishop and his presbyterate."

Here in the second sentence of LG 29, the council made its most compelling theological statement about a re-created diaconate. The sentence about deacons merits repetition: "Empowered, in fact, by sacramental grace, they serve the people of God in the *diaconia* of the liturgy, of the word, and

[20] Borras called the council's statements about the diaconate "une théologie de fortune." See Alphonse Borras, *Le diaconat au risque de sa nouveauté* (Brussels: Éditions Lessius, 2007), 54, 206; Alphonse Borras, "Le diaconat, cinquante ans après Vatican II," *Pistis & Praxis: Teologia e Pastoral* 7, no. 2 (2015): 313; Alphonse Borras, "Le diaconat permanent: questions et perspectives," *Nouvelle revue théologique* 138, no. 4 (2016): 571.

[21] Hervé Legrand, "Le diaconat dans sa relation à la théologie de l'Église et des ministères: Réception et devenir du diaconat depuis Vatican II," in *Diaconat, XXIe siècle*, 19.

[22] AS 2/1: 235.

[23] AS 2/1: 235.

of charity in communion with the bishop and his presbyterate."[24] This statement lays an authoritative theological foundation for the diaconate as a ministry in a synodal church.

Everything depends on the sacramentality of the diaconate or on "the sacramental character of the diaconate," as Jean Beyer, the eminent Jesuit canon lawyer, contended in 1980.[25] Beyer rejected the sacramentality of the diaconate before the Second Vatican Council,[26] and, afterwards, he argued that the council did not conclusively and convincingly assert it.[27] That deacons were, according to LG 29, ordained "not for the priesthood, but for ministry," raised for Beyer the question whether the diaconate "is sacramental inasmuch as the sacrament of order is the priesthood."[28] He characterized LG 29's claim that deacons were "empowered by sacramental grace"[29] as "fainthearted."[30] That modest claim, however, has sufficiently underwritten a growing theological and ecclesial consensus in support of the sacramentality of the diaconate.

The recognition of grace was and remains fundamental. The council affirmed that God's self-communication through the church's sacrament of order is the foundation of diaconal ministry. As a variation on the sacramentality of the diaconate, in the proposed homily of the post-conciliar ordination rite of deacons, the ordaining bishop refers to them as "empowered (*roborati*) by the gift of the Holy

[24] Tanner, *Decrees*, 2: 874.

[25] Jean Beyer, "De diaconatu animadversiones," *Periodoca de re morali, canonica, liturgica* 69, nos. 3–4 (1980): 458.

[26] Jean Beyer, "Nature et Position du Sacerdoce," *Nouvelle revue théologique* 76, no. 4 (1954): 371–72.

[27] Beyer, "De diaconatu animadversiones," 449–60.

[28] Jean Beyer, "Il diaconato permanente nell'attuale vita ecclesiale," trans. G. Sarzi Sartori, *Quaderni di diritto ecclesiale* 10 (1997): 135.

[29] Tanner, *Decrees*, 2: 874.

[30] Beyer, "De diaconatu animadversiones," 449.

Spirit."[31] Sacramental grace is for service in and to the church, a service of leadership that deacons exercise, not as absolutely autonomous ministers, but as ministers in communion with other ministers: the diocesan bishop and the priests of the local church. Theirs is a graced ministerial communion, for all ordained ministers receive the self-gift of the Spirit in the sacrament of order for service to the people of God. Matthias Remenyi observed: "Ministry is service to service for the gospel."[32] Service is the calling of all the baptized who make the people of God a servant people, and who, co-responsibly in the power of the Spirit, continue the liberating and evangelizing mission of Jesus Christ.

The Holy Spirit is the protagonist of a synodal church, as Pope Francis reminded the church.[33] Gifted by the Spirit, the baptized are co-responsible for carrying out the church's mission of proclaiming Christ's gospel of God's reign to the world. The Spirit unifies the church, the people of God, "both in communion and ministry" (LG 4).[34] In this graced, Spirit-wrought communion, the baptized listen to what the Spirit tells the churches (Rev 2:7, 11, 17, 29; 3:6, 13, 22) for the church's mission through a co-responsible discernment of the signs of the times (GS 4, 11).[35] Recognizing attentiveness to the Spirit among the people of God gathered "in synodal assemblies" is essential to a deliberative ecclesial communion, the International Theological Commission maintained: "In the synodal Church, the whole community,

[31] *Pontificale Romanum* (1990), 105, no. 199.

[32] Matthias Remenyi, "Die Autorität des Dienens. Der Diakonat als Paradigma des kirchlichen Amtes," in *Amt und Autorität: Kirche in der späten Moderne*, ed. Matthias Remenyi (Paderborn: Ferdinand Schöningh, 2012), 173.

[33] Jos Moons, "The Holy Spirit as the Protagonist of the Synod: Pope Francis's Creative Reception of the Second Vatican Council," *Theological Studies* 84, no. 1 (March 2023): 64.

[34] Tanner, *Decrees*, 2: 850.

[35] Tanner, *Decrees*, 2: 1070, 1075.

in the free and rich diversity of its members is called together to pray, listen, analyse, dialogue, discern and offer advice on taking pastoral decisions which correspond as closely as possible to God's will."[36]

In response to the recommendation by the Synod on Synodality (2021–2024) to explore "more deeply" the council's teaching on the diaconate,[37] I examine in this book the three principal theological motifs of the second sentence of LG 29: sacramental grace, ministerial communion, and service to the people of God. The first chapter proposes that the sacramentality of the diaconate overcomes a *Geistvergessenheit* implicit in a subordination of the diaconate to the episcopate. The council's recourse to the ancient formula that deacons are ordained "not for priesthood, but for ministry"—a formula regularly repeated owing to its conciliar revival—should not underpin a definition of diaconal ministry as an extension of episcopal ministry. At the prayer of the people of God expressed by the ordaining bishop, deacons receive the self-gift of the Spirit for the ministry of Christ and of the Spirit exercised in communion with the bishop and priests.

The Synod on Synodality held that a bishop works "with Priests and Deacons in a way that reflects their common sacramental bond," and thus "they are co-responsible with him for ministerial service in the local Church."[38] Yet, as the second chapter of the book demonstrates, the common

[36] International Theological Commission, *Synodality in the Life and Mission of the Church*, no. 68, March 2, 2018, Vatican website, https://www.vatican.va/roman_curia/congregations/cfaith/cti_documents/rc_cti_20180302_sinodalita_en.html.

[37] Francis and XVI Ordinary General Assembly of the Synod of Bishops, *For a Synodal Church: Communion, Participation, Mission—Final Document*, 26, no. 73, November 24, 2024, Vatican website, https://www.synod.va/content/dam/synod/news/2024-10-26_final-document/ENG---Documento-finale.pdf.

[38] Francis and XVI Ordinary General Assembly of the Synod of Bishops, *For a Synodal Church*, 25, no. 69.

conceptualization of the diaconate as a ministry auxiliary and ancillary to the episcopate and presbyterate contradicts co-responsible ministerial service. A supply ministry is incompatible with a ministerial communion, empowered by the Spirit and grounded in three commonalities: service to the people of God, evangelization, and the exercise of the threefold office of Christ. Efforts by the magisterium to reserve to bishops and priests the sacramental representation of Christ the head of the church also frustrate a communion of these ministers with deacons in service to the people of God.

In its reflection on "Charisms, Vocations and Ministries for Mission," the Synod on Synodality called the people of God "this dynamism in the Spirit."[39] Dismissing obstacles to "leadership roles in the Church" for women, the Synod appealed to an unstoppable Holy Spirit.[40] Matching the Synod's pneumatic ecclesiology, the book's third chapter envisions the ministering people of God as the sacrament of the improvising Spirit, who bestows charisms on all the baptized for the church's mission, especially to the poor and marginalized at its threshold. The diaconate is not a threshold ministry mediating between a bishop and the laity for an ecclesial *diaconia* of charity. Instead, deacons minister with other minsters, ordained and instituted, in a diaconal communion open to new expressions of threshold ministry, thanks to the guidance of the Spirit. By virtue of their ordination, deacons also exercise leadership of threshold communities, inspiring community members to contribute to the formation of their community in the various ways in which the Spirit has gifted them.

In harmony with the admission by the Synod on Synodality that "the ministry of Deacons remains unknown to many

[39] Francis and XVI Ordinary General Assembly of the Synod of Bishops, *For a Synodal Church*, 22, no. 58.

[40] Francis and XVI Ordinary General Assembly of the Synod of Bishops, *For a Synodal Church*, 22, no. 60.

Christians,"[41] the book's conclusion takes up the theme of a theologically unsettled diaconate. The endurance of the transitional diaconate and the reservation of the diaconate to men in the Roman Catholic Church perturb the integrity of the diaconate as a distinctive ministry in communion with the episcopate and the presbyterate. The *Geistvergessenheit* in the theology of ministry that challenges the diaconate can find a partial remedy in the revision of the consecratory prayers for bishops, priests, and deacons that recognizes a graced communion of ordained ministers in service to the people of God, blessed with a rich variety of charisms for the church's mission.

In an article published in 1961, in the same year in which Dilschneider coined the term *Geistvergessenheit*, Karl Rahner, the great theological pioneer of the diaconate, formulated *die atkuelle Frage*—the question of the hour: "Should the diaconate as a sacramental share in the one sacrament of order be so renewed in the contemporary situation that it can again exercise an actual and discrete function in the church, and, in fact, in such a way that celibacy is not associated with it?"[42] Rahner was primarily interested in the ecclesial present, not the past, of the diaconate. Thus, he asked: "What can one do today and what may and should one do today in the matter of the diaconate?"[43] Although he never mentioned the Holy Spirit in his article, Rahner, of course, knew the pneumatic relevance of a sacramental diaconate. In his first article on the diaconate, published in 1957, he wrote that it was "an established fact in the church that

[41] Francis and XVI Ordinary General Assembly of the Synod of Bishops, *For a Synodal Church*, 26, no. 73.

[42] Karl Rahner, "Erwägungen über Inhalt und Aufbau eines Sammelwerkes über die zeitgemäße Erneuerung des Diakonates," in Rahner, *Sämtliche Werke*, vol. 16: *Kirchliche Erneuerung: Studien zur Pastoraltheologie und Struktur der Kirche*, ed. Albert Raffelt (Freiburg im Breisgau: Herder, 2005), 357.

[43] Rahner, "Erwägungen," 357.

ordained ministry (*das Amt*) can only be *properly* exercised in the Spirit (*im Pneuma*)."[44]

Rahner's emphasis on "today" carries pneumatic value. The Spirit guides Christ's church today in the present circumstances of the world. What the diaconate once was in the earliest centuries of the church cannot therefore exclusively determine what it can and must be today.

By contrast, James Barnett argued that preaching did not constitute a function of the ancient diaconate.[45] A restoration of ministry to "its original organic character" should not allow for deacons to preach today to safeguard a distinction "between the functions of the deacon and the presbyter due to the now centuries-old concept that the totality of ministry essentially belongs to the presbyter."[46] Thus, for the church to make preaching a function of the modern diaconate, contrary to the practice of early Christianity, "is neither helpful nor desirable," according to Barnett.[47] The historical record is open to debate, however. Some scholars have provided evidence that deacons of the ancient church did preach.[48]

[44] Karl Rahner, "Dogmatische Vorbemerkungen für eine richtige Fragestellung über die Wiedererneuerung des Diakonats," in *Theologie in Geschichte und Gegenwart: Michael Schmaus zum sechzigsten Geburtstag*, ed. Johann Auer and Hermann Volk (Munich: Karl Zink Verlag, 1957), 136, emphasis in the original. For more on Rahner, see Hilmar M. Pabel, "Karl Rahner's Theology of the Diaconate: A Reappraisal," *Journal for the History of Modern Theology* 31, no. 1 (May 2024): 43–72.

[45] James Monroe Barnett, *The Diaconate: A Full and Equal Order*, rev. ed. (Valley Forge, PA: Trinity Press International, 1995), 80–82.

[46] Barnett, *The Diaconate*, 191.

[47] Barnett, *The Diaconate*, 211.

[48] Johann Nepomuk Seidl, *Der Diakonat in der katholischen Kirche, dessen hieratische Würde und geschichtliche Entwicklung: Eine kirchenrechts-geschichtliche Abhandlung* (Regensburg: Georg Joseph Manz, 1884), 148–53; Bart J. Koet, *The Go-Between: Augustine on Deacons* (Leiden: Brill, 2019), 102–3; Doru Costache, "Athanasius on Deacons and the Diaconate," in *Deacons and Diakonia in Late Antiquity*, ed. Bart J. Koet, Edwina Murphy, and Esko Ryökäs (Tübingen: Mohr Siebeck, 2024), 71–72; Andreas Müller, "The Diaconate according to John Chrysostom," in *Deacons and Diakonia in*

Yet even if Barnett were indisputably correct that deacons in the early centuries of the church did not preach, that fact alone should not deny them the ministry of preaching God's word today as part of their *munus docendi*. History does not own the triune God or God's church. Reform in and of the church does not lead backward to a past that supposedly functions as an absolute measure of ecclesial perfection for today. Seewald thus maintained: "To expect from history directives for the present and to limit the sphere of what may be done and believed to what was already once done or believed in the past would be to demand too much of history and of the historical scholarship that attends to it."[49] Such an expectation also misdirects theology's task of reformative clarification. Authentic reform moves forward with tradition, not backward, as the Holy Spirit guides the church in the face of new, contemporary challenges. The Spirit's guidance may prove unsettling, and appropriately so because of the diaconate, for, as one French bishop told Alain Desjonquères: "One of the main graces of the diaconate is precisely to disturb."[50] The pages that follow will disturb several assumptions, ideas, and arguments about the diaconate.

I disturb common parlance by deliberately not qualifying deacons and the diaconate as "permanent." To refer to deacons as permanent or transitional makes no sense since there is only one sacramental diaconate, as Deacon William Ditewig has correctly contended.[51] Both the concepts of a

---

Late Antiquity, 119; Enrique A. Eguiarte, "Liturgical Roles of the Deacon in Augustine: A Punic-Speaking Deacon is Needed (*Ep.* 84)," in *Deacons and Diakonia in Late Antiquity*, 293–98.

[49] Michael Seewald, *Reform—Dieselbe Kirche anders denken* (Freiburg im Breisgau: Herder, 2018), 118.

[50] Alain Desjonquères, *Être diacre permanent, pourquoi?* (Paris: Éditions Salvator, 2019), 115: "Une des principales grâces du diaconat est justement de déranger."

[51] William Ditewig, *Courageous Humility: Reflections on the Church, Diakonia, and Deacons* (New York: Paulist Press, 2022), 219.

permanent and transitional diaconate perpetuate the clerical *cursus honorum*, the structure of hierarchical advancement, which has no place in a diaconal and synodal church, in which ordained ministers exercise servant-leadership as fellow pilgrims with all the baptized in the church's mission of proclaiming the gospel of Jesus Christ. Before the Second Vatican Council, the rite of ordination of deacons presumed their hierarchical inferiority. The bishop prayed to God for the newly ordained deacons "that with worthy successes from a lower step (*de inferiori gradu*) they might merit through your grace to attain better things (*potiora*)," an implied ascent to the priesthood, to which deacons were eventually ordained.[52] The differentiation between deacons after the council suggests that permanent deacons are "stuck" where they are on the lowest step of the hierarchy, while transitional deacons anticipate rising higher to the priesthood after a brief period of exercising diaconal functions. Permanence and transience suggest an unhealthy hierarchy within the diaconate, unlikely to foster a graced communion of ministers within a local church: bishop, priests, and deacons.

Some readers will find disturbing that I refer only briefly and tangentially to the currently controversial question of ordaining women as deacons, a question that the Synod on Synodality determined was still "open."[53] Even after the Holy See's second Commission on the Study of the Female Diaconate was not able to recommend the ordination of women as deacons on the basis of historical evidence, its president, Cardinal Giuseppe Petrocchi informed Pope Leo XIV on September 18, 2025, that "the issues relating to the diaconal ordination of women remain open to further

[52] Manlio Sodi and Alessandro Toniolo, eds., *Pontificale Romanum: Editio Typica, 1961–1962* (Vatican City: Libreria Editirice Vaticana, 2008), 44.

[53] Francis and XVI Ordinary General Assembly of the Synod of Bishops, *For a Synodal Church*, 22, no. 60.

theological and pastoral exploration."[54] Yet, given the exclusion of women from the diaconate, Paul Zulehner correctly observed: "The diaconate touches a deep wound of the church: the positioning of women in ecclesial processes of decision-making and ministries."[55] While the ordination of women to the diaconate undoubtedly requires separate theological treatment,[56] the debate about women as deacons ought to benefit from a theology of the diaconate that seeks to rescue deacons from ecclesial marginalization. Petrocchi believed that the success of discerning whether women should be ordained as deacons depended on "a rigorous and expansive critical examination carried out on the perspective of the 'diaconate in itself,' namely on its sacramental 'identity,' and on its ecclesial 'mission,' clarifying certain 'structural' and pastoral aspects that currently do not happen to be completely defined."[57] Women should be able to exercise diaconal ministry underpinned by a theology that emphasizes the sacramentality of the diaconate in a ministerial and ecclesial communion, not as a form of subservience, especially to ordained men.

Women's subordination to men in the church represents a past and present reality. In its Synthesis Report, released after its first session in October 2023, the Synod on Synodality recorded the gratitude of women to bishops and priests but also registered the critique of Catholic women: "They also spoke of a Church that wounds. Clericalism, a

[54] Giuseppe Petrocchi, "Sintesi della Commissione di Studio sul Diaconato Femminile," December 4, 2025, Vatican website, https://press.vatican.va/content/salastampa/it/bollettino/pubblico/2025/12/04/0950/01725.html.

[55] Paul M. Zulehner, *Dienende Männer – Anstifter zur Solidarität: Diakone in Westeuropa* (Ostfildern: Schwabenverlag, 2003), 134–35.

[56] Karl Lehmann, "Die Entwicklung des Ständigen Diakonats. Beobachtungen und Überlegungen aus der Sicht des bischöflichen Amtes," in *Ortsbestimmungen: Der Diakonat als kirchlicher Dienst*, ed. Richard Hartmann, Franz Reger, and Stefan Sander (Frankfurt am Main: Verlag Josef Knecht, 2009), 25.

[57] Petrocchi, "Sintesi."

chauvinist mentality and inappropriate expressions of authority continue to scar the face of the Church and damage its communion."[58] Synodal delegates expressed their desire "to promote a Church in which men and women dialogue together, in order to understand more deeply the horizon of God's project, that sees them together as protagonists, without subordination, exclusion and competition."[59] The elaboration of a theology of the diaconate that privileges communion over subordination will benefit not only the men who are or will be ordained to the diaconate, but also women, if and when the church decides to ordain them as deacons.

The sacramental premise of a theology of the diaconate departs from the semantic analysis, championed by John Collins, of the Greek nouns *diakonos* and *diakonia* and the cognate verb *diakonein*. Collins insisted that modern notions of deacons as humble ministers of loving service to the poor in the form of ecclesial social workers conceptually undermine the appropriation by the New Testament and the early church of the Greek cognates.[60] *Diakonoi* were intermediaries between the gods/God and human beings, or official agents of the state who acted in accordance with a commission that they received and who were responsible to the divine or human source of that commission. Christian *diakonia* originated with a divine mandate or exercised a mission on

[58] XVI Ordinary General Assembly of the Synod of Bishops, *A Synodal Church in Mission: Synthesis Report*, no. 9f, October 28, 2023, Vatican website, https://www.synod.va/content/dam/synod/assembly/synthesis/english/2023.10.28-ENG-Synthesis-Report.pdf.

[59] XVI Ordinary General Assembly of the Synod of Bishops, *A Synodal Church in Mission*, no. 9h.

[60] John N. Collins, *Diakonia: Re-interpreting the Ancient Sources* (New York: Oxford University Press, 1990), 45, 67, 194, 195, 254, 255; John N. Collins, *Deacons and the Church: Making Connections between Old and New* (Leominster, Herefordshire: Gracewing; Harrisburg, PA: Morehouse Publishing, 2002), 13, 26, 65, 66, 68–69, 120–21, 122, 132, 136.

behalf of a Christian community or of one of its leaders.[61] In early Christian communities, deacons functioned as assistants of the bishop and presbyters or "auxiliaries of the bishop."[62] Anni Hentschel has argued, however, against a presumed absolute subordination of *diakonoi* to *episkopoi*, maintaining, based on Philippians 1:1, 1 Timothy 3:8-13, the *Didache*, and 1 Clement, that deacons were not hierarchical inferiors but rather exercised roles of teaching, of preaching, and thus of leadership in Christian communities.[63] These roles suggest themselves, too, in the letters of Ignatius of Antioch, who combined the superiority of the bishop with a collegiality among bishop, presbyters, and deacons.[64]

Yet, etymology and exegesis must yield to sacramentality for a fundamental theology of the diaconate. Not semantics, but grace, the self-gift of the Spirit in the sacrament of order grounds deacons in their ministry in the contemporary context of the needs of their local church. Sacramental grace, furthermore, establishes a communion of ministers—bishops, priests, and deacons, who are all ordered toward or ordained for service to the people of God. If *diakonia* did not originally and semantically connote ministry to the poor, the ancient church regarded deacons as ministers to the marginalized: to the sick, travellers, widows, orphans, the destitute, catechumens requiring support and instruction, migrants, and refugees. Moreover, deacons were to keep the local church informed about those who were poor.[65] In

[61] For the varied semantic field of the Greek cognates, see Collins, *Diakonia*, 77–234.

[62] Collins, *Diakonia*, 236, 237, 238, 239, 240; Collins, *Deacons*, 93, 94, 100, 101, 126; quotation: John N. Collins, *Are All Christians Ministers?* (Collegeville, MN: Liturgical Press, 1992), 144.

[63] Anni Hentschel, *Diakonia im Neuen Testament: Studien zur Semantik unter besonderer Berücksichtigung der Rolle von Frauen* (Tübingen: Mohr Siebeck, 2007), 175, 176, 400, 402, 403, 408, 410, 414, 416.

[64] Hentschel, *Diakonia*, 419–20, 422–23, 428.

[65] Ignatius Ephraem II Rahmani, ed., *Testamentum Domini Nostri Jesu Christi* (Mainz: Franz Kirchheim, 1899), 81.

the contemporary synodal church that places the poor at its "heart" and that answers the divine call "to be poor with those who are poor,"[66] *diakonia*, in the current ecclesial and theological vocabulary, expresses the church's sacramental reality as a sign, in Christ, of God's communion with all human beings and of the communion that human beings have with each other (LG 1),[67] especially for the sake of the majority who are poor.

The church looks to God as its guide through history. In a slight adaptation of the ancient consecratory prayer of the ordination rite of deacons, the ordaining bishop invokes God: "remaining in yourself, you renew all things, and, arranging all things through your word, power, and wisdom, Jesus Christ, your Son, our Lord, you steward them to be adapted to each and every time."[68] The diaconate remains open today to God's renewal and adaptive

[66] Francis and XVI Ordinary General Assembly of the Synod of Bishops, *For a Synodal Church*, 10, no. 19.

[67] Tanner, *Decrees*, 2: 849.

[68] *Pontificale Romanum* (1990), 121, no. 207 (ordination of more than one deacon); 137, no. 235 (ordination of one deacon): "qui in te manens innovas omnia, et sempiterna providentia cuncta disponens, per verbum, virtutem sapientiamque tuam Iesum Christum, Filium tuum, Dominum nostrum, singulis quibusque temporibus aptanda dispensas." This invocation in the most recent edition of the Roman Pontifical revises the relevant passage in the oldest record of the consecratory prayer from the fifth or sixth century, which appears in the Verona Sacramentary, by deleting one verb (*praeparas*), changing one verb (*dispones*) into a gerund (*disponens*), and making the ablative of means (*sempiterna providentia*) dependent on *disponens*. For the original passage, see Leo Cunibert Mohlberg, ed., *Sacramentarium Veronense*, 2nd ed. (Rome: Herder, 1966), 121: "Qui in te manens innouas omnia, et cuncta dispones per uerbum, uirtutem sapientiamque tuam Iesum Christum filium tuum dominum nostrum, sempiterna prouidentia praeparas et singuilis quibusque temporibus aptanda dispensas." The original passage remained unchanged in the revisions of the Roman Pontifical in 1961–1962 and 1968. See Sodi and Toniolo, , *Pontificale Romanum*, 40–41; *Pontificale Romanum ex decreto sacrosancti oecumenici Concilii Vaticani II instauratum auctoritate Pauli PP. VI promulgatum: De ordinatione diaconi, presbyteri et episcopi*

stewardship of creation. The Second Vatican Council did not resuscitate the ancient diaconate; as an expression of synodality, it re-created the diaconate "under the assistance of the Holy Spirit" (DV 8),[69] who continues to renew the church as a synodal communion. For the diaconate, the question of the hour is what it means for deacons today to be empowered by sacramental grace to serve the people of God in communion with their bishop and the priests of a local church, to be empowered by the Spirit as ministers of an ecclesial communion that serves as a sacramental sign of Christ's love for the poor.

(Vatican City: Libreria Editrice Vaticana, 1968), 26, no. 21 (ordination of more than one deacon); 84, no. 21 (ordination of one deacon).

[69] Tanner, *Decrees*, 2: 974.

Chapter 1: Sacramental Grace

A Cautious Beginning

By its own admission, the Doctrinal Commission of the Second Vatican Council proceeded "cautiously" in expressing the sacramentality of the diaconate when it transformed the 1963 schema, *De Ecclesia*, into the document that in 1964 became *Lumen Gentium*.[1] The section on deacons in the second chapter of the former document listed only their functions without relating these to the sacrament of order.[2] In 1964, the commission justified recognizing the sacramental nature of the diaconate with reference to the Council of Trent's sixth canon on the sacrament of order and Pope Pius XII's apostolic constitution *Sacramentum Ordinis* (1947).[3] The canon from the twenty-third session of Trent (July 15, 1563) condemned anyone who denied that bishops, priests, and "ministers" constituted the hierarchy of the Catholic Church "by divine ordinance."[4] Even if one were to equate "ministers" with deacons, as Karl Rahner did in 1964,[5] the canon made no pronouncement about the sacramentality of any

[1] AS 3/1: 260.

[2] AS 2/1: 235.

[3] AS 3/1: 260.

[4] Tanner, *Decrees*, 2: 744.

[5] Karl Rahner, "Diakonat und Diakon," in *Handbuch der Pastoraltheologie: Praktische Theologie der Kirche in ihrer Gegenwart*, vol. 1, ed. Franz Xaver Arnold, Karl Rahner, Viktor Schnurr, Leonhard M. Weber (Freiburg im Breisgau: Herder, 1964), 190.

ordained minister. In 1563, the defined teaching of the church did not regard the episcopate as sacramentally conferred. Pius XII recognized "the diaconate, the presbyterate, and the episcopate" as "holy orders" and redefined the matter and form of the ordination to these orders.[6] The commission did not want to give the impression, however, that the Second Vatican Council condemned "those few recent authors"—unnamed—who doubted the sacramental nature of diaconal ordination.[7]

Although the Doctrinal Commission did not elaborate on its appeal to *Sacramentum Ordinis*, the apostolic constitution represented an important stage of development in the theology of the diaconate. Pius XII's aim was to clarify the theological uncertainty about what constituted the matter and form of ordinations to the episcopate, presbyterate, and diaconate. His decision also responded to the worries about the validity of their ordination that disturbed priests who were unsure if the explanatory rite of the *traditio instrumentorum*—"the handing over of the instruments," namely the chalice and patten—had been observed correctly. The pope declared that henceforth the laying on of hands by the ordaining bishop was to be the matter for all three ordinations. Thus, he excluded the *traditio instrumentorum* from the matter. His declaration contradicted the position of Thomas Aquinas and the Decree for the Armenians at the Council of Florence (1439).[8] Pius XII specified which words of the consecratory prayer in the three ordination rites established

[6] Pius XII, "Sacramentum Ordinis," *Acta Apostolicae Sedis* 40 (1948): 6–7, nos. 4–5, quotation: 6.

[7] AS 3/1: 260.

[8] Pius XII, "Sacramentum Ordinis," 6, no. 5, 7, no. 6; Franz Hürth, "Commentarius ad Const. Apostolicam," *Periodica de re morali canonica liturgica* 37, no. 1 (1948): 14–15; Matthias Daufratshofer, "Did Pius XII Change a Dogma in 1947? The Apostolic Constitution *Sacramentum ordinis* and its Underestimated Potential," *Journal of Modern and Contemporary Christianity* 3, no. 1 (April 2024): 252–53.

the form of the ordination.[9] The apostolic constitution seemed to assume the sacramentality of all three orders, *pace* Jean Beyer, who pointed out that the pope never identified any of the three as sacramental.[10] When the pope explicitly presupposed the "unity and identity" of the sacrament of order,[11] the sacrament's unity and identity presumably encompassed a unity in a threefold diversity. In arguing for the sacramentality of the episcopate, Ephrem Boularand observed in 1953 that, thanks to *Sacramentum Ordinis*, the episcopate shared with the diaconate and the presbyterate "all the elements of the sacrament of order: one matter, one form, the signification and the conferral of a power of order and of the grace of the Holy Spirit."[12] At the first International Congress on Pastoral Liturgy held in Assisi in 1956, Francisco Miranda Vicente, the auxiliary bishop of Toledo, Spain, and the president of the liturgical commission of the Spanish bishops, understood: "The Apostolic Constitution only deals with the orders that are truly sacramental, namely the episcopate, the priesthood, and the diaconate."[13] *Sacramentum Ordinis* did not address the subdiaconate and the four minor orders, those of porter, lector, exorcist, and acolyte. In treating the other three orders together, Pius XII provided an authoritative foundation not only for their sacramentality but also for their communion in the one sacrament of order.

Despite the authoritative sources identified by the Doctrinal Commission, *Lumen Gentium* only obliquely formulated the sacramentality of the diaconate without mentioning

[9] Pius XII, "Sacramentum Ordinis," 7, no. 5.

[10] Jean Beyer, "Nature et Position du Sacerdoce," *Nouvelle revue théologique* 76, no. 4 (1954): 358, n. 6.

[11] Pius XII, "Sacramentum Ordinis," 5, no. 2.

[12] Ephrem Boularand, "La consécration épiscoplae est-elle sacramentelle?," *Bulletin de littérature ecclésiastique* 54, no. 1 (January–March 1953): 33–34.

[13] Francisco Miranda Vicente, "Signification théologique de la Constitution *Sacramentum Ordinis*," *La Maison-Dieu* 47–48 (1956): 199.

the sacrament of order: *gratia . . . sacramentali roborati*. Deacons are "empowered by sacramental grace" (LG 29).[14] By contrast, the Dogmatic Constitution on the Church taught that "by episcopal consecration the fullness of the sacrament of order is conferred" and that "it is the duty of bishops to receive the newly elected into the episcopal body through the sacrament of order" (LG 21).[15] Furthermore, presbyters "by the power of the sacrament of order are consecrated to the image of Christ, the supreme and, moreover, eternal priest for preaching the gospel and nurturing the faithful and celebrating divine worship" (LG 28).[16] What in conciliar teaching was explicit for bishops and priests was only implicit for deacons, even though the intention of the oblique statement was to communicate the sacramentality of the diaconate.

The cautious approach of the Doctrinal Commission was surprising. Even if arguments for and against married deacons, and not the sacramentality of the diaconate, constituted "the emotional climax" of the conciliar debate on the diaconate in October 1963,[17] most bishops who addressed sacramentality favored it. In its analysis of the debates, the Doctrinal Commission in 1964 noted that an appeal to the teaching of the Council of Trent did not convince two bishops of the sacramentality of the diaconate. Two other bishops responded by asserting that nobody doubted that the diaconate was as much a sacrament as the episcopate.[18] Some bishops took the sacramentality of the diaconate for granted.[19] Others commented on it. Precisely because the

[14] Tanner, *Decrees*, 2: 874.

[15] Tanner, *Decrees*, 2: 865.

[16] Tanner, *Decrees*, 2: 872.

[17] Stefan Sander, *Das Amt des Diakons: Eine Handreichung*, rev. ed. (Freiburg im Breisgau: Herder, 2013), 103.

[18] AS 3/1: 263.

[19] AS 2/2: 317, 319 (speech of Cardinal Leo Joseph Suenens, Archbishop of Mecheln-Brussels), 347 (speech of Cardinal Paul Richaud, Archbishop of Bordeaux), 431 (speech of Archbishop Paul Yu Pin of Nanking), 536

diaconate was a sacrament, it was akin to the priesthood and therefore required celibacy, according to Bishop Petar Čule of Mostar-Duvno (-Trebinje e Mrkan) in Bosnia and Herzegovina.[20] For Juan Hervás y Benet, the titular Bishop of Dora and the Prelate of Ciudad Real in Spain, the strength of the argument for sacramental grace was not enough to support the necessity and suitability of the restoration of a stable diaconate.[21] In his defense of such a diaconate, Archbishop Josef Clemens Maurer, the German-born archbishop of Sucre in Bolivia, used the traditional terminology of the sacramental character mediated by ordination: "The diaconate, according to the unquestionably common teaching, imprints a permanent and indelible character on the soul."[22] That the schema *De Ecclesia* said "nothing about the sacramental character of diaconal ordination" surprised Narciso Jubany Arnau, auxiliary bishop of Barcelona. It needed to be affirmed "after the solemn promulgation of the sacramentality of the episcopate" and after a reaffirmation of the "sacramentality of the presbyterate."[23] Inherent in Jubany's demand was a recognition of a sacramental communion of the three forms of ordained ministry. *Lumen Gentium* did not meet his demand that "the sacramentality of the diaconate be clearly affirmed in the text."[24] In 1967, in his *motu proprio, Sacrum Diaconatus Ordinem*, Pope Paul VI partially addressed Jubany's request by presenting the diaconate as "enriched with its own indelible character and its own special, distinctive grace."[25]

(in the longer text of the speech of Bishop Jorge Kémérer of Posadas, Brazil, speaking for twenty Latin American bishops).

[20] AS 2/2: 518.

[21] AS 2/2: 784.

[22] AS 2/2: 411.

[23] AS 2/2: 580.

[24] AS 2/2: 582.

[25] Paul VI, "Sacrum Diaconatus Ordinem," *Acta Apostolicae Sedis* 59 (1967): 698.

Both Archbishop Armando Fares of Catanzaro in southern Italy and Cardinal Julius Döpfner, the archbishop of Munich, appealed to the Council of Trent to justify the sacramentality of the diaconate. According to Fares, most authors were convinced that "ministers" in the sixth Tridentine canon on the sacrament of order referred only to deacons. He concluded that the Dogmatic Constitution on the Church could opportunely declare the sacramentality of the diaconate and thus bestow completion on "the structure (*ratio*) of the hierarchical order that is in the church."[26] Cardinal Döpfner, in a speech drafted by Rahner, held that the "tripartite hierarchy," consisting of the "episcopate, presbyterate, and diaconate, is of divine right and in essence characteristic of the church's constitution."[27] Rahner, too, assimilated the "divine ordinance" of the sixth canon with the "divine right" that constitutionally established three ordained ministries.[28] The tripartition of the hierarchy, Döpfner continued, made possible a "stable diaconate" and furnished "those principles, which already until now (*iam hucusque*) were contained in the teaching of the church, especially also in the decrees of the Council of Trent, which, as noted, asserted the sacramentality of the diaconate and also required that the ministries of the diaconate should be exercised only by those who have in fact been constituted in the said order."[29] This statement alluded to the Trent's seventeenth canon of reform of the sacrament of order, which addressed "the functions of holy orders from the diaconate to that of porters." The bishops at Trent demanded that "from now on ministries of this type should be exercised only by those

[26] AS 2/2: 530–31.

[27] AS 2/2: 227. For the fact that Rahner drafted Döpfner's speech, see Herbert Vorgrimler, *Understanding Karl Rahner: An Introduction to His Life and Thought*, trans. John Bowden (New York: Crossroad, 1986), 175; Declan Marmion, "Karl Rahner, Vatican II, and the Shape of the Church," *Theological Studies* 78, no. 1 (March 2017): 30, n. 18.

[28] Rahner, "Diakonat und Diakon," 190.

[29] AS 2/2: 227.

constituted in the said orders."[30] Ministry was therefore ordered and relational. It drew together ministers who shared functions proper to their order.

For Döpfner a stable order of deacons, albeit not ordained, already existed in the church, in effect exercising ecclesiastical office. They should receive, he insisted, "the respective sacramental grace" for a more worthy and more complete exercise of their office.[31] After dismissing the argument that married deacons undermined priestly celibacy, Döpfner asked, "why should sacramental grace, which is present of its own accord, be denied" to all those already exercising diaconal ministry?[32]

Here Rahner's voice spoke again. In 1962, he declared that "the office of deacon exists in the church," while conceding that it existed "anonymously." As proof he pointed to those who served within the church as full-time catechists, welfare workers, and administrators.[33] Conferral of sacramental ordination on these anonymous deacons was therefore opportune, of benefit for those who exercise diaconal office and "for the church itself."[34] The sacramental rite of conferring office finds its "ultimate justification" in the office itself, and not vice versa, Rahner maintained.[35] Diaconal ministry therefore qualified as sacramental.

In written submissions, two conciliar bishops understood the necessary relationship between sacramental ordination and diaconal ministry. Bishop Joseph Nkongolo of Luebo in Congo appreciated the many married men "among the faithful" who demonstrated moral "integrity." He foresaw married deacons as leading "small Christian communities

[30] Tanner, *Decrees*, 2: 750.

[31] AS 2/2: 228.

[32] AS 2/2: 229.

[33] Karl Rahner, "Die Theologie der Ereneuerung des Diakonats," in *Diaconia in Christo: Über die Erneuerung des Diakonates*, ed. Karl Rahner and Herbert Vorgrimler (Freiburg im Breisgau: Herder, 1962), 298.

[34] Rahner, "Die Theologie der Ereneuerung des Diakonats," 300.

[35] Rahner, "Die Theologie der Ereneuerung des Diakonats," 296.

that a priest can visit only rarely." The presence of a deacon in these communities would ensure that they "would not be deprived of any sacred minister, who would be sacramentally appointed for this office (*munus*)."[36] Bishop Charles Herman Helmsing of Kansas City-Saint Joseph, who favored married deacons, believed that "supported with both the sacramental character and grace," deacons "could in the future serve the church much better and more widely."[37] He again echoed Döpfner and Rahner when he wrote:

> The leaders of catechists [operate] in regions where the church is at first planted. If already there exist those aptly qualified as men proven in the cultivation of the interior life and of fraternal charity, what stands in the way of their ordination as deacons, who, empowered by a sacramental character and sacramental grace, similarly may daily better serve the church[?]

Helmsing anticipated the formula chosen by the Doctrinal Commission to convey the sacramentality of the diaconate in *Lumen Gentium*: *gratia sacramentali roborati*.[38]

After *Lumen Gentium*, the conciliar bishops improved their articulation of the sacramentality of the diaconate. The Decree on the Pastoral Office of Bishops in the Church understood that deacons, "ordained for ministry, serve the people of God in communion with the bishop and his presbyterate" (CD 15).[39] Ordination, of course, refers exclusively

[36] AS 2/2: 828.

[37] AS 2/2: 781.

[38] AS 2/2: 781: "Duces catechistarum in regionibus ubi Ecclesia primo plantatur. Si iam sint bene probati uti viri cultu vitae interioris et fraternae caritatis probati, quid prohibet tales ordinari ut diaconi qui similiter charactere sacramenti et gratia sacramentali roborati melius in dies Ecclesiae inserviant."

[39] Tanner, *Decrees*, 2: 926.

to the sacrament of order (CCC 1538).[40] The Decree on the Missionary Activity of the Church recognized "the sacramental grace of the diaconate" (AG 16).[41]

Caution eventually yielded to confidence in asserting the sacramentality of the diaconate, which "has become," as Alphonse Borras observed, "not only a common doctrine but a doctrinal certainty (*une doctrine certaine*) in Catholic theology."[42] Two documents published in concert by the Holy See in 1998 repeatedly demonstrated Borras's point. In English, they are known as the *Basic Norms for the Formation of Permanent Deacons* and the *Directory for the Ministry and Life of Permanent Deacons*. The Congregation for Catholic Education produced the former and the Congregation for the Clergy the latter document to clarify the nature and purpose of the diaconate after an "*explosion*" of ordinations had occasioned "considerable differences in both the initial as well as the ongoing formation of deacons and in the exercise of their ecclesial ministry."[43] One reference to each document will suffice. By "the laying on of hands," the *Basic Norms* stated, the deacon "is sustained by a specific sacramental grace which inserts him into the sacrament of Orders."[44] The *Directory* borrowed phrases from the conciliar articulation of the sacramentality of priests in the Decree on the Ministry and Life of Priests and applied them to deacons: "The Sacrament of Holy Orders confers upon deacons a new consecration to God, through which they are 'consecrated by the anointing of the Holy Spirit and sent by

[40] *Catechism of the Catholic Church*, 2nd ed. (Washington, DC: United States Catholic Conference; Vatican City: Libreria Editrice Vaticana, 2000), 384.

[41] Tanner, *Decrees*, 2: 1026.

[42] Alphonse Borras, *Le diaconat au risque de sa nouveauté* (Brussels: Éditions Lessius, 2007), 87.

[43] Enzo Petrolino, *Il Concilio Vaticano II e il Diaconato: La Chiesa mistero di commune e di servizio* (Vatican City: Libreria Editrice Vaticana, 2013), 59, emphasis in the original.

[44] *Basic Norms*, no. 4 in *Basic Norms/Directory*, 24.

Christ' [PO 12] into the service of the people of God for the building up of the body of Christ (Eph 4:12)."[45] Eliding the sacramentality of priests and deacons presupposes a sacramental, ministerial communion between them.

The ordination rite for deacons serves as an ideal, although only recently investigated, "source for a theology of the diaconate," and especially its sacramentality.[46] At an ordination, the local church at prayer invokes the Holy Spirit, whose self-gift is the sacramental grace that empowers ordained ministers to serve the people of God. The graced ministry of deacons competes, as this chapter will show, with an ancient formula of diaconal ministry that separates it from priesthood and subordinates it to the episcopate. This separation, and especially this subordination, risks a *Geistvergessenheit*, a forgetting of the self-gift of the Spirit to deacons at the cost of function, namely a diaconal extension of episcopal ministry. The best way to remedy this forgetfulness of grace is a theological reassertion of the grace of the diaconate. Deacons are Christ's heralds, as the ordination rite makes clear.[47] Their ministry, not specified in the epiclesis of the rite, opens them to the freedom of the Spirit as discerned by a local church.

[45] Congregation for the Clergy, "Directorium pro ministerio et vita diaconorum permanentium," *Acta Apostolicae Sedis* 90 (1998): 904, no. 44. Here and in other references to the *Directorium* and the *Ratio fundamentalis* (*Basic Norms*), I preferred my translation as more accurate than that of *Basic Norms/Directory*. I supplied in square brackets the reference to PO 12. For the passage in PO 12, see Tanner, *Decrees*, 2: 1057.

[46] Klemens Ambrunster and Matthias Mühl, "Geweiht für was? – Die Weihe des Bischofs, der Priester und der Diakone. Ein Vergleich," in *Bereit wozu? Geweiht für was? Zur Diskussion um den ständigen Diakonat*, ed. Klemens Ambrunster and Matthias Mühl (Freiburg im Breisgau: Herder, 2009), 122.

[47] *Pontificale Romanum ex decreto sacrosancti oecumenici Concilii Vaticani II renovatum auctoritate Pauli PP. VI editum Ioannis Pauli PP. II cura recognitum: De ordinatione episcopi, presbyterorum et diaconorum*, 2nd ed. (1990; repr., Vatican City: Libreria Editrice Vaticana, 2011), 125, no. 210 (ordination of more than one deacon); 139, no. 238 (ordination of one deacon).

Liturgical Prayer in and for the Spirit

The official prayer of the church is a *locus pneumaticus*, a presence of the Holy Spirit among the people of God. To give priority to the church as this people or as the "mystical body of Christ, which is primarily constituted through the unity of the justified in the Holy Spirit" over the church as a social institution, has consequences for its liturgical life, according to Rahner.[48] Its liturgy "encompasses not merely external ceremony, but all the grace and glory that must be ascribed to it, that belongs to the church as a whole, if it is more than a juridical organization."[49] Rahner insisted: "The officially ordered prayer of the church as a society can only be the ordering of the prayer of the church as the people of God in the Holy Spirit." Liturgical prayer depends on "a pneumatic reality of the capacity for prayer" and on "prayer as the ground of possibility."[50] Rahner identified this prayer as "the prayer of the people of God and the body of Christ," the prayer which makes liturgical prayer possible, just as grace makes possible the sacraments.[51] The Spirit bestows sacramental grace on deacons and on all ordained ministers in and through the rite of ordination, which the prayerful people of God makes its prayer by virtue of the Spirit. A rite devised by a committee of liturgical experts becomes a pneumatic event when a local church community prays for the Spirit's self-gift upon those whom the Spirit chooses as the Spirit's own ministers of Christ.

Officially published in 1968, a revised rite of ordination of deacons, priests, and bishops appeared as the first

[48] Karl Rahner, "Das Gebet des Einzelnen und die Liturgie der Kirche," in *Strukturen christlicher Existenz: Beiträge zur Erneuerung des geistlichen Lebens*, ed. H. Schlier, E. von Severus, J. Sudbrack, and A. Pereira (Würzburg: Echter-Verlag, 1968), 196.

[49] Rahner, "Das Gebet des Einzelnen und die Liturgie der Kirche," 196.

[50] Rahner, "Das Gebet des Einzelnen und die Liturgie der Kirche," 196.

[51] Rahner, "Das Gebet des Einzelnen und die Liturgie der Kirche," 196.

post-conciliar "liturgical book."[52] Dissatisfaction soon emerged with this Roman Pontifical. Critics drew attention to "a series of terminological imprecisions," an ascent of orders from deacon to bishop that missed the descent of orders beginning with the bishop, and the consecratory prayer for priests that emphasized the Old Testament notion of priesthood at the expense of Christ's high priesthood.[53] After an intermittent and therefore protracted process of revision that began in 1973, a final text was ready in June 1988, which Pope John Paul II approved on May 10, 1989. The Vatican Press published the new Pontifical one year later.[54]

Prefatory remarks (*praenotanda*) and a reversed order in ordination rites represented the immediately obvious features of change in the new Pontifical. The instructions for all ordinations (*praenoanda generalia*) drew attention to the conspicuous conferral of "the gift of the Holy Spirit by the laying on of hands and by the consecratory prayer (*Prece Ordinationis*)."[55] The laying on of hands may not be omitted and the consecratory prayer is inalterable.[56] According to Pierre Jounel, beginning with episcopal and ending with diaconal ordinations removed the impression of an ascent through clerical ranks and emphasized the role of the bishop as the leader of the local church.[57] The decree from the Congregation for Divine Worship and the Discipline of the Sacraments, dated June 29, 1989, and inserted as a preface in the new Roman Pontifical, offered a different explanation,

[52] Jerzy Stefanski, "Die römischen Ordinationsriten von 1968 and 1990: Eine geschichtlich-liturgische Studie," trans. Sebastian Zgraja, in *Manifestatio Ecclesiae: Studien zu Pontifikale und bischöflicher Liturgie*, ed. Winfried Haunerland, Otto Mittermeier, Monika Selle, and Wolfgang Steck (Regensburg: Verlag Friedrich Pustet, 2004), 148.

[53] Stefanski, "Die römischen Ordinationsriten von 1968 and 1990," 149.

[54] Stefanski, "Die römischen Ordinationsriten von 1968 and 1990," 149–55.

[55] *Pontificale Romanum* (1990), 2, no. 6.

[56] *Pontificale Romanum* (1990), 3, no. 11f.

[57] Pierre Jounel, "La nouvelle édition typique du rituel des ordinations," *La Maison-Dieu* 186 (1991): 9.

suggesting an all-absorbing episcopal ministry: "The arrangement of the book has been altered so that, at first, beginning with the bishop, who has the fullness of sacred order, it might be better understood how presbyters are his collaborators (*cooperatores*) and deacons are ordained for his service (*ad eius ministerium*)."[58]

Textual changes in the ordination prayers for priests and deacons, the decree indicated, will provide those chosen for ordination and the rest of Christ's faithful with "a richer idea of the presbyterate and diaconate, inasmuch as they flow forth from Christ the priest (*a Christo sacerdote*)."[59] That deacons, as well as priests, should derive their sacramental identity from Christ the priest seems surprising, given the adoption in LG 29 of the ancient formula that deacons are ordained *non ad sacerdotium, sed ad ministerium* ("not for the priesthood, but for ministry").[60] While textual changes to the ordination prayer for deacons were slight,[61] the decree understated the significance of changes to corresponding prayer for priests. The latter prayer gained in pneumatological and christological import. Jounel observed: "Ministers of Christ to sanctify his people and to make his message reach every part of the world, priests are men of the Spirit."[62]

The experience of a stable diaconate has registered little effect on the ordination rite. A correspondence between the church's prayer and "a tradition of lived experience of the diaconate as a permanent order within the Church" could not have existed in 1968.[63] That correspondence remained limited in 1990, after a generation of the ordination of married men. While the first post-conciliar Roman Pontifical did not distinguish between married and celibate *ordinandi*,

[58] *Pontificale Romanum* (1990), iii, no. 2.

[59] *Pontificale Romanum* (1990), iv, no. 3.

[60] Tanner, *Decrees*, 2: 874.

[61] Jounel, "La nouvelle édition typique du rituel des ordinations," 11.

[62] Jounel, "La nouvelle édition typique du rituel des ordinations," 21.

[63] Susan K. Wood, *Sacramental Orders* (Collegeville, MN: Liturgical Press, 2000), 148–49.

the promise of celibacy that unmarried men make before the ordaining bishop in accordance with the rite published in 1990 elicited recommendations for adding a promise of commitment to their marriage by married deacons.[64]

For all the emphasis in the ecclesial discourse on the diaconate as a ministry especially dedicated to the poor, the ordination rites of 1968 and 1990 made only a glancing reference to this presumably defining aspect of diaconal ministry. The post-conciliar ordination prayer for a deacon is, as Susan Wood pointed out, "essentially the ancient consecratory prayer of the Sacramentary of Verona (fifth or sixth century)."[65] Interpolated into this ancient prayer, a modern petition expresses the wish that "care for the sick and also the poor might overflow" in deacons.[66] That petition is the

[64] Franz Kohlschein, "'Sende auf sie herab den Heiligen Gest . . .': Zur Ordination der Diakone in der Kirche," *Liturgisches Jahrbuch* 46, no. 2 (1990): 85–86; Jan Michael Joncas, "The Public Language of Ministry Revisited: *De Ordinatione Episcopi, Presbyterorum et Diaconorum* 1990," *Worship* 68, no. 5 (September 1994): 395; Helmut Hoping, "Der dreifache Tischdienst des Diakons und die Einheit des Ordosakraments: Theologische Beobachtungen zur Liturgie der Diakonenweihe," in *Manifestatio Ecclesiae: Studien zu Pontifikale und bischöflicher Liturgie*, 198; W. Shawn McKnight, *Understanding the Diaconate: Historical, Theological, and Sociological Foundations* (Washington, DC: The Catholic University of America Press, 2018), 267; William T. Ditewig, *Courageous Humility: Reflections on the Church, Diakonia, and Deacons* (New York: Paulist Press, 2022), 176, 178.

[65] Wood, *Sacramental Orders*, 156.

[66] *Pontificale Romanum ex decreto sacrosancti oecumenici Concilii Vaticani II instauratum auctoritate Pauli PP. VI promulgatum: De ordinatione diaconi, presbyteri et episcopi* (Vatican City: Libreria Editrice Vaticana, 1968), 26, no. 21; *Pontificale Romanum* (1990), 122, no 207: "Abundet in eis evangelicae forma virtutis, dilectio sine simulatione, sollicitudo infirmorum ac pauperorum, auctorias modesta, innocentiae puritas et spiritualis observantia disciplinae." The relevant passage in the Verona Sacramentary reads: "Abundet in eis totius forma uirtutis, auctoritas modesta, pudor constans, innocentiae puritas et spiritalis obseruantia disciplinae." See Leo Cunibert Mohlberg, ed., *Sacramentarium Veronense*, 2nd ed. (Rome: Herder, 1966), 121.

only reference in the ordination rite to a diaconal ministry of charity.

In German-speaking countries, the Pontifical adds a question in the ordaining bishop's examination of candidates for the diaconate: "Are you resolved to support the sick and the poor and to help migrants and the destitute?"[67] This question in the German liturgy approximates the question prescribed by the Roman Pontificals in 1968 and 1990 in the ordination of a bishop: "Are you resolved to show kindness and mercy to the poor and to migrants and to all the destitute because of the name of the Lord?"[68] Since the German liturgy poses the same question about care for the sick, the poor, the migrants, and the destitute to prospective priests and deacons, Winfried Haunerland held that the ministry of charity "can scarcely express a special emphasis of diaconal office."[69] Alternatively, a common commitment to serving the poor made by bishops, priests, and deacons at their ordinations would express the communion of ordained ministry in the leadership of a church for the poor that must also become a church of the poor in faithfulness to its sacramental expression of Christ's liberative communion with the poor.[70]

[67] Quoted in Hoping, "Der dreifache Tischdienst des Diakons und die Einheit des Ordosakraments," 192: "Seid ihr bereit, den Armen und Kranken beizustehen und den Heimatlosen und Notleidenden zu helfen?"

[68] *Pontificale Romanum* (1968), 66, no. 19; *Pontificale Romanum* (1990), 14, no. 40: "Vis pauperibus et peregrinis omnibusque indigentibus propter nomen Domini affabilem et misericordiam te praebere?"

[69] Winfried Haunerland, "Das Amt des Diakons nach den Zeugnissen der römischen Liturgie," in *Der Diakonat: Geschichte und Theologie*, ed. Manfred Hauke and Helmut Hoping (Regensburg: Verlag Friedrich Pustet, 2019), 93.

[70] Ignacio Ellacuría, "The Church of the Poor: Historical Sacrament of Liberation," trans. Margaret D. Wilde, in Ignacio Ellacuría, *Essays on History, Liberation, and Salvation*, ed. Michael E. Lee (Maryknoll, NY: Orbis Books, 2013), 228–53.

The common structure of the post-conciliar ordination rites for bishops, priests, and deacons evinces, as scholars have observed, the unity of the three ordained ministries in the one sacrament of order.[71] Theologically, the most important shared element is the epiclesis, as Helmut Hoping has noted.[72] The petition for the bestowal of the Holy Spirit on those to be ordained constitutes the form of the sacrament in all three rites. The epiclesis belongs to the consecratory prayer, which follows the laying on of hands, the matter of the sacrament.

In the pre-conciliar ordination rites, only the consecratory prayers for deacons and priests had an epiclesis with an explicit reference to the Holy Spirit. The epiclesis remained unchanged in the post-conciliar rites. In the ordination rite for a deacon, the bishop prayed and prays: "Send upon him, we ask, Lord, the Holy Spirit, so that by the gift of your sevenfold grace [the Spirit] may empower him to carry out faithfully the work of ministry."[73] Invoking the Spirit for a priest, the ordaining bishop prayed and prays: "Grant, we ask, almighty Father, to this your servant the dignity of a presbyter. Renew in his heart the Spirit of holiness. May he worthily hold the office, received from you, God, and may

[71] Matthieu Cnudde, "L'ordination des diacres," *La Maison-Dieu* 98 (1969): 83; Otto Nußbaum, "Theologie und Ritus der Diakonenweihe," in *Der Diakon: Wiederentdeckung und Erneuerung seines Dienstes*, ed. Josef G. Plöger and Hermann Johann Weber (Freiburg im Breisgau: Herder, 1980), 136; Stefanski, "Die römischen Ordinationsriten von 1968 and 1990," 145; Wood, *Sacramental Orders*, 149; Hoping, "Der dreifache Tischdienst des Diakons und die Einheit des Ordosakraments," 200.

[72] Hoping, "Der dreifache Tischdienst des Diakons und die Einheit des Ordosakraments," 199–201.

[73] Manlio Sodi and Alessandro Toniolo, eds., *Pontificale Romanum: Editio Typica, 1961–1962* (Vatican City: Libreria Editirice Vaticana, 2008), 43; *Pontificale Romanum* (1968), 84, no. 21; *Pontificale Romanum* (1990), 138, no. 235.

he gain the esteem of good character by the example of his conduct."[74]

In the post-conciliar Roman Pontifical, the consecratory prayer for the bishop underwent a considerable change. The new rite replaced the pre-conciliar prayer with the consecratory prayer of a bishop from the *Apostolic Tradition*, a church order consisting of layers of thinking from the second to the fourth centuries.[75] In 1947, Pius XII had designated the following petition, which alluded to the Holy Spirit metaphorically as the "dew of heavenly anointing," as the form of the sacrament: "Complete in your priest the supremacy of your ministry and with the dew of heavenly anointing sanctify him, equipped with the ornaments of all glorification."[76] In the post-conciliar rite of the ordination of a bishop, the prayer recovered from the *Apostolic Tradition* included an unmistakably obvious epiclesis, appropriate for episcopal sacramentality: "And now, pour out upon this chosen one that power, which is from you, the governing Spirit (*Spiritum principalem*), whom you gave to your beloved Son Jesus Christ, whom he bestowed on the holy apostles, who have constituted the church in each and every place as your sanctuary for the glory and unfailing praise of your name."[77] According to Bernard Botte, the Holy Spirit as *Spiritus principalis* corresponds to the bishop as "the leader of the church."[78]

[74] Sodi and Toniolo, *Pontificale Romanum*, 43; *Pontificale Romanum* (1968), 92, no. 22; *Pontificale Romanum* (1990), 93, no. 159.

[75] Paul F. Bradshaw, *Rites of Ordination: Their History and Theology* (Collegeville, MN: Liturgical Press, 2013), 58.

[76] Pius XII, "Sacramentum Ordinis," 7, no. 5; Sodi and Toniolo, *Pontificale Romanum*, 72.

[77] Hippolytus of Rome, *La tradition apostolique d'après les anciennes versions*, 2nd ed., rev., trans. and ed. Bernard Botte, Sources Chrétiennes vol. 11/2 (Paris: Les Éditions du Cerf, 1984), 44; *Pontificale Romanum* (1968), 75, no. 26; *Pontificale Romanum* (1990), 24–25, no. 47.

[78] Bernard Botte, "'Spiritus principalis' (formule de l'ordination épiscopale)," *Notitiae* 100 (December 1974): 411. Paul Bradshaw has translated the reference to the Spirit as "the princely Spirit" and "the spirit of leadership."

The epicletic reform of the ordination rite for bishops makes liturgically evident a "communion of the Holy Spirit" (2 Cor 13:13) among ordained ministers. This communion is vertical and horizontal. Vertically, as Joseph Komonchak explained, "the invocation of the Holy Spirit . . . in an ordination symbolizes the Church's conviction that it does not derive its life from itself but from Christ and the Spirit and that the ministries which communicate, sustain, develop, and express its life derive their power, not from the community and not from the individuals selected, but from God."[79] Sacramental grace, the gift of the Spirit, empowers ordained ministers for a horizontal communion of service to the people of God. Ministry, or office in the church, is a charism, as Rahner insisted. "The charismatic" or "the supra-official" of ministry designates it as graced, and thus Catholics usually speak of "the support (*Beistand*) of the Holy Spirit for office and its bearers."[80] Put differently, from an Orthodox perspective, John Zizioulas wrote that the "*immediacy* of divine action in ordination is what safeguards the charismatic nature of the ministry."[81] Bishops, priests, and deacons all minister by virtue of the Spirit, by virtue of grace or of the "immediacy of divine action" in the sacrament of order. Their ministerial "communion of the Holy Spirit" (2 Cor 13:13) ought to serve as the theological foundation for the question asked in the rite of ordination for a

---

See Paul F. Bradshaw, *Ordination Rites of the Ancient Churches of East and West* (New York: Pueblo Publishing Company, 1990), 107 ("the princely Spirit"); and Paul F. Bradshaw, Maxwell E. Johnson, and L. Edward Phillips, *The Apostolic Tradition: A Commentary*, ed. Harold W. Attridge (Minneapolis: Fortress Press, 2002), 30; Bradshaw, *Rites of Ordination*, 62 ("the spirit of leadership").

[79] Joseph A. Komonchak, "The Permanent Diaconate and the Variety of Ministries in the Church," *Diaconal Quarterly* 4, no. 1 (1978): 19.

[80] Karl Rahner, *Das Dynamische in der Kirche* (Freiburg im Breisgau: Herder, 1959), 40.

[81] John D. Zizioulas, *Being as Communion: Studies in Personhood and the Church* (Crestwood, NY: St. Vladimir's Seminary Press, 1985), 219, emphasis in the original.

bishop: "Are you resolved to cherish and lead into the way of salvation the holy people of God with your fellow ministers (*cum comministris tuis*), the presbyters and deacons?"[82] The three ministries are ecclesially interrelational and interdependent.[83]

At its fullest extent, the "communion of the Holy Spirit" (2 Cor 13:13) is the communion of the baptized. Ministerial communion exists only within ecclesial communion. For Komonchak, the ordination of deacons made ultimate sense owing to "the conviction that the fellowship of the Holy Spirit cannot be ministered to except in and through the power of the Spirit."[84] When, led by the ordaining bishop, the people of God prays for the Spirit to empower a deacon "to carry out faithfully the work of ministry," all the baptized expect that graced ministry to be fruitful among and for them.

The Gift and Gifts of the Spirit

The gift of God's "sevenfold grace" by which the Holy Spirit empowers deacons for ministry is a rare liturgical reference to the seven gifts of the Spirit. Commenting on another liturgical reference point, the medieval hymn *Veni, Sancte Spiritus* intended to be sung at Mass on Pentecost, Alfred Delp, the Jesuit martyr, called the Spirit "the dispenser . . . of the so often forgotten, of the unknown seven gifts of the Holy Spirit." Delp equated the seven gifts with "the equipping of the human person with new capabilities and skills for living."[85] Sung at an episcopal ordination in

[82] *Pontificale Romanum* (1968), 66, no. 19; *Pontificale Romanum* (1990), 13, no. 40.

[83] Zizioulas, *Being as Communion*, 222.

[84] Komonchak, "The Permanent Diaconate," *Diaconal Quarterly* 4, no. 1 (1978): 22.

[85] Alfred Delp, "Veni Sancte Spiritus," in Alfred Delp, *Gesammelte Schriften*, vol. 4, ed. Roman Bleistein (Frankfurt am Main: Verlag Josef Knecht, 1984), 267.

accordance with Roman Pontifical of 1990, the hymn *Veni, Creator Spiritus* acclaims the Spirit as "sevenfold in gift."[86] As the bishop extended his hands towards those about to receive the sacrament of confirmation in the rite before the Second Vatican Council, he prayed for God to send upon them "your sevenfold Spirit, the Holy Paraclete, from heaven." Quoting the Vulgate version of Isaiah 11:2-3, he specified: "the Spirit of wisdom and of understanding," "the Spirit of counsel and of fortitude," "the Spirit of knowledge and of piety," and "the Spirit of the fear of the Lord."[87] The revised rite of confirmation of 1971 left out the reference to piety, presumably in a faithful translation of the original Hebrew text, which does not mention this gift.[88]

Of course, the Spirit is gift both within and of the Trinity. As a substantial relation, the Spirit is the self-giving communion in love of the Father and of the Son, a trinitarian communion revealed to the church for the church to be the loving communion of the baptized. Augustine, the great proponent of the Holy Spirit as the self-giving gift of love between Father and Son, wrote in *De Trinitate* (5.14.15): "the

[86] *Pontificale Romanum* (1990), 9, no. 35; 37, no. 71; 227 (text of the hymn). The rubrics of the 1968 ordination rite for more than one priest or for one priest called for the singing of the *Veni, Creator Spiritus* as a priest was invested with his stole and as the bishop anointed the priest's hands. For an ordination of one or more bishops the rubrics expressly mentioned only the hymn, *Te Deum laudamus*, appointed to follow the post-Communion prayer. See *Pontificale Romanum* (1968), 44, no. 25 (for more than one priest); 102, no. 29 (for one priest); 77, no. 38 (for one bishop); 112, no. 38 (for more than one bishop).

[87] Sodi and Toniolo, *Pontificale Romanum*, 9–10.

[88] At the laying on of hands in the post-conciliar rite of confirmation, the bishop prays: "Give them the spirit of wisdom and understanding, the spirit of right judgment and courage, the spirit of knowledge and reverence. Fill them with the spirit of wonder and awe in your presence." Clearly, "wonder and awe" extend the concept of "reverence," a modern equivalent for "fear of the Lord." See International Commission on English in the Liturgy, *The Rites of the Catholic Church: Study Edition*, 2 vols. (Collegeville, MN: Liturgical Press, 1990), 1: 490.

Holy *Spirit* is called not only [the Spirit] *of the Father and of the Son* who gave [the Spirit], but ours too, who have received [the Spirit]."[89] As communion, the Spirit for Augustine "has a fundamentally ecclesiological meaning,"[90] to quote Joseph Ratzinger. The church, "a creation of the Spirit,"[91] has received the Spirit whom the Father and the Son have given. Pneumatology and ecclesiology converge.[92] The Spirit is in the gifts for the church.[93]

Thomas Aquinas understood the seven gifts of the Holy Spirit as divinely inspired perfections that render human beings capable of responding to the promptings of God, or of the Spirit, *prompte*—readily or eagerly.[94] With these gifts as *habitus*, or abiding dispositions, human beings, through whom the Spirit acts, freely act as the Spirit's instruments.[95] Since the Spirit's gifts "govern" (*regulant*) the virtues, these gifts exceed them in spiritual value.[96] They are necessary for salvation because, more than and beyond reason, they dispose human beings to the guidance of the Spirit towards

[89] CCSL 50: 223: "*spiritus* sanctus non tantum *patris et filii* qui dederunt, sed etiam noster dicitur qui accepimus," emphasis in the original.

[90] Joseph Ratzinger, "The Holy Spirit as Communio: Concerning the Relationship of Pneumatology and Spirituality in Augustine," trans. Peter Casarella, *Communio* 25, no. 2 (Summer 1998): 327.

[91] Ratzinger, "The Holy Spirit as Communio," 325.

[92] Ratzinger, "The Holy Spirit as Communio," 327.

[93] Ratzinger, "The Holy Spirit as Communio," 334–35.

[94] Thomas Aquinas, *Summa Theologiae*, 1a2ae, q. 68, art. 1, art. 3, art. 4. See Thomas Aquinas, *Summa Theologiae*, vol. 24: *The Gifts of the Spirit (Ia2ae. 68–70)*, trans. and ed. Edward D. O'Connor (1974; repr., Cambridge: Cambridge University Press, 2006), 8–9, 18–19, 20–21.

[95] Thomas Aquinas, *Summa Theologiae*, 1a2ae, q. 68, art. 2, obj. 2, ad 2. See Thomas Aquinas, *Summa Theologiae*, vol. 24: *The Gifts of the Spirit (Ia2ae. 68-70)*, 18.

[96] Thomas Aquinas, *Summa Theologiae*, 1a2ae, q. 68, art. 8. See Thomas Aquinas, *Summa Theologiae*, vol. 24: *The Gifts of the Spirit (Ia2ae. 68-70)*, 38.

"the final supernatural end" of salvation.[97] Interdependent, the seven gifts "refresh each other."[98] Consequently, liturgical prayer conceives of and requests all seven gifts together.

In accordance with the theology of Aquinas, the church in its liturgy prays for deacons as reliable instruments of the Spirit, responsive to the Spirit's promptings in and for ecclesial ministry. The Spirit's gifts are not simply for the salvation of individuals but for persons as members of the ecclesial communion bound in duty to it.[99] For the work of ministry, deacons require the intellectual dispositions of wisdom, understanding, and knowledge to grasp conceptually and with insight what a given ministry demands. With counsel and strength, they make prudent ministerial decisions and carry them out. Piety and fear of the Lord orient deacons to God, whose Spirit empowers them for ministry. But precisely because the Spirit's gifts are for ministry, they orient deacons to their fellow human beings in need. The material and spiritual relief offered by deacons mediate grace, and thus their *diaconia*, an expression of the sacramentality of the diaconate, becomes salvific.

Two messianic figures serve as examples for deacons as Spirit-prompted ministers, equipped with discernment and committed to a divine mission for the poor. First, the resting of the manifold Spirit on the messianic shoot growing out of the stump of Jesse yielded this assessment of God's anointed: "He shall not judge by what his eyes see, or decide by what his ears hear; but with righteousness he shall judge

[97] Thomas Aquinas, *Summa Theologiae*, 1a2ae, q. 68, art. 2. See Thomas Aquinas, *Summa Theologiae*, vol. 24: *The Gifts of the Spirit (Ia2ae. 68-70)*, 14.

[98] Thomas Aquinas, *Summa Theologiae*, 1a2ae, q. 68, art. 5. See Thomas Aquinas, *Summa Theologiae*, vol. 24: *The Gifts of the Spirit (Ia2ae. 68-70)*, 24.

[99] Michael Schmaus, "Gaben des Heiligen Geistes," in *Sacramentum Mundi: Theologisches Lexikon für die Praxis*, ed. Karl Rahner et al., vol. 2 (Freiburg im Breisgau: Herder, 1968), col. 153.

the poor, and decide with equity for the meek of the earth" (Isa 11:3-4). Reading aloud from Isaiah in the synagogue, Jesus made the prophetic anointing of God's Spirit his own and thus understood that the Spirit empowered him "to bring good news to the poor . . . to proclaim release to the captives and recovery to the sight of the blind, to let the oppressed go free, to proclaim the year of the Lord's favor" (Luke 4:18-19).

A recognition of the empowerment of deacons by the self-gift and gifts of the Spirit raises a problem that the ordination rite does not address and suggests an interpretation of diaconal ministry at odds with a pneumatic diaconate. The rite does not concretely apply the "sevenfold grace" to ministerial activity. More vexingly, the proposed homily of the rite resonates with an ancient and enduring emphasis on the subordination of deacons to priests and especially to their bishop that risks diminishing the significance of the grace of the diaconate.

Non ad sacerdotium, sed ad ministerium

The consecratory prayer for deacons affords little insight into what constitutes the work of ministry, mentioned in the epiclesis. The petition immediately preceding the epiclesis places diaconal office in apposition with liturgical ministry: "Look kindly, we ask, Lord, also on these your servants, whom we humbly dedicate as future ministers at your altars for the office of the diaconate."[100] After the epiclesis, the consecratory prayer identifies dispositions in which deacons should overflow or excel, dispositions that correspond to the gifts of piety and of counsel, but do not specify functions beyond ministry to the sick and the

[100] *Pontificale Romanum* (1968), 26, no. 21; *Pontificale Romanum* (1990), 122, no. 207: "Super hos quoque famulos tuos, quaesumus, Domine, placatus intende, quos tuis sacris altaribus servituros in officium diaconii suppliciter dedicamus."

poor: "In them may overflow the pattern of evangelical virtue, love without pretense, care for the sick and also the poor, prudential authority (*auctoritas modesta*), purity of innocence, and the observance of spiritual discipline."[101] The prayer continues by positioning deacons as worthy of imitation: "May your commandments be resplendent in their way of life so that by the example of their conduct they may obtain the imitation of the holy people."[102] Emphasizing their exemplary status, the prayer does not indicate a decisive ministerial outlet for the qualities that the church wishes to admire in deacons.

The consecratory prayer also raises the problem of whose work of ministry deacons will and must faithfully discharge. The earliest ordination rite of deacons appeared in the *Apostolic Tradition*, which, according to Gregory Dix, launched "an attack on deacons."[103] It stipulated: "In ordaining a

[101] *Pontificale Romanum* (1990), 122, no. 207. The revised consecratory prayer gives a Christian expression of diaconal virtue in conformity with the gospel (*evangelicae forma virtutis*), whereas in 1968, the consecratory prayer, in accordance with the Verona Sacramentary, referred to *totius forma virtutis*—"the pattern of all virtue." See *Pontificale Romanum* (1968), 26, no. 21; Mohlberg, ed., *Sacramentarium Veronense*, 121. The usual English translation of *auctoritas modesta* in the ordination rite renders *modesta* modestly: "unassuming authority." See International Commission on English in the Liturgy, *The Rites of the Catholic Church*, 2: 35. But for Cicero *modestia* was a virtue akin to prudence. In the *De Officiis* (1.40), he called it *scientia opportunitatis idoneorum ad agendum temporum*—"the science of doing the right thing at the right time." See Marcus Tullius Cicero, *De Officiis*, trans. Walter Miller (London: William Heinemann; New York: G. P. Putnam's Sons, 1928), 146, 147. I quoted Miller's translation.

[102] *Pontificale Romanum* (1990), 122, no. 207. In recognition that deacons can be married ministers, the revised rite substituted exemplary chastity with a more general exemplary behavior. Chastity, of course, is a virtue for all people, but often its association is with celibacy. The petition in 1968 read: "In moribus eorum praecepta tua fulgeant, ut suae castitatis exemplo imitationem sanctae plebis acquirant." See *Pontificale Romanum* (1968), 26.

[103] Gregory Dix, ed., *The Treatise on the Apostolic Tradition of St. Hippolytus of Rome, Bishop and Martyr*, rev. ed. (London: S.P.C.K., 1968), xxxv.

deacon, only the bishop lays on hands since he is ordained not in the priesthood, but in the ministry of the bishop (*non in sacerdotio ordinatur, sed in ministerio episcopi*), so that he should do what he is commanded by him."[104] Presumably, since the diaconate was not a priestly order, deacons did not participate in the advisory body of the clergy, suggesting, as Paul Bradshaw, Maxwell Johnson, and L. Edward Phillips have commented, that they did not belong to the clergy.[105] A deacon, according to the *Apostolic Tradition*, did not receive "the common spirit of the presbyterate . . . but whatever has been entrusted [to him] under the power of the bishop."[106] The consecratory prayer in the *Apostolic Tradition* presented the deacon as a minister of the church, however, and not of the bishop, for it called upon God: "bestow your Holy Spirit of grace and solicitude and diligence upon this your servant, whom you have chosen to serve (*ministrare*) your church."[107] The prayer did not specify the deacon's ecclesial ministry, however.[108]

The *Statuta ecclesiae antiqua* of late fifth-century Gaul borrowed from the description of diaconal ministry in the *Apostolic Tradition*. It decreed: "When a deacon is ordained, only the bishop, who blesses him, lays a hand upon his head, since he is consecrated not for the priesthood but for ministry (*non ad sacerdotium sed ad ministerium*)."[109] Unlike the *Apostolic Tradition*, however, the Gallic *Statutes* did not specify that a deacon was ordained for the ministry of the bishop. The suppression of the reference to the bishop as the object of diaconal ministry in the *Statutes* reflected the priestly author's suspicions about "the excesses of episcopal

[104] Hippolytus of Rome, *La tradition apostolique*, 58.

[105] Hippolytus of Rome, *La tradition apostolique*, 60; Bradshaw, Johnson, and Phillips, *The Apostolic Tradition: A Commentary*, 65.

[106] Hippolytus of Rome, *La tradition apostolique*, 60.

[107] Hippolytus of Rome, *La tradition apostolique*, 62.

[108] Bradshaw, Johnson, and Phillips, *The Apostolic Tradition: A Commentary*, 65–66.

[109] CCSL 148: 181.

monarchy" and signaled that a deacon was "the priest's servant" as well as that of the bishop.[110] An earlier canon in the *Statutes* explained: "A deacon should know that he is as much the servant of the presbyter as of the bishop."[111] Three more canons reinforced "the deacon's subordination to the priest."[112] A deacon was obliged to obtain the permission of a presbyter to distribute the Eucharist "when a presbyter was present" and, "if necessity demanded" it, to sit where a presbyter indicated, and to speak when questioned "in an assembly of presbyters."[113] By distinguishing *sacerdotium* and *ministerium*, ancient church orders invested the priesthood with theological significance while denying it to ministry.[114]

The homily proposed for the bishop to preach at the ordination of deacons in the rite mandated after the Second Vatican Council perpetuates the ancient Christian perspective of diaconal subordination. Speaking of deacons to the people of God, the bishop teaches: "Empowered by the gift of the Holy Spirit, they offer help (*adiumentum*) to the bishop and his presbyterate in the ministry of the word, of the altar, and of charity, presenting themselves as the servants of all."[115] Another allusion to the sacrament of order implied that deacons served the bishop and the pastor of a parish: "Consecrated by the imposition of hands, handed down from ancient times (*inde*) by the apostles and bound more

[110] Bernard Botte, "Le Rituel d'ordination des Statuta Ecclesiae antiqua," *Recherches de théologie ancienne et médiévale* 11 (July 1939): 227, 228.

[111] CCSL 148: 175: "Diaconus ita se presbyteri ut episcopi ministrum nouerit."

[112] Botte, "Le Rituel d'ordination des Statuta Ecclesiae antiqua," 227.

[113] CCSL 148: 176.

[114] Paul De Clerck, "Note sur l'expression *non ad sacerdoctium, sed ad ministerium (episcopi)*: De l'évolution du sens des mots et des choses," *La Maison-Dieu* 249 (2007): 58–59.

[115] *Pontificale Romanum* (1968), 14, no. 14; *Pontificale Romanum* (1990), 105, no. 199.

closely to the altar, they will fulfill the ministry of charity in the name of the bishop or of the parish priest."[116]

LG 29 resuscitated the ancient formula *non ad sacerdotium, sed ad ministerium*. Thus, in 1964, the Second Vatican Council restored a phrase that the Sacred Congregation of Rites had in 1950 removed from the rubric of the rite of diaconal ordination that instructed the bishop to lay his hand on the head of the ordinand.[117] Furthermore, in the relevant footnote (74), *Lumen Gentium* referred perplexingly not to the *Statuta ecclesiae antiqua* but to another ancient church order, the fourth-century *Constitutiones ecclesiae aegyptiacae*.[118] Following the *Apostolic Tradition*, these Egyptian *Constitutions* answered the question why the ordaining bishop alone lays hands on the deacon. Reproducing the answer of the *Apostolic Tradition*, the *Constitutions* explained: "This is the reason: he should be ordained not for the priesthood, but for the ministry of the bishop, so that he might do those things that are enjoined upon him."[119]

It seems that *Lumen Gentium* deliberately chose only what it wanted from the statement in the *Constitutions*, but the Doctrinal Commission suggested otherwise. The Second Vatican Council formally adopted *Lumen Gentium* at its fifth public session on November 21, 1964. Four days earlier, on November 17, the Doctrinal Commission responded in a *Relatio generalis* to comments on and proposals for a revision of chapter 3 of *Lumen Gentium* on the ecclesiastical hierarchy. The *Relatio* stated: "Two Fathers consider the phrase *non ad sacerdotium sed ad ministerium* to be ambiguous, for

[116] *Pontificale Romanum* (1968), 14, no. 14; *Pontificale Romanum* (1990), 106, no. 199.

[117] Bruno Kleinmeyer, "Der Diakon im Lichte der römischen Weiheliturgie," in *Diaconia in Christo: Über die Erneuerung des Diakonates*, ed. Karl Rahner and Herbert Vorgrimler (Freiburg im Breisgau: Herder, 1962), 80.

[118] AS 3/8: 810.

[119] Franz Xaver Funk, ed., *Didascalia et constitutiones apostolorum*, vol. 2: *Testimonia et scripturae propinquae* (Paderborn: Ferdinand Schoeningh, 1905), 103.

priesthood is a ministry." The commission replied: "The words are taken from the *Statuta ecclesiae antiqua*, as it says in note 74 on page 79, and indicate that deacons are not ordained to offer the body and blood of the Lord but to the *service of charity* in the church."[120]

Clearly, the Doctrinal Commission and *Lumen Gentium* were literally not on the same page for the source of the ancient Latin formula. More important, the commission's *Relatio* revealed disquiet about the inherent disjunction in the formula between priesthood and ministry, a disjunction that the commission justified and that through the final version of *Lumen Gentium* has endured to encumber the theology of the diaconate. Ironically, LG 29, in the council's vision of a renewed diaconal ministry, emphasized sacramental and liturgical functions, such as the ordinary administration of baptism and Communion, previously associated with the priesthood, not the ministry of charity.[121]

Still in force at the Second Vatican Council, the 1917 Code of Canon Law stipulated that a priest (*sacerdos*) was the ordinary minister of baptism (c. 738 §1) and of Communion (c. 845 §1). Only with the permission of the local ordinary or the parish priest (*parochus*) could a deacon administer baptism (c. 741) or Communion (c. 845 §2). Such an "extraordinary" diaconal ministry was exceptional, occurring only when permission was lawfully conceded "for a just cause" in the case of necessity (c. 741) or was "lawfully presumed for a grave cause" in the "case of necessity" (c. 845 §2).[122] LG 29 changed canon law by giving ministries to deacons that had been the ordinary prerogative of priests. Even though the celebration of the Eucharist at Mass remained an exclusively priestly function, the functions that

[120] AS 3/8: 101, emphasis in the original.

[121] Tanner, *Decrees*, 2: 874.

[122] *Codex iuris canonici Pii X Pontificis Maximi iussu digestus, Benedicti Papae XV auctoritate promulgatus* (Roma: Typis Polyglottis Vaticianis, 1917), 220, 221, 244.

the council accorded to deacons called into question the formula that separated priesthood from ministry.

By the "meaningless" formula *non ad sacerdotium, sed ad ministerium*, LG 29 reversed, with commensurately baleful effect, Jesus's observation about how not to patch clothes and fill wineskins (Matt 9:16-17).[123] The Dogmatic Constitution on the Church put an old patch on a new cloak and poured old wine into new wineskins as the conciliar bishops wished to restore the diaconate as "a permanent grade of the hierarchy" (LG 29) with functions, such as assisting at marriages and presiding at prayer and worship services, which deacons had never exercised before.[124] In its original sense, the formula aptly extended the first remark about deacons in LG 29, namely that they occupied a lower step in the hierarchy: *In gradu inferiori hierarchiae sistunt Diaconi, quibus "non ad sacerdotium, sed ad ministerium" manus imponuntur*—"On a lower step of the hierarchy stand the deacons, upon whom hands are laid 'not for priesthood, but for ministry.'"[125] Although Stefan Sander denied that the Second Vatican Council offered "a plausible justification for the hierarchical gradation" of the diaconate,[126] the separation of priesthood and ministry reinforced the deacon's subordinate status among ordained ministers.

This separation in the hierarchical favor of the priesthood conflicts with an often-cited passage in *Lumen Gentium*. Priesthood and ministry elide in LG 10, which distinguishes between a "ministerial priesthood" (*sacerdotium ministeriale*) and the "common priesthood of the faithful." The two priesthoods "differ in essence and not only by degree."[127] To which priesthood do deacons belong? To situate deacons within the "common priesthood of the faithful," and not

[123] Sander, *Das Amt des Diakons*, 128, referred to "die sinnentleerte und verkürzte Formel der *Statuta Ecclesiae antiqua*."

[124] Tanner, *Decrees*, 2: 874.

[125] Tanner, *Decrees*, 2: 874.

[126] Sander, *Das Amt des Diakons*, 118.

[127] Tanner, *Decrees*, 2: 857.

within the ministerial priesthood, undermines the sacramentality of the diaconate, established by the self-gift of the Spirit in the sacrament of order. Conscious that the formula, *non ad sacerdotium, sed ad ministerium*, was "not very clear" and that a deacon assisted at the celebration of the Eucharist, Serafino Lanzetta maintained that "one cannot exclude the deacon from the ministerial priesthood in the broader sense."[128] Such an exclusion would identify deacons as laypeople.[129] It would discredit them as ordained ministers. Enzo Petrolino recommended that LG 10 should not be read as excluding deacons "from a participation in the ministerial priesthood of Christ, but rather as a clarification of ministerial 'assignments,'" which did not include the celebration of the Eucharist and of the sacrament of reconciliation, and "a distinction" between "the sacramental adherence to Christ" of deacons and the baptismal relation to Christ of other Christians.[130]

For several reasons Gianfranco Ghirlanda maintained that a deacon "did not remain in the common priesthood but has a certain participation, albeit to a highly restricted degree, in the ministerial or hierarchical priesthood."[131] The incapacity to celebrate the Eucharist, to absolve people of sins sacramentally, and to exercise pastoral care limited the diaconate in relation to the episcopate and presbyterate.[132] Yet, as a "minister of sacramentals" (c. 1168) a deacon is a cleric with a sacred power, which laypeople do not possess.[133] Furthermore, as ordained ministers, deacons

[128] Serafino Lanzetta, "Die Erneuerung des ständigen Diakonats auf dem Zweiten Vatikanum: Anliegen, Ergebnisse und Probleme," in *Der Diakonat: Geschichte und Theologie*, 138, 139.

[129] Lanzetta, "Die Erneuerung des ständigen Diakonats auf dem Zweiten Vatikanum," 139.

[130] Petrolino, *Il Concilio Vaticano II e il Diaconato*, 95.

[131] Gianfranco Ghirlanda, *Il sacramento dell'ordine e la vita dei cherici (Cann. 1008-1054; 232 297)*, 2nd ed. (Rome: Edizioni Studium, 2024), 56.

[132] Ghirlanda, *Il sacramento dell'ordine*, 55, 56–57.

[133] Ghirlanda, *Il sacramento dell'ordine*, 56.

participate in the *munus* of the one apostolic ministry with "its ontological participation in the consecration and mission of Christ."[134] But Ghirlanda's reasoning indicates that their participation is one of dependence on the bishop, into whose ministry deacons are ordained,[135] and from whom they receive a "limited participation in the *munus* of the apostolic ministry with regard to preaching the gospel and celebrating sacramentals."[136] Ghirlanda's response to his demand for an explanation of LG 29's assertion that deacons are not ordained for the priesthood[137] paradoxically located them, if even in a limited way, within the ministerial priesthood. As the third chapter of this book will show, diaconal ministry should not be restricted to preaching and sacramentals.

The relationship of the diaconate to the priesthood surfaced also in LG 41. Situated in the fifth chapter of *Lumen Gentium*, "On the universal vocation to holiness in the church," the article began by recognizing that all in the church pursue "one holiness in the various types and responsibilities of life." In their ministry, which they must carry out "in the image of the supreme and eternal priest (*ad imaginem summi et aeterni sacerdotis*)," pastors, namely bishops, will find "for themselves an exceptionally important means of sanctification."[138] While associating bishops with Christ the priest, LG 41 related presbyters to an expression of Christ the savior. "Through Christ the eternal and unique mediator," they share "by grace" in the responsibilities of bishops.[139] After discussing the sanctification of priests, LG 41, in a new, fourth, paragraph, began: "But

[134] Ghirlanda, *Il sacramento dell'ordine*, 57.

[135] Ghirlanda, *Il sacramento dell'ordine*, 54, 55. Ghirlanda clearly preferred the more ancient designation that deacons are ordained *ad ministerium episcopi* to the abbreviation of this designation: *ad ministerium*.

[136] Ghirlanda, *Il sacramento dell'ordine*, 57.

[137] Ghirlanda, *Il sacramento dell'ordine*, 52.

[138] Tanner, *Decrees*, 2: 881.

[139] Tanner, *Decrees*, 2: 881.

ministers of a lower order, especially deacons, also participate in their own way in the mission and grace of the supreme priest (*missionis autem et gratiae supremi sacerdotis*), and, serving the mysteries of Christ and of the church, they ought to keep themselves free from every vice and, furthermore, to please God, and to make available every good thing in the presence of human beings." The paragraph continued by mentioning clerics preparing for ministry and ended by adding a reference to "laypeople, chosen by God, who, to dedicate themselves completely to apostolic works, are called by the bishop and labor in the field of the Lord with great fruit."[140]

Given the differentiation of the ministerial and common priesthood in LG 10, the question arises: in which priesthood do deacons participate in view of LG 41? Without answering this question directly, the International Theological Commission (ITC) offered an interpretation of LG 41 that could situate deacons within the ministerial priesthood. First, LG 41 attributed "to deacons a special share in the mission and grace of the High Priest."[141] Second, what makes this participation "special" seems to be the diaconate's "constitutive link with the priestly ministry to which it lends its aid (cf. *LG* 41)." The ITC explained: "It is not just any service which is attributed to the deacon in the Church: his service belongs to the sacrament of Holy Orders, as a close collaboration with the bishop and the priests, in the unity of the same ministerial actualization of the mission of Christ."[142] While the ITC referred to the mission, and not

[140] Tanner, *Decrees*, 2: 882. Tanner's edition does not format a separate fourth paragraph devoted to clerics and laypeople. For an official documentation of this fourth paragraph, see AS 3/8: 819.

[141] International Theological Commission (ITC), *From the Diakonia of Christ to the Diakonia of the Apostles*, chapter VII, section III.3, 2002, Vatican website, https://www.vatican.va/roman_curia/congregations/cfaith/cti_documents/rc_con_cfaith_pro_05072004_diaconate_en.html.

[142] ITC, *From the Diakonia of Christ to the Diakonia of the Apostles*, chapter VII, section V.

also to the priesthood, of Christ, it collated the ministry of deacons, priests, and bishops in the one sacrament of order and in the one and the same "ministerial actualization" of Christ's mission. That unity of ordained ministry in Christ's mission suggested a threefold participation of bishops, priests, and deacons in the ministerial priesthood.

Helmut Hoping replaced the ITC's suggestive with a decisive interpretation of LG 41. For Hoping, the participation of deacons "in the mission and grace of the supreme priest"[143] necessitated a participation in the ministerial priesthood, since LG 41's reference to deacons, who were ordained ministers, could not be interpreted as a reference to the common priesthood of all the baptized. Furthermore, LG 41 required a reinterpretation of the formula *non ad sacerdotium, sed ad ministerium*, which could not mean that deacons were excluded from a share in priesthood.[144]

Martin Troupeau contested the assimilation of a diaconal share in Christ's priesthood in LG 41 with the ministerial priesthood for two main reasons. First, Troupeau aligned the reference to Christ's priesthood in the fourth paragraph of LG 41 with LG 34, which associated laypeople with "the supreme (*supremus*) and eternal priest, Christ Jesus."[145] Second, the inclusion of lay ministers in the fourth paragraph of LG 41 meant that the priesthood at issue in this paragraph was the common priesthood of all the baptized, not the ministerial priesthood.[146] Troupeau drew what he believed

143 Tanner, *Decrees*, 2: 882.

144 Helmut Hoping, "Der dreifache Tischdienst des Diakons und die Einheit des Ordosakraments," 202–3; Helmut Hoping, "Die liturgische Verortung des Diakonats und seine Stellung innerhalb des sakramentalen Ordo: Ein Beitrag aus römisch-katholischer Sicht," *Internationale kirchliche Zeitschrift* 95, no. 4 (2005): 258; Helmut Hoping, "Das Priestertum des geistlichen Dienstamtes—Diakonat und Presbyterat," in *Der Diakonat: Geschichte und Theologie*, 291.

145 Tanner, *Decrees*, 2: 877; Martin Troupeau, "La question des diacres en *Lumen gentium* 41," *Nouvelle revue théologique* 143, no. 3 (2021): 404.

146 Troupeau, "La question des diacres en *Lumen gentium* 41," 404–6.

was the necessary conclusion of his analysis: "for the diaconate, the only passage that evokes the link to Christ, the sovereign priest, is LG 41 §4, which is decisively inscribed in the category of baptismal priesthood."[147]

Troupeau's argument is not as decisive as he believed. The articulation of Christ's priesthood in LG 34 and LG 41 cannot easily correspond to the categories of ministerial and common priesthood in LG 10. The "supreme and eternal priest" mentioned in LG 34 aligns with the "supreme and eternal priest" with whom LG 41 associated bishops and with whom LG 28 associated priests. In article 28, *Lumen Gentium* taught that presbyters, "by virtue of the sacrament of order are consecrated to the image of Christ the supreme and, moreover, the eternal priest (*ad imaginem Christi summi atque aeterni sacerdotis*) to preach the gospel, to nurture the faithful, and to celebrate divine worship."[148] The only difference was the Latin adjective translated as "supreme"—*supremus* in LG 34 and in LG 41's reference to deacons, and *summus* in LG 28 and LG 41's reference to bishops. Surely, the lexical difference between two Latin synonyms cannot underpin an important theological claim for the differentiation of the ministerial and common priesthood.

What distinguished the reference to deacons is that LG 41 referred only to Christ's supreme, not his eternal, priesthood. A facetious reading of *Lumen Gentium* might justify the marginalization of deacons, associated merely with Christ's supreme priesthood, because of their exclusion from the noble company of laypeople, presbyters, and bishops, who have Christ, the supreme *and* eternal priest, on their side. A serious observation of the association of deacons with Christ's priesthood in LG 41 might lead one to wonder what priesthood deacons share with bishops and presbyters since they have all received the one sacrament of order. Thus, like presbyters, are deacons "consecrated to

[147] Troupeau, "La question des diacres en *Lumen gentium* 41," 407.
[148] Tanner, *Decrees*, 2: 872.

the image of Christ the supreme and, moreover, the eternal priest" (LG 28)[149] for the same purpose of exercising Christ's threefold office of teaching, governing, and sanctifying? The second chapter of his book will address this question.

For now, it is enough to realize how difficult the interpretation of the documents of the Second Vatican Council can be, especially with reference to the diaconate. The resuscitation in LG 29 of the formula *non ad sacerdotium, sed ad ministerium* raises questions about the participation of deacons in Christ's priesthood. Since the diaconate did not exist as a stable ordained ministry at the time of council, the bishops and theological experts at the council could not draw on any meaningful experience of diaconal ministry, exercised in communion with the episcopate and presbyterate, for theological guidance. The development of the diaconate requires the interdependence of theological reflection and magisterial teaching.

For this development, William Ditewig proposed a return to the original formula of the *Apostolic Tradition*: *non ad sacerdotium sed in ministerio episcopi*, a restoration that suggests that the "work of ministry" for which deacons are ordained belongs to the bishop. He explained: "The deacon on whom hands are laid by the bishop alone to signify the unique relationship between the bishop and his deacons is ordained specifically and concretely *into* the ministry of the bishop."[150] Such a specification of diaconal ministry, in Ditewig's view, would resolve "the problem of a generic and unspecific *ministerium*" in the abbreviated formula from the Gallic *Statutes* that the Second Vatican Council and the Roman Pontifical preserved. With the regrettable axiom *non ad sacerdotium, sed ad ministerium*, "the deacon could be expected to act for the bishop, for the presbyter, for just about anyone!"[151] Yet, recovering "the traditional and ancient

[149] Tanner, *Decrees*, 2: 872.

[150] Ditewig, *Courageous Humility*, 160, emphasis in the original.

[151] Ditewig, *Courageous Humility*, 80–81.

relationship of the deacon and the bishop" affords, for Ditewig, definitive purpose: "The deacon is ordained to assist and to extend the mission of the bishop himself."[152] This clarity of purpose invites a challenge, however, in determining a deacon's ministerial identity. How does a deacon by ordination into the bishop's ministry enter "a unique and dependent relationship with the bishop" while having "his own proper duties and responsibilities" since "he is not simply a substitute when another minister is unavailable"?[153]

The notion that deacons are ordained into the ministry of a bishop risks the presupposition of an all-absorbing episcopal sacramental grace. The conciliar teaching that bishops by virtue of their ordination have "the fullness of the sacrament of order" (LG 21)[154] must be explained in such a way that the sacramentality of the episcopate does not render redundant the ordination of priests and deacons. The revaluation by the Second Vatican Council of episcopal ministry as sacramentally graced needs to be reconciled with the integrity of the ordination of priests and deacons, who receive the self-gift of the Spirit without measure. Grace is impervious to gradation.

The all-absorbing sacramentality of the bishop found expression in October 1963 at the Second Vatican Council in the written speech of Carlos Eduardo de Saboia Bandeira de Mello, the Bishop of Palmas. The Brazilian prelate held that the episcopate contained "the presbyterate, diaconate, subdiaconate, and also the minor orders."[155] He wanted the council to define that "the episcopate in itself, apart from all other grades [of order], contains the complete and full priesthood and comprises all of its grades within itself." Consequently, he asserted that "the presbyterate comes from a human being (the bishop)." The various grades of ministers "make up the one sacrament, namely of order,

[152] Ditewig, *Courageous Humility*, 99.
[153] Ditewig, *Courageous Humility*, 210.
[154] Tanner, *Decrees*, 2: 865.
[155] AS 2/2: 119.

immediately *instituted in the episcopate* by Christ Jesus (or in the apostolate of the twelve, to which it succeeds)."[156] If, according to James Barnett, an "omnivorous priesthood" had in the past rendered the diaconate ineffectual by absorbing diaconal ministries,[157] ordaining deacons into the ministry of a bishop risks the presupposition of an "omnivorous episcopate."

Susan Wood interpreted the sacramental plenitude of the episcopate in relation to a bishop's membership in the episcopal college by virtue of his ordination. A bishop represents the communion of his local church within the hierarchical communion of bishops with and under the pope as the bishop of Rome, "a communion of communions" that represents the universal church.[158] Priesthood determines the relationship of presbyters to their bishop. Since he represents the local church, a bishop has the "fullness of priesthood," in which presbyters participate by presiding at the Eucharist of an altar community, usually a parish, within the diocese.[159] Wood acknowledged that priesthood was not subject to gradation, for "the concept of a partial or incomplete priesthood" is incompatible with "a presbyter's ability to represent Christ and the community eucharistically."[160] Presumably, a presbyter completely represents his community and Christ. Priestly fullness becomes a confusing concept when presbyters and bishops possess that fullness.

Deacons as well as presbyters participate in a bishop's "fullness of orders."[161] The little that Wood had to say about the participation of deacons implied an episcopal fullness of diaconate: "The bishop, because he has the fullness of

[156] AS 2/2: 120, emphasis in the original.

[157] James Monroe Barnett, *The Diaconate: A Full and Equal Order*, rev. ed. (Valley Forge, PA: Trinity Press International, 1995), 154.

[158] Wood, *Sacramental Orders*, 75–77, quotation: 76.

[159] Wood, *Sacramental Orders*, 125.

[160] Wood, *Sacramental Orders*, 124.

[161] Wood, *Sacramental Orders*, 168.

orders, has the ultimate responsibility towards the poor, the weak, and the persecuted, but historically this responsibility was exercised with diaconal assistance."[162] This episcopal "ultimate responsibility" raises the question of whether the diaconate is subject to gradation. Is the diaconate or the *diaconia* of deacons a partial and incomplete participation in the fullness of episcopal *diaconia*?

Dario Vitali would probably answer this question affirmatively. Upholding the formula *non ad sacerdotium, sed ad ministerium*, Vitali separated priestly and ministerial "functions" and rooted them in the bishop. Deacons carry out the bishop's "ministry of the care for the ecclesial body." From him they receive "the specific task of manifesting and rendering concrete his solicitude for the people of God entrusted to him."[163] Vitali added: "Deacons are taken up into the sacrament of order (*asunti nell'Ordine*) by reason of their bond with the bishop who associates them with his care for the people of God."[164] Not surprisingly, Vitali promoted the formula from the *Apostolic Tradition* that deacons are ordained "for the ministry of the bishop" as "the purpose" of diaconal ministry.[165]

Christological and Pneumatological Approaches

A christological approach to the sacramentality of the diaconate liberates the diaconate from functioning as a subservient extension of episcopal ministry. Since, according to conciliar teaching, Christ "is present in the sacraments by his power" (SC 7),[166] Walter Kasper appropriately held that Christ is the "actual minister of the sacrament of order." Christ's presence in this sacrament has several consequences. Those who receive the sacrament are configured

[162] Wood, *Sacramental Orders*, 173.
[163] Dario Vitali, *Diaconi: che fare?* (Milan: San Paolo, 2019), 180.
[164] Vitali, *Diaconi: che fare?*, 181.
[165] Vitali, *Diaconi: che fare?*, 160.
[166] Tanner, *Decrees*, 2: 822.

"in a special way to Christ, the one high priest, shepherd, and bishop."[167] Thus, Kasper continued, the sacrament of order and those ordained "are withdrawn from the bishop's absolute power of control." The "immediacy of Christ's presence" (*Christusunmittelbarkeit*) afforded by the sacrament bestows upon ordained ministers "a certain autonomy (*Eigenständigkeit*) and individual responsibility that the bishop must respect."[168]

The German noun *Eigenständigkeit* means "autonomy" or "independence," literally the quality of standing on one's own. The related adjective, *eigenständig*, can thus be translated as "discrete" or "separate" as well as "autonomous." The synod of West Germany's Catholic dioceses, held in Würzburg between 1971 and 1975, repeatedly described diaconal ministry as *eigenständig*. The Second Vatican Council, the synod affirmed, had renewed the diaconate "as an autonomous, sacramentally conferred ministry."[169] Of course, deacons ministered within an ecclesial context; their autonomy was not absolute. "The diocesan leadership" assigned to them their "separate areas of responsibility."[170] The synod insisted: "The autonomous diaconate is no mere substitute for a lack of priests." Only by exception, therefore, could deacons "assume specific functions of parish leadership in the name of the pastor and of the bishop."[171] The synod justified its support for the ordination of women as deacons in part because the diaconate represented "a

[167] Walter Kasper, "Der Diakon in ekklesiologischer Sicht angesichts der gegenwärtigen Herausforderungen in Kirche und Gesellschaft," in Walter Kasper, *Theologie und Kirche*, vol. 2 (Mainz: Matthias-Grünewald-Verlag, 1999), 147.

[168] Kasper, "Der Diakon," 147.

[169] L. Bertsch, Ph. Boonen, R. Hammerschmidt, J. Homeyer, F. Kronenberg, and K. Lehmann, eds., *Gemeinsame Synode der Bistümer der Bundesrepublik Deutschland: Offizielle Gesamtausgabe*, new ed. (Freiburg im Breisgau: Herder, 2012), 614, no. 4.1.1.

[170] L. Bertsch et al., *Gemeinsame Synode*, 618, no. 4.3.3.

[171] L. Bertsch et al., *Gemeinsame Synode*, 616, no. 4.1.3.

discrete expression of the sacrament of order that differs theologically and functionally from priestly service."[172]

Its sacramentality establishes the diaconate as a relatively autonomous ordained ministry. As a sacrament, the diaconate is autonomous because it is a discrete representation of Christ in the church. Its autonomy is relative to priests and especially the diocesan bishop, who determines the specific ministries that deacons exercise.

As ordained ministers sharing in different ways in "the one mission of Jesus Christ," a bishop, priests, and deacons rely on "fraternal and collegial cooperation," as Kasper explained. Their "correlation to the bishop" does not make deacons his "mere flunkies."[173] They minister in their own right but always in communion with their bishop, who leads the local church, and with priests, who exercise their own forms of ministerial leadership. They are Christ's deacons, not the bishop's deacons. In the proposed homily for the rite of diaconal ordination, the bishop equates deacons with "the ministers of Jesus Christ."[174]

Didier Gonneaud preferred the formula *non ad sacerdotium, sed ad ministerium* without the objective genitive, *episcopi*. The Second Vatican Council encouraged thinking about the sacrament of order in terms of "both its unity and diversity" and not of an absorbing or centralizing "figure," whether a bishop or a priest. While Gonneaud thought it "prudent to define the sacramentality of the diaconate as a participation in sacramental fullness of the bishop," an emphasis on this definition "could diminish the sacramentality of the diaconate," of which the bishop "is not the source, nor the foundation, but the instrument."[175] The bishop is Christ's ordaining instrument.

[172] L. Bertsch et al., *Gemeinsame Synode*, 617, no. 4.2.2.

[173] Kasper, "Der Diakon," 147.

[174] *Pontificale Romanum* (1990), 106, no. 99.

[175] Didier Gonneaud, "La sacramentalité du ministère diaconal," *Revue théologique* de *Louvain* 36 (2005): 8.

The ordaining bishop, who represents Christ in the church's rite of ordination, affirms the immediacy of the relationship between Christ and Christ's deacons and "the capacity for representing Christ" beyond "human control."[176] After the prayer of consecration, in the explanatory rite, the bishop places the book of the gospels in the hands of the deacon with this command: "Receive the gospel of Christ, whose herald you have become, and see to it that you believe what you read, that you teach what you believe, and that you practice what you teach."[177] The corresponding exhortation in the pre-conciliar rite was functional, not christological, reflecting the medieval notion of ordination that emphasized the bestowal of sacred power for individual possession: "Receive the power of reading the gospel in the church of God both for the living and the dead."[178] Having transformed deacons from lectors into evangelists, the post-conciliar rite of ordination recognizes them as Christ's direct ministers by virtue of their faith in, proclamation of, and witness to Christ's gospel.

Pope Paul VI offered another way of conceptualizing the christological foundation of the sacramentality of the diaconate. He may have taken inspiration from the Italian Episcopal Conference, which in 1971 had approved a document in favor of restoring the diaconate in Italy. The Italian bishops described the diaconate as a "sacramental sign, and thus a representative and stimulus (*animatore*) of the vocation to service, proper to Christ, servant of YHWH (cf. Isa 53), who came 'not to be served, but to serve and to give his

[176] Hermman Johann Weber, "Zur theologischen Ortsbestimmung des Diakonats im einen Weihesakrament," in *Der Diakon: Wiederentdeckung und Erneuerung seines Dienstes*, 114.

[177] *Pontificale Romanum* (1968), 28, no. 24; *Pontificale Romanum* (1990), 125, no. 210.

[178] Bradshaw, *Rites of Ordination*, 145–46 (medieval notion of ordination); Sodi and Toniolo, *Pontificale Romanum*, 44 (liturgical exhortation).

life as a ransom for many' (Matt 20:28)."[179] In his *motu proprio, Ad Pascendum* (1972), the pope declared that the diaconate was "a sign or sacrament of Christ the Lord himself, *who did not come to be served, but to serve* (*qui non venit ministrari, sed ministrare*)."[180]

Deacons receive in the sacrament of order not only a configuration to Christ, but, empowered by the Spirit in the sacrament, they also express in their ministry the minister who is Christ and thus, in making Christ present, they make present the grace that they signify. They are Christ's deacons, ordained into his ministry. As graced, and therefore not arbitrary, signs of Christ, they must be willed by Christ to be his sacramental representation: tangible and effective bearers and expressions of his ministering presence.[181] As sign or symbol or sacrament of Christ, deacons, furthermore, make present in their ministry the ministering Christ in his church, specifically in the tangible, local manifestations of the church, for, as Paul VI wrote, the diaconate is "the catalyst (*instimulator*) of the service or *diaconia* of the church within local Christian communities."[182] The diaconate thus does not only render Christ sacramentally present, but it also symbolizes or renders sacramentally expressive the church as the ministering church of the ministering Christ. But the diaconate can only symbolize the church because the church expresses itself sacramentally in the diaconate. The sacrament of order is a sacrament of the church,

[179] Italian Episcopal Conference, "La restaurazione del diaconato permanente in Italia," no. 5, in *Enchiridion sul diaconato: Le fonte e i documenti ufficiali della chiesa*, ed. Enzo Petrolino (Vatican City: Libreria Editrice Vaticana, 2009), 474.

[180] Paul VI, "Ad Pascendum," *Acta Apostolicae Sedis* 64 (1972): 536, emphasis in the original.

[181] The foundation for this explication of the diaconate as a sacrament of Christ is Karl Rahner's ontology and theology of the symbol. See Karl Rahner, "Zur Theologie des Symbols," in Rahner, *Schriften zur Theologie*, vol. 4 (Einsiedeln: Benziger Verlag, 1960), 275–311.

[182] Paul VI, "Ad Pascendum," 536.

by which, as in the case of all the sacraments, the church realizes itself as the sacrament of Christ and makes Christ sacramentally present in the world for the salvation of all people.[183] Of course, deacons are not the only sacramental expressions of Christ and his church, for, as Ditewig unfolded the concept of the servant church, "all members of the church, initiated into Christ, share in Christ's ministry of service across the threefold *munus* of teaching, sanctifying, and ruling."[184] Yet, empowered by the grace of the sacrament of order, deacons evince their own "certain autonomy and individual responsibility"[185] in symbolizing Christ as his ministers in their own specific way, and not as ministers in extension of the bishop, but in communion with him.

Christ is present in the church and in its sacraments by the power of the Spirit. Empowered by the Spirit, he ministered to the marginalized during his earthly life. The risen Christ continues to minister through the Spirit in all who have received him and his Spirit in the sacraments of the church. Given the importance of the epiclesis as the form of the sacrament of order, the sacramentality of the diaconate deserves a pneumatological identity.

Empowered by sacramental grace, deacons are also the ministers of the Spirit. They, like the apostle Paul, who asserted his own *diakonia* as divinely commissioned, serve in "the ministry of the Spirit"—*hē diakonia tou pneumatos* (2 Cor 3:8) with a "fitness" or "qualification" (*hikanotēs*) for ministry that is "from God" (2 Cor 3:5).[186] Rahner called this

[183] Karl Rahner, *Kirche und Sakramente* (Freiburg im Breisgau: Herder, 1960), 21.

[184] William T. Ditewig, *The Emerging Diaconate: Servant Leaders in a Servant Church* (New York: Paulist Press, 2007), 198.

[185] Kasper, "Der Diakon," 147.

[186] On Paul's divinely commissioned *diakonia* in 2 Corinthians 3, see John N. Collins, *Diakonia: Re-interpreting the Ancient Sources* (New York: Oxford University Press, 1990), 198, 202, and, especially, Anni Hentschel,

qualification "the grace of office"[187] and "the charism of office."[188] The sacrament of order, "the sacrament of leadership in the church," confers, Rahner wrote, the "power of ministry" and "the claim upon the corresponding grace for the proper exercise of office." Grace empowers ministry. The appropriate actualization of ministry occurs only "in the Spirit (*im Pneuma*)."[189] The Spirit alone, and not any human regulation, guarantees "the infallibly correct practice of office."[190] As ordained ministers, deacons have the grace of office. They carry out their ministry in the Spirit and, as the church prays, with the Spirit's sevenfold grace.

Paul wrote: "where the Spirit of the Lord is, there is freedom" (2 Cor 3:17). For Rahner the church constitutes the setting, the "where," of the Spirit of freedom. The church realizes itself as "the effective sign of pneumatic freedom" in the proclamation of Christ's gospel, in the mediation of the Spirit in the sacraments, in the love of its members for God, and in their loving service of human beings.[191]

As imprecise as "the work of ministry" sounds in the church's invocation of the Spirit in the ordination of deacons, the vague formula that relates graced diaconal office serves as an opportunity for the church's "pneumatic freedom." Attentive to the Spirit (Rev 2:7, 11, 17, 28; 3:6, 13, 22), local churches can and should determine the forms of diaconal ministry that they require in their own historical circumstances to signify and make effective the "ministry of

---

Diakonia im Neuen Testament: *Studien zur Semantik unter besonderer Berücksichtigung der Rolle von Frauen* (Tübingen: Mohr Siebeck, 2007), 100–112.

[187] Rahner, "Die Theologie der Ereneuerung des Diakonats," 316.

[188] Rahner, *Das Dynamische in der Kirche*, 38.

[189] Karl Rahner, "Dogmatische Vorbemerkungen für eine richtige Fragestellung über die Wiedererneuerung des Diakonats," in *Theologie in Geschichte und Gegenwart: Michael Schmaus zum sechzigsten Geburtstag*, ed. Johann Auer and Hermann Volk (Munich: Karl Zink Verlag, 1957), 136.

[190] Rahner, *Das Dynamische in der Kirche*, 41.

[191] Karl Rahner, "Die Freiheit in der Kirche," in Rahner, *Schriften zur Theologie*, vol. 2 (Einsiedeln: Benziger Verlag, 1958), 104.

the Spirit." As a structure of the church—by "divine ordinance" according to the Council of Trent[192]—the diaconate belongs to what Rahner called "the historically tangible life in the church as the symbolic embodiment of the Spirit of God and of the inner history of the dialogue between God's free love and human freedom."[193] In the pneumatic dialogue of freedom, which constitutes a synodal church, the people of God discerns prudently the deployment of its ministries and ministers to be the local church in the time and place that God has given. As the Italian bishops stated in 1993 in their directory for deacons, "the ministry of deacons must remain open to the promptings that come from the Spirit and from the signs of the times to the church and its mission."[194] The "work of ministry" for which deacons are ordained is that of the church because it is that of Christ and of his Spirit.

The Value of Ordination

Commenting on the ordination rite for deacons, Franz Kohlschein asked: "What value does a diocese attach to deacons and their ordination?"[195] The *Basic Norms* (*Ratio fundamentalis*) for diaconal formation require a diocesan bishop, after deciding to restore the diaconate, "to promote a timely catechesis" on the diaconate, "whether among laypeople or among priests and religious, in such a way that diaconal ministry may be correctly and thoroughly understood."[196] That understanding in the local church begins with an appreciation of sacramental grace, God's

[192] Tanner, *Decrees*, 2: 744.

[193] Rahner, "Zur Theologie des Symbols," 300–301.

[194] Italian Episcopal Conference, "I diaconi permanenti in Italia: Orientamenti e norme," no. 40, in *Enchiridion sul diaconato*, ed. Petrolino, 519.

[195] Kohlschein, "'Sende auf sie herab den Heiligen Gest . . . ,'" 82.

[196] Congregation for Catholic Education, "Ratio fundamentalis institutionis diaconorum permanentium," *Acta Apostolicae Sedis* 90 (1998): 850, no. 16.

bestowal of the Spirit on the ordained. At an ordination, all the baptized pray with the ordaining bishop in the Spirit and for the Spirit to empower the deacons to be ordained for the "work of ministry." At the beginning of the rite, they manifest their approval of the candidates in the rite of election.[197] In this way, they express their consent that those about to be ordained may minister among them. Here begins what Kevin Coyle called the "recognition model" of ordination—the recognition by the community of the Spirit's presence that culminates in the laying on of hands.[198] And to this climactic gesture, the matter of the sacrament, one must add the form: the epiclesis in the consecratory prayer. Valuing the primacy of grace in deacons and in their ordination disposes the local church to an openness to the unpredictable Spirit, to a cooperation with the Spirit in discerning the ministerial priorities of deacons and all ministers.[199]

Grace implies communion, an ecclesial communion with God in Christ through the power of the Spirit and a sacramental communion among the people of God owing to a common baptism. Ordination repositions the deacon, and any ordained minister, within the ecclesial communion.[200] The classical doctrine of the indelible character imprinted on the ordained makes sense only relationally.[201] The grace of ordination is not for a private, sundered sacrality, but for "the work of ministry," which grounds deacons in relationships with Christ and with the Spirit and within the church.

The interpretation of the relational value of diaconal ministry presents tensions. Does ordination reposition deacons

[197] Wood, *Sacramental Orders*, 150.

[198] J. Kevin Coyle, "The Laying on of Hands as Conferral of the Spirit: Some Problems and a Possible Solution," *Studia Patristica* 18, no. 2 (1989): 349.

[199] Coyle, "The Laying on of Hands as Conferral of the Spirit," 350.

[200] Richard R. Gaillardetz, "Towards a Contemporary Theology of the Diaconate," *Worship* 79, no. 5 (September 2005): 431.

[201] Sander, *Das Amt des Diakons*, 120–21.

to serve the bishop and his presbyterate, as the *Catechism of the Catholic Church* teaches (CCC 1554)?[202] The Spirit does not subordinate deacons to the ministry of their bishop and to priests but empowers deacons for the "work of ministry," a graced ministry, the ministry of Christ and of the Spirit, that deacons freely offer for and among the people of God in communion with their bishop and with priests. To understand the repositioning of deacons within this ecclesial communion, a claim for their position within an ordained ministerial communion is in order. This chapter has already indicated the basis for such a communion in the sacramental invocation of the Holy Spirit. Staking a claim for deacons in an ordained ministerial communion, the subject of the next chapter, values what the council teaches, namely that deacons "serve the people of God in the *diaconia* of the liturgy, of the word, and of charity in communion with their bishop and his presbyterate" (LG 29).[203]

[202] *Catechism of the Catholic Church*, 2nd ed. (Washington, DC: United States Catholic Conference, 2000), 388.

[203] Tanner, *Decrees*, 2: 874.

Chapter 2: Ordained Ministerial Communion

Communion vs. *Suppléance*

In 1996, at their annual plenary meeting in Lourdes, the French bishops adopted several resolutions on the diaconate. Some of these revealed desired dimensions of diaconal ministry in France, including the view that ideal candidates for ordination should "respond to the local needs of the mission of the church."[1] Although the bishops agreed to pay special attention to candidates "already living in solidarity with the abandoned, the excluded, [and] the youngest people," the resolutions never expressly identified the ministry of charity or ministry to and among the poor as the defining diaconal ministry. Nor did they elaborate on the social structures of "professional work," volunteerism, family, and communal life that represented "the most important settings of the mission of deacons." Nevertheless, the French bishops resolved "to ordain to the diaconate men having significant commitments in these different domains."[2] Since the church's "sacramental life" and the preaching of homilies belonged to diaconal ministry, the

[1] Conference of the Bishops of France, "Diaconat: Points d'attention votés en Assemblée," *Documentation Catholique* 93, no. 2149 (December 1, 1996): 1012, Fiche 1,1.

[2] Conference of the Bishops of France, "Diaconat," 1012, Fiche 1.2; Fiche 4.

bishops committed themselves to providing deacons with a "biblical, liturgical, and sacramental formation" that would "nourish their liturgical ministry." Those deacons with the requisite charism should receive formation for the ministry of "spiritual accompaniment."[3]

In the resolutions, the ecclesial articulation of diaconal ministry led to an expression of the ideal relationship between deacons and priests. Wishing "to respect the specificity of presbyteral ministry and that of diaconal ministry," the French bishops decided "to avoid generalizing the situations in which deacons would receive a participation in the exercise of pastoral ministry, understood as parish ministry." Instead, they identified "the life of Christian communities," without further specification, as the object of diaconal ministry. The next resolution stated: "The bishops will ensure that the image given by deacons is not that of the substitution (*suppléance*) for priests but of communion with them in the exercise of the sacrament of order."[4] Ordination established a relationship of graced communion between deacons and priests, who ministered in differentiated settings.

Communion suggested a harmonious relationship of equals. The French bishops aimed at "a fraternal and reciprocal collaboration between deacons and priests," sustained by "a better knowledge of diaconal ministry" on the part of priests.[5] *Suppléance*, however, implied subordination, a relationship of unequals, in which deacons stood in for priests.

The French bishops did not imagine a category for their own relationship with deacons. Yet, two tasks, co-evaluation and dialogue, that brought together deacons and their bishop, or his representative, pointed to a communion of ministers. A deacon's co-evaluation of his ministry "with

[3] Conference of the Bishops of France, "Diaconat," 1012, Fiche 2.1, 2.2; Fiche 8.3.

[4] Conference of the Bishops of France, "Diaconat," 1012, Fiche 3.1, 3.2.

[5] Conference of the Bishops of France, "Diaconat," 1013, Fiche 10.2.

the bishop or one of his collaborators" should take place at the end of a term set for the ministry.[6] The bishops had more to say about obedience. Obedience, presumably to the bishop, necessitated dialogue:

> For obedience to be life-giving and to promote unity, a trusting and regular dialogue is necessary between the deacon and the bishop or his close collaborators, [such as the] vicar general [or] episcopal vicar. This dialogue is particularly indispensable at important moments of change: a change of profession or of domicile, the arrival of retirement, [and] other assigned ministries, especially if they are difficult.[7]

In France, ideally, deacons could speak evaluatively and freely with their bishop in an environment of respect about the ministries to which he had assigned them.

The disjunction between communion and *suppléance*, posed by France's Catholic bishops, establishes an interpretive key to understand the statement in LG 29 that deacons, "empowered by sacramental grace, serve the people of God in the *diaconia* of the liturgy, of the word, and of charity in communion with the bishop and his presbyterate."[8] Inhabiting a graced communion of ordained ministers, deacons are not ministers of supply for priests or for their bishop. Not only is diaconal ministry not substitutionary; it is also not auxiliary. Nor is it ancillary. Deacons, priests, and bishops receive the empowering self-gift of the Spirit to be ministers, servant-leaders for and among the people of God. The liberating grace of ordination does not create a diaconal underclass of helpers to ease or complete the ministry of bishops and priests.

[6] Conference of the Bishops of France, "Diaconat," 1012, Fiche 5.
[7] Conference of the Bishops of France, "Diaconat," 1012, Fiche 9.
[8] Tanner, *Decrees*, 2: 874.

Consequently, a change is necessary in the promises deacons make in response to questions posed by the ordaining bishops. The current rite of ordination requires the bishop to ask: "Are you resolved to fulfill the office of the diaconate with humble charity in aid of the priestly order and for the benefit of the Christian people?"[9] This question could be reformulated as: "Are you resolved to fulfill the office of the diaconate with humble charity in communion with me, your bishop, and with the priests ministering in this diocese for the benefit of the Christian people?"

Authoritative documents of the Holy See, however, have interpreted ministerial communion as the diaconate's service to the episcopate and presbyterate. The Holy See's *Directory* for deacons (1998) began a section on deacons as "servants of the people of God" by remarking: "By virtue of the sacrament of order, the deacon, in communion with the bishop and the diocesan presbyterate, also participates in these pastoral offices but exercises them in a different way, indeed by serving and helping the bishop and the presbyters."[10] The Holy See's *Directory for the Pastoral Ministry of Bishops* (2004) understood diaconal ministry as service to God "and in God's name, to the brethren," but it added: "the diaconate is also a service to the episcopate and to the presbyterate, to which the order of deacons is joined by bonds of obedience and communion, according to canonical discipline."[11]

[9] *Pontificale Romanum ex decreto sacrosancti oecumenici Concilii Vaticani II renovatum auctoritate Pauli PP. VI editum Ioannis Pauli PP. II cura recognitum: De ordinatione episcopi, presbyterorum et diaconorum*, 2nd ed. (1990; repr., Vatican City: Libreria Editrice Vaticana, 2011), 108, no. 200 (ordination of more than one deacon); 134, no. 228 (ordination of one deacon).

[10] Congregation for the Clergy, "Directorium pro ministerio et vita diaconorum permanentium," *Acta Apostolicae Sedis* 90 (1998): 898, no. 37.

[11] Congregation for Bishops, *Directory for the Pastoral Ministry of Bishops: "Apostolorum Successores"* (Vatican City: Libreria Editrice Vaticana, 2004), 104, no. 92.

In reducing deacons to "ancillary service" and marginality in pastoral care,[12] a model of hierarchical subordination transgresses a communion of ministers that is a communion in grace. Such a communion ought to embrace "an equivalence of ministries" in a differentiation of ordained ministries, according to Stefan Sander.[13] The communion of ordained ministers is at odds, therefore, with the gambit of LG 29: the placement of deacons "on a lower step of the hierarchy."[14]

The auxiliary status of deacons suffuses the ecclesial and theological discourse on the diaconate. That status found support at the Second Vatican Council in *Lumen Gentium*, which described bishops taking up "the ministry of the community with presbyters and deacons as helpers" (LG 20).[15] In their *Framework for Permanent Deacons*, the German bishops reinforced this statement with an appeal to antiquity: "Since ancient times, the deacon with the priest has been regarded as the bishop's helper." The *Framework* proceeded to point out, without elaborating on help for the bishop, that a deacon receives his ministerial assignments from the bishop.[16]

Promoting its renewal in 1962, on the eve of the Second Vatican Council, Karl Rahner conceived of the diaconate as exercised "in the service and the *diaconia* of the office of the

[12] Stefan Sander, *Das Amt des Diakons: Eine Handreichung*, rev. ed. (Freiburg im Breisgau: Herder, 2013), 138.

[13] Sander, *Das Amt des Diakons*, 153.

[14] Tanner, *Decrees*, 2: 874.

[15] Tanner, *Decrees*, 2: 864.

[16] German Conference of Bishops, "Rahmenordung der Deutschen Bischofskonferenz vom 22. Januar 1979 für Ständige Diakone," *Archiv für katholisches Kirchenrecht* 148, no. 1 (September 1979): 161, no. 1.1. The statement remains unchanged in the most recent edition of the document. See German Conference of Bishops, *Rahmenordnung für Ständige Diakone in den Bistümern der Budesrepublik Deutschland, 19. Mai 2015* (Bonn: Sekretariat der Deutschen Bischofskonferenz, 2016), 8, no. 1.1.

bishop and of the priest."[17] It remained for the church to decide the relationship between the diaconate and the priesthood: whether the diaconate and the priesthood were two coordinate ministries emanating from the episcopate or whether the deacon should be understood as the priest's "helper."[18] In practice, it depended on the bishop whether he should assign a deacon as "help" for a priest or as "help" for himself.[19]

Fifteen years later, in 1977, Rahner, wrestling with the difficulty of delineating a difference between the diaconate and priesthood, adopted a different position. It seemed advisable, he thought, "not to understand the mission (*Aufgabe*) of the diaconate as an abbreviated partial function of the priest under the priest."[20] Thus, Rahner placed the deacon "with his independent mission *next* to the priest"; although in a community led by a priest, the deacon also stood under the priest's leadership.[21]

Rahner wrote to address the "problem of formidable weight in pastoral theology" of relating the diaconate and lay pastoral assistants to the priesthood in the wake of a recent regulation of pastoral ministries by the German Conference of Bishops.[22] Earlier in 1977, the German bishops had issued principles governing these ministries. The bishops, in their theological analysis of the diaconate, wrote:

[17] Karl Rahner, "Die Theologie der Ereneuerung des Diakonats," in *Diaconia in Christo: Über die Erneuerung des Diakonates*, ed. Karl Rahner and Herbert Vorgrimler (Freiburg im Breisgau: Herder, 1962), 310.

[18] Rahner, "Die Theologie der Ereneuerung des Diakonats," 313–14, quotation: 314.

[19] Rahner, "Die Theologie der Ereneuerung des Diakonats," 315–16.

[20] Karl Rahner, "Pastorale Dienste und Gemeindeleitung," *Stimmen der Zeit* 195, no. 11 (November 1977): 735.

[21] Rahner, "Pastorale Dienste und Gemeindeleitung," 735, emphasis in the original.

[22] Rahner, "Pastorale Dienste und Gemeindeleitung," 733 and 743, n. 1.

> Deacons are commissioned and through sacramental grace are empowered in their service to the word, the liturgy, and Christian charity (*in ihrem Dienst der Verkündigung, der Liturgie und der christlichen Bruderliebe*) to support the bishop and the priest. As much as bishops and priests are obliged to witness through their words and actions that Christ has become the servant of all, so little, however, can they bear the love of Christ to all on their own. Especially, in this task (*Aufgabe*), deacons help them in ministerial mission and power (*in amtlicher Sendung und Vollmacht*). Above all, they attend to people in need, and they contribute to the development and formation of fraternal communities and to the empowerment of all for the *diaconia* of Christ.[23]

While deacons had their own contributions to make, the bishops associated diaconal ordination with the support of episcopal and priestly ministries. Deacons completed the *diaconia* of bishops and priests.

The Holy See's *Directory* for deacons reinforced the notion of a subservient diaconal completion of the ministry of charity that belongs to bishops and priests: "The works of charity, diocesan or parochial, which are among the principal responsibilities (*officia*) of a bishop and presbyters, are transferred (*transmittuntur*) by them, in keeping with the witness of the church's tradition, to the servants of the ecclesiastical ministry, that is, to deacons." A supporting footnote for this statement referenced the consecratory prayer of the ordination of deacons in the revised rite of 1990.[24] Presumably, the *Directory* meant the prayer's anamnestic recourse to Acts 6:1-6. At the prompting of the Holy Spirit, the apostles chose seven men to help them in their "daily ministry" and laid

[23] German Conference of Bishops, "Grundsätze der Deutschen Bischofskonferenz vom 2. März 1977 zur Ordnung der Pastoralen Dienste," *Archiv für katholisches Kirchenrecht* 147, no. 2 (November 1978): 492, no. 3.1.

[24] Congregation for the Clergy, "Directorium," 899, no. 38.

hands upon them for "the ministry of the tables."[25] The prayer changes course, however, when it moves on to the ordinand: "Look kindly, Lord, we ask, also upon this your servant, whom we dedicate for service to your holy altars in the office of the diaconate."[26] This petition places the deacon in God's service, in the service of worship, transferring attention from the table of charity to the eucharistic altar. Certainly, charity and liturgy combine in deacons. But the church's prayer does not envision deacons as servants of their bishop and of priests, taking on and over their ministry of charity, as if bishops and priests could delegate their own ministry of charity to deacons.

The International Theological Commission (ITC) also accorded to deacons an auxiliary role in the ministry of charity. Deacons did not occupy a unique place in this ministry. "Charitable works" could not be understood "as being specific to the diaconate, because they are also properly the responsibility of the bishops and the priests, whose auxiliaries the deacons are."[27] Diaconal participation "in the one mission of Christ," the ITC also concluded, fulfilled "this mission in the manner of an auxiliary service." And yet this auxiliary service was also collaborative, for the deacon's service "belongs to the sacrament of Holy Orders, as a close collaboration with the bishop and the priests, in the unity of the same ministerial actualization of the mission of Christ."[28]

The image of Christ as servant, whom, according to the *Directory*, deacons represent in their ministry of charity,[29]

[25] *Pontificale Romanum* (1990), 137, no. 235.

[26] *Pontificale Romanum* (1990), 138, no. 235.

[27] International Theological Commission (ITC), *From the Diakonia of Christ to the Diakonia of the Apostles*, chapter VII, section IV.1, 2002, Vatican website, https://www.vatican.va/roman_curia/congregations/cfaith/cti_documents/rc_con_cfaith_pro_05072004_diaconate_en.html.

[28] ITC, *From the Diakonia of Christ to the Diakonia of the Apostles*, chapter VII, section V.

[29] *Directory*, no. 38 in *Basic Norms/Directory*, 101.

has led to two different confirmations of an auxiliary diaconate. On the one hand, the way in which deacons reflect Christ the servant led Tim O'Donnell to consider them as "particularly serving the bishop, but also priests in their role of standing in for the bishop in the local community."[30] On the other hand, Dario Vitali maintained that "in the church it is the bishop, and not the deacon, who is the image (*figura*) of Christ the servant." It would be absurd, therefore, for the bishop, who fully represents Christ as "teacher, high priest, and shepherd" in his diocese, not to represent "the aspect of *diaconia*, with which the deacon would be invested in an exemplary way. This is impossible."[31] Thus destined for service to the bishop, the deacon allows for the conceptualization of "a ministry of help for the bishop."[32]

Dissociating communion and *suppléance* remains a theological challenge. Theological grounds for a communion of deacons with bishops and priests exist in a common service to the people of God, in evangelization, and in discharging Christ's threefold office of sanctifying, teaching, and leading. These dimensions of ministry have their source in the self-gift of the Spirit in the sacrament of order. While grace constitutes ministerial communion, efforts of the church's magisterium have frustrated this communion through an appeal to grace, namely an invocation of a representation of Christ in ministry that aims to separate bishops and priests from deacons. A co-responsible ministerial communion, purified of all vestiges of diaconal *suppléance*, remains theologically precarious while the unfortunate and unhelpful perception persists that "among the ministers of the church, the deacon occupies a subordinate position,"

[30] Tim O'Donnell, *The Deacon: Icon of Christ the Servant, Minister of the Threshold* (New York: Paulist Press, 2020), 92.

[31] Dario Vitali, *Diaconi: che fare*? (Milan: San Paolo, 2019), 138.

[32] Vitali, *Diaconi: che fare*?, 160.

functioning as "a sort of auxiliary (*supplétif*), who can provide some services."[33]

Grounds for Communion

Ecclesial communion means unity in Christ for a mission empowered by the Spirit, a mission in which all the baptized take part. What determines the etymology of the word is not the combination of *cum* and *unio*, an emphasis on unity, but *cum* and *munus*, a shared responsibility. While Yves Congar and Alphonse Borras both agreed on this etymology, they understood communion differently. For Borras, communion meant the participation in the sacraments by the people "sanctified by the grace of God." Its agency found expression in general and lyrical terms as a communal movement towards God's reign: "This people on the move at the heart of history towards the kingdom takes shape through an attachment of faith in the gospel of grace and the participation in the gift of self that Christ makes to the Father in the Spirit."[34] For Congar, communion signified "the participation in a common task." A sacramental "participation in the same Christ, in the same Spirit" signaled "a call and a duty" to translate a eucharistic communion into "a prior reconciliation between oneself and God" and into "the sharing in and the concrete exercise of a true fraternal charity."[35] More than that, communion is also a participation of all the baptized in the mission of the church to proclaim the gospel in the world for the salvation of all people.

[33] Alain Desjonquères, *Être diacre permanent, pourquoi?* (Paris: Éditions Salvator, 2019), 121.

[34] Alphonse Borras, *Le diaconat au risque de sa nouveauté* (Brussels: Éditions Lessius, 2007), 72–73.

[35] Yves Congar, "Le diaconat dans la théologie des ministères," in *Le diacre dans l'Église et le monde d'aujourd'hui*, ed. Paul Winninger and Yves Congar (Paris: Les Éditions du Cerf, 1966), 136.

The purpose of all ministries is "for the nurturing (*ad pascendum*) and constant increase of the people of God" as LG 18 says in its first sentence. That is why Christ established "in the church its various ministries" (LG 18).[36] Here the Second Vatican Council supplied the beginnings of what amounts to a "dogmatic definition" of ministry: plural and diversified in reality, originating with Christ and not with the church, and intended for the church's benefit.[37] While *pascere* means, as Borras pointed out, "to lead,"[38] a qualification is necessary. The leadership of ministry is a leadership of care, a leadership that nurtures. Exercising leadership in and for the church is a dimension of all ministries, including that of laypeople and of deacons.

The function of leadership in diaconal ministry continues to be contested and reasserted. As archbishop of Freiburg and president of the German Bishops Conference, Robert Zollitsch noted that "deacons do not as a rule assume an (inherent) ecclesial leadership function, as is the case with the bishop and with priests."[39] Sherri Vallee found leadership and service theologically incompatible: "Theologically, deacons are less able to symbolize Christ the servant if they do not appear to be servants, but rather appear to be leaders."[40] Similarly suggesting that service and leadership were antithetical terms, Matthew Glover, in an analysis of the canons that relate to deacons, proposed "that the notion of diaconal leadership is somewhat of an oxymoron." Thus,

[36] Tanner, *Decrees*, 2: 862.

[37] Peter Hünermann, "Theologischer Kommentar zur dogmatischen Konstitution über die Kirche *Lumen gentium*," in *Herders Theologischer Kommentar zum Zweiten Vatikanischen Konzil*, ed. Peter Hünermann and Bernd Jochen Hilberath, vol. 2 (Freiburg im Breisgau: Herder, 2004), 406.

[38] Borras, *Le diaconat au risque de sa nouveauté*, 103.

[39] Robert Zollitisch, "Der Diakonat – ein modernes Amt," in *Bereit wozu? Geweiht für was? Zur Diskussion um den ständigen Diakonat*, ed. Klemens Ambrunster and Matthias Mühl (Freiburg im Breisgau: Herder, 2009), 375.

[40] Sherri L. Vallee, "The Restoration of the Permanent Diaconate: A Blending of Roles," *Worship* 77, no. 6 (November 2003): 550.

a deacon's ministry of service contradicted "diaconal leadership or diaconal governance."[41] On the contrary, William Ditewig insisted that "leadership and governance are not alien to the diaconate."[42] In asserting the ministerial leadership of deacons, Ditewig cited LG 29, which foresaw the possibility of assigning the care of souls to deacons, and c. 517 §2, which gave priority to deacons for the pastoral care of a parish community in the absence of a resident parish priest.[43]

The second sentence of LG 18 refers to ordained ministers, to "ministers, who exercise a sacred power." It develops the concept of ministry, stated in the first sentence, in the direction of service. Ordained ministers "serve their brothers [and sisters] so that all who belong to the people of God and thus enjoy true Christian dignity, acting together in freedom and in an orderly fashion towards the same goal, might attain salvation."[44] A dynamic and ordered communion of free subjects in the people of God forms the ecclesial environment for the service that fundamentally characterizes ordained ministry.

The service of ordained ministry implies what Rahner called "*theological* essential limits" to this ministry in a lecture he gave in 1966, "On the Meaning of Church Office."[45] Charisms constituted one of these limits. All members of the church, not simply the clergy, receive gifts from the Holy Spirit, which "belong to the abiding essence of the church."[46] The hierarchy of the church must recognize that without

[41] Matthew A. Glover, "The Permanent Diaconate: A Holy Order in Search of (Canonical) Reality," *Proceedings of the Canon Law Society of America Convention* 81 (2019): 205.

[42] William T. Ditewig, *The Deacon's Ministry of Charity and Justice* (Collegeville, MN: Liturgical Press, 2015), 138.

[43] Ditewig, *The Deacon's Ministry of Charity and Justice*, 139–40, 145–47.

[44] Tanner, *Decrees*, 2: 862.

[45] Karl Rahner, *Vom Sinn des kirchlichen Amtes* (Freiburg im Breisgau: Herder, 1966), 29, emphasis in the original.

[46] Rahner, *Vom Sinn des kirchlichen Amtes*, 33.

these charisms "the life of the church would be perverted into a bureaucratic factory and would lose the sheen of the saints and the power of a youthful future."[47] Rahner insisted that the ordained minister's representation of Christ did not dictate the Spirit's work in the church. Consequently, ordained ministry or "office (*Amt*) is not the master of the Spirit and the Spirit's charisms, but their servant."[48] Ordained ministers should serve the flourishing of charisms among all the people of God.

Service to the people of God grounds the communion of deacons with priests and their bishop, as LG 29 specifies, and, of course, service or *diaconia* is a fundamental characteristic of all the baptized. Consequently, as Francis Deniau wrote, "the *diaconia* of the church, as the service of humanity, is not the exclusive preserve of deacons, nor their specialty."[49] Bishops and priests are not exclusively dispensers of sacraments who relegate to deacons the ministry of charity. Before *Lumen Gentium* described the ministry of deacons as *diaconia*, it did so first for bishops (LG 24).[50] In the exercise of their pastoral office, diocesan bishops should appear among their people "as those who serve" (CD 16).[51] Here *Christus Dominus*, the Second Vatican Council's Decree on the Pastoral Office of Bishops in the Church, alluded to Jesus's self-identification as a servant among his disciples at the Last Supper (Luke 22:27). As teachers of the faith, bishops should devote special attention to "the poor and marginalized (*tenuiores*), to whom the Lord sent them to proclaim the gospel" (CD 13).[52] To say that a deacon should

[47] Rahner, *Vom Sinn des kirchlichen Amtes*, 34.

[48] Rahner, *Vom Sinn des kirchlichen Amtes*, 35.

[49] Francis Deniau, "Le diaconat à la lumière des trois 'fonctions' du Christ et de l'Église, selon Vatican II," in *Diaconat, XXIe siècle: Actes du Colloque de Louvain-la-Neuve (13–15 septembre 1994)*, ed. André Haquin and Philippe Weber (Brussels: Éditions Lumen Vitae, 1997), 106.

[50] Tanner, *Decrees*, 2: 868.

[51] Tanner, *Decrees*, 2: 926.

[52] Tanner, *Decrees*, 2: 925.

have nothing to do with "sacramental ministry because that would get in his way of being of service to the world, which should not enter into the *modus operandi* of priests" offends priests, Deniau insisted, since priests "have neither the desire nor the mission of being confined to sacramental ministry."[53] In *Presbyterorum Ordinis*, its Decree on the Ministry and Life of Priests, the council applied to priests what it had already said of bishops, namely that priests should minister especially to "the poor and marginalized, with whom the Lord himself demonstrated closeness and whose evangelization serves as a sign of messianic mission" (PO 6).[54] In their formation of a Christian community, priests should realize that the celebration of the Eucharist becomes "genuine and complete" when it leads "as much to various works of charity and mutual assistance as to missionary action and various forms of Christian witness too" (PO 6).[55] The self-gift of the Spirit in the sacrament of order unites ordained ministers in *diaconia*, in what the Holy See's *Directory* for deacons called "a service of charity, whose objective is to help and motivate all members of a particular church to be able to participate in the life and mission of the church in a spirit of communion and according to their charisms."[56]

From the perspective of an ecclesiology of communion, *diaconia* is, according to Walter Kasper, "not one, but *the* essential dimension of the church."[57] The church is a communion of all the baptized, of course. Through baptism and

[53] Francis Deniau, "Diacres et prêtres en France: des années 1970 aux transformations actuelles," in *Le diaconat permanent: Relecture et perspectives*, ed. Bruno Dumons and Daniel Moulinet (Paris: Les Éditions du Cerf, 2007), 302.

[54] Tanner, *Decrees*, 2: 1049.

[55] Tanner, *Decrees*, 2: 1050.

[56] Congregation for the Clergy, "Directorium," 898, no. 37.

[57] Walter Kasper, "Der Diakon in ekklesiologischer Sicht angesichts der gegenwärtigen Herausforderungen in Kirche und Gesellschaft," in Walter Kasper, *Theologie und Kirche*, vol. 2 (Mainz: Matthias-Grünewald-Verlag, 1999), 152; emphasis in the original.

confirmation, all Christians accept the responsibility of loving and serving their neighbors, and the sacrament of order repeats this requirement for all ordained ministers.[58] Thus, every Christian community as a local manifestation of the church must make *diaconia* a reality. The profession of faith, the proclamation of the gospel, and the liturgical celebration of the Eucharist "must be oriented towards *diaconia*."[59] Deacons cannot exercise "the entire *diaconia* of the church," Kasper affirmed, but they can "inspire, motivate, and train" fellow Christians for *diaconia*.[60] Nevertheless, deacons can do so only because the Spirit has already bestowed "varieties of service" on all who profess "the same Lord" (1 Cor 12:4). The *diaconia* of ecclesial communion grounds the *diaconia* of the diaconate and the communion of all ordained ministers.

The Holy See's *Directory* equated the "service of charity" with the authority of deacons, which they "exercised in hierarchical communion with the bishop and his presbyters."[61] Locating deacons in a "hierarchical communion" represented a terminological development. This new theologoumenon first figured in *Lumen Gentium* in reference to the members of the college of bishops under the headship of the pope (LG 21, 22).[62] *Christus Dominus* repeated this meaning of the term (CD 4, 5).[63] *Presbyterorum Ordinis* extended hierarchical communion to priests in two ways. First, the "unity of consecration and mission" of priests "requires their hierarchical communion with the order of bishops" (PO 7).[64] Second, priests carry out their ministry "in the hierarchical communion of the whole

[58] Kasper, "Der Diakon," 149.
[59] Kasper, "Der Diakon," 153.
[60] Kasper, "Der Diakon," 155.
[61] Congregation for the Clergy, "Directorium," 898, no. 37.
[62] Tanner, *Decrees*, 2: 865, 866.
[63] Tanner, *Decrees*, 2: 922.
[64] Tanner, *Decrees*, 2: 1050.

body" of the church (PO 15).[65] The *Directory* limited hierarchical communion to ordained ministers. According to the *Directory*, a deacon's love for the church makes him "actively labor for the building up of the church through dedication to his ministerial responsibilities, through fraternity and hierarchical communion with his own bishop and the presbyterate."[66]

The *Directory*, however, also related diaconal ordination and service to the church with hierarchical communion to indicate the auxiliary and subordinate nature of diaconal liturgical ministry. It stated:

> The deacon receives the sacrament of order so that, as a minister, he serves the sanctification of the Christian community in hierarchical communion with the bishop and presbyters. To the ministry of the bishop and, subordinately, to the ministry of presbyters, the deacon offers assistance that is sacramental (*auxilium sacramentale*) and thus also intrinsic, organic, and completely unalloyed (*a confusione alienum*).[67]

These characteristics of a deacon's "sacramental assistance" presumably reinforced the next point in the *Directory*: in the liturgy, the ministry of deacons sets them apart from laypeople and from priests. Diaconal liturgical ministry differs "essentially from whatever liturgical ministry that pastors could entrust to the Christian faithful who are not ordained" and it differs "equally from ordained priestly ministry itself."[68] In the *Directory*, hierarchical communion had, at least liturgically, a differentiating effect among ordained ministers in the subordination of deacons and between deacons and lay ministers. This approach to ministry risked the "inferiorization" that Alphonse Borras and Bernard Pottier

[65] Tanner, *Decrees*, 2: 1061.
[66] Congregation for the Clergy, "Directorium," 911, no. 57.
[67] Congregation for the Clergy, "Directorium," 893, no. 28.
[68] Congregation for the Clergy, "Directorium," 893, no. 28.

wanted to avoid in the articulation of ordained and lay ministries.[69]

Pope Paul VI produced an early, if not the first, post-conciliar statement about the relationship between a communion of ordained ministers and the sacrament of order that signaled cooperation, not subordination. Significantly, he did so in his apostolic exhortation on evangelization, *Evangelii Nuntiandi* (1975). He committed all the clergy to "the work of evangelization," beginning with himself, the bishops of local churches, and then "presbyters and deacons joined with their bishops, whose cooperators they are through the communion that originates from the sacrament of sacred order and from the charity of the church."[70] Owing to their sacramental communion, priests and deacons, while under obedience to their bishops, work with them in the church's mission to spread the gospel. At their ordination, deacons receive from the bishop the book of the gospel to become Christ's heralds.[71]

According to Paul VI, preaching the gospel was impossible *sine Sancti Spiritus munere*—"without the commission of the Holy Spirit."[72] The Second Vatican Council had articulated the threefold *munus* of Christ—the office of sanctifying, teaching, and governing—in which ministers and all the baptized shared. In *Evangelii Nuntiandi*, Paul VI in effect attributed an evangelizing office to the Holy Spirit. Jesus and the apostles were beneficiaries of that office.[73] So too was Stephen, who, "full of the same Spirit," was "chosen

[69] Alphonse Borras and Bernard Pottier, *La grâce du diaconat: Questions actuelles autour du diaconat latin* (Brussels: Éditions Lessius, 1998), 199.

[70] Paul VI, "Evangelii Nuntiandi," *Acta Apostolicae Sedis* 68 (1976): 58, no. 68.

[71] *Pontificale Romanum* (1990), 125, no. 210 (ordination of more than one deacon); 139, no. 238 (ordination of one deacon).

[72] Paul VI, "Evangelii Nuntiandi," 64, no. 75.

[73] Paul VI, "Evangelii Nuntiandi," 64, no. 75.

as deacon" and shed a martyr's blood.[74] The pope continued that "today" the Spirit "works in each and every herald of the gospel" who takes the Spirit as guide. Only with the Spirit's inspiration can the various "arts of evangelization" attain value, the preparation for preaching achieve effectiveness, the power of reasoning move human beings, and the contributions of sociology and psychology find relevance. Paul VI drew the obvious conclusion: the Holy Spirit takes the "leading role in spreading the gospel." Since the Spirit moves the preacher and prepares human hearts "to receive and understand the word of salvation," the Spirit deserves to be called "the aim and also the end of all evangelization."[75]

Although Paul VI considered all the baptized as called into the Spirit's evangelizing office, ordained ministers certainly exercised this office by virtue of what the Holy See's *Basic Norms* for the diaconate called "a special outpouring of the Spirit" in the sacrament of order.[76] "Deacons," the Holy See's *Directory* affirmed, "enjoy the faculty to preach everywhere under the conditions foreseen by law. And this faculty proceeds from the sacrament," presumably the sacrament of order.[77] Their "*diaconia* of the word" obliges deacons "to cooperate with the bishop and the presbyters in the exercise of a ministry not of their own wisdom but of the word of God, inviting all to conversion and holiness."[78]

The second edition of the American *Directory* for deacons aptly expressed a communion of ordained ministers in the service of God's word, especially between deacons and priests:

[74] Paul VI, "Evangelii Nuntiandi," 65, no. 75. Here Paul VI implicitly recognized Acts 6:1-6 as the institution of the diaconate, although in *Ad Pascendum* he neglected this traditional biblical *locus*, favoring instead Philippians 1:1 and 1 Timothy 3:8-13 as scriptural sources for the diaconate. See Paul VI, "Ad Pascendum," *Acta Apostolicae Sedis* 64 (1972): 534.

[75] Paul VI, "Evangelii Nuntiandi," 65–66, no. 75.

[76] *Basic Norms*, no. 5 in *Basic Norms/Directory*, 24.

[77] Congregation for the Clergy, "Directorium," 890–91, no. 24.

[78] Congregation for the Clergy, "Directorium," 890, no. 23.

> Priests and deacons are bonded closely together in their common ministry of the Word. All deacons receive the Holy Gospels from the diocesan bishop on their ordination day. This powerful sign of cooperation with the ministry of the diocesan bishop, and its connection to Christ's own mandate (Lk 24:45-49) places the ministry of deacon and priest within a shared communion of obedience to and love of the Word, which together they labor to proclaim. It is laudatory for priests and deacons to deepen their communion, as brothers in Holy Orders, by way of their shared prayer and reflection on the Word of God.[79]

In the referenced passage from Luke, Jesus "opened the minds" of his disciples "to understand the scriptures," whose message is of the suffering and resurrection of the Messiah and the proclamation of the gospel in his name: "repentance and forgiveness of sins." For their witness to the gospel Jesus assured the disciples of the empowerment of the Spirit, the promise of the Father, and "the power from on high," with which they would be invested. With the gift of the Spirit in the sacrament of order, deacons, priests, and their bishop minister in communion, cooperatively to continue Christ's charge to witness to and proclaim the gospel in the power of the Spirit.

Evangelization belongs to the *diaconia* of the word in the threefold *diaconia* of the liturgy, of the word, and of charity that deacons exercise in communion with their bishop and fellow priests (LG 29).[80] Does the threefold *diaconia* express Christ's threefold office of sanctification, teaching, and governance? *Lumen Gentium* expressly attributed these three *munera* to bishops in LG 21.[81] For presbyters it rearranged

[79] United States Conference of Catholic Bishops, *The National Directory for the Formation, Ministry, and Life of Permanent Deacons in the United States of America*, 2nd ed. (Washington, DC: United States Conference of Catholic Bishops, 2021), 37, no. 55.

[80] Tanner, *Decrees*, 2: 874.

[81] Tanner, *Decrees*, 2: 865.

their order when referring to their consecration "for preaching the gospel, and for nurturing the faithful, and for celebrating divine worship" (LG 28).[82] It recognized Christ's bestowal of the correlative office of priest, prophet, and king on laypeople (LG 34–36).[83]

Pope John Paul II connected the threefold *diaconia* and the threefold *munera* in a speech of March 16, 1985, to Italian deacons. After expounding the significance of each of the three *diaconiae*, the pope continued:

> The deacon in his degree personifies Christ, servant of the Father, participating in the threefold function of the sacrament of order. He is a *teacher* since he proclaims and illuminates the word of God. He is a *sanctifier* since he administers the sacrament of baptism, of the Eucharist, and the sacramentals. He is a *leader* (*guida*) since he is a facilitator (*animatore*) of community or sectors of ecclesial life. In this way, the deacon contributes to giving birth to the church as a reality of communion, of service, [and] of mission.[84]

The Italian bishops incorporated this statement as a papal teaching in their directory of the diaconate in 1993.[85] In 1998, both the Holy See's *Basic Norms* and *Directory* correlated the three *diaconiae* with the three *munera* consistent with John Paul II's statement, which the *Directory* explicitly referenced.[86] The *Basic Norms* (*Ratio fundamentalis*) elaborated on

[82] Tanner, *Decrees*, 2: 872.

[83] Tanner, *Decrees*, 2: 877–79.

[84] John Paul II, "Discorso ai Diaconi Italiani," in *Enchiridion sul diaconato: Le fonte e i documenti ufficiali della chiesa*, ed. Enzo Petrolino (Vatican City: Libreria Editrice Vaticana, 2009), 174, emphasis in the original.

[85] Italian Episcopal Conference, "I diaconi permanenti nella chiesa in Italia. Orientamenti e norme," no. 6, in *Enchiridion sul diaconato*, ed. Petrolino, 506.

[86] *Basic Norms*, no. 9, and *Directory*, no. 22 in *Basic Norms/Directory*, 27, 88, 88, n. 46.

the deacon's *munus regendi*, pointing out that it is "exercised through dedication to works of charity, through the offer of assistance, through the development of religious life in a community or in its individual associations with special consideration retained for charity, which constitutes the preeminent focus of diaconal ministry."[87] Without expressly mentioning the three *munera*, both editions of the American *Directory* for deacons revealed their theological debt to John Paul II by identifying the deacon as "evangelizer and teacher," "sanctifier," and "witness and guide."[88]

The Holy See's *Directory* associated a deacon's "virtue of obedience" with a subservient exercise of the *munera*. The *Directory* related the sacramentality of the diaconate to Christ's mission statement: "The Son of Man did not come to be served but to serve and to give his life a ransom for many" (Matt 20:28). Then it affirmed:

> In this way, the deacon exercises in the midst of his ministry and otherwise (*et per aliud*) the virtue of obedience. When he faithfully carries out the offices (*munera*) entrusted to him, he serves the bishop and presbyters in the offices (*in muneribus*) that belong to the mission of Christ. In this way, he discharges his pastoral ministry for the good of human beings.[89]

The *Directory* understood service in Christ's office of teaching, sanctification, and governance in the church as a theological justification for deacons to serve bishops and priests

[87] Congregation for Catholic Education, "Ratio fundamentalis institutionis diaconorum permanentium," *Acta Apostolicae Sedis* 90 (1998): 848, no. 9.

[88] United States Conference of Catholic Bishops, *National Directory for the Formation, Ministry, and Life of Permanent Deacons in the United States* (Washington, DC: United States Conference of Catholic Bishops, 2005), 18, 20; United States Conference of Catholic Bishops, *National Directory* (2021), 25, 26, 27.

[89] Congregation for the Clergy, "Directorium," 904, no. 44.

rather than as means for a communion of collaborative ordained ministers.

Conceptualizing the *munus regendi* generated ministerial imparity. Bishops and priests exercised a presidential prerogative in the celebration of the Eucharist that deacons did not share and thus necessitated the subordination of deacons to the superior episcopal and presbyteral exercise of the *munus regendi*. How could this imparity in ministerial function be reconciled with the unity of the sacrament of order, which conferred on all the ordained the three *munera*?

Didier Gonneaud proposed a solution that separated bishops and priests from deacons. Bishops and priests hold and exercise all three *munera* integrally and concurrently because they form one priestly college, one *presbyterium*. This type of exercise affords bishops and priests their leadership of a community, their *munus regendi*. Deacons, however, who are ordained into an *ordo* without a collegial structure, exercise only one or another *munus* at the commission of their bishop.[90] They exercise "the three *munera* fundamental to the sacrament of order not in their unity, but in their diversity."[91] Since deacons do not exercise the three *munera* in concert, their ministry, Gonneaud argued, cannot be a pastoral ministry because it lacks "the radical unity of the three *munera*" that makes the ministry of bishops and priests pastoral, or, in other words, that gives them the leadership of a community.[92]

[90] Didier Gonneaud, "Pour le quarantième anniversaire du rétablissement de l'ordo diaconal: réflexions autour d'une maxime doctrinale," *Nouvelle revue théologique* 126, no. 4 (2004): 563–64; Didier Gonneaud, "La sacramentalité du ministère diaconal," *Revue théologique de Louvain* 36 (2005): 17–18; Didier Gonneaud, "Diaconat et ministères," in *Le diaconat permanent: Relecture et perspectives*, ed. Bruno Dumons and Daniel Moulinet (Paris: Les Éditions du Cerf, 2007), 231–35.

[91] Gonneaud, "Pour le quarantième anniversaire du rétablissement de l'ordo diaconal," 564.

[92] Gonneaud, "Diaconat et ministères," 232.

Gonneaud's proposal suffers from several deficiencies. It undermines "the profound unity of the three *munera*" that Gonneaud approvingly attributes to the teaching of the Second Vatican Council.[93] The source of Christ's threefold office in ordained ministry is the sacrament of order, the gift of the Spirit to all ordained ministers. The contention that only bishops and priests, but not deacons, exercise the threefold office in concert disrupts its "profound unity." While teaching, sanctifying, and leading each has its "own logic" in expressing "the totality and identity of Christ," they all have an interdependent coherence for the ordained minister. Gonneaud acknowledged that an ordained minister cannot exercise one *munus* without also exercising the other. To teach means to sanctify and to lead, and interchangeably.[94] To limit deacons to one or another *munus* disrupts again the profound unity of the *munera*, whose source is Christ in the power of the Spirit, and not a bishop or priest. The Holy See's *Directory* affirms that, while "the three fields of diaconal ministry" will take up more or less of a given deacon's "activity," all three together, however, "constitute a certain unity of service in the divine economy of redemption: the ministry of the word leads to the ministry of the altar, which, in turn, impels movement beyond the liturgy into the life that blossoms into charity."[95]

Dividing the *munera* between integral and selective exercise signals two more disruptions. First, it divides Christ and his action in the church. He cannot be a teacher, sanctifier, and guide in some Christians, but not in others. Christ cannot be more or less Christ, depending on one's ministerial status. Anthony Barratt's proposal to relate the presbyter and the bishop in an integration of a unity of ontology (the sacramental relationship to Christ and the church) and a diversity of ministerial function could apply to all the

[93] Gonneaud, "Diaconat et ministères," 228.

[94] Gonneaud, "Pour le quarantième anniversaire du rétablissement de l'ordo diaconal," 563.

[95] Congregation for the Clergy, "Directorium," 900, no. 39.

baptized.[96] They equally express Christ and his mission through sacramental grace (baptism, confirmation, and, for some, the sacrament of order), but they do so through various forms of service and ministry. A theological integration of sacramental ontology and ministerial function must still explain, however, why all the baptized and all ordained ministers may not exercise the same ministries. Second, Gonneaud's proposal disrupts the communion of ordained ministers, rooted in the one sacrament of order and thus in grace, by setting bishops and priests in one completely effective ministerial college and deacons in an *ordo* of limited effect.

The graced vertical ministerial communion establishes a graced horizontal communion in which bishops, priests, and deacons share integrally in the prophetic, priestly, and royal office of Christ. *Pace* Gonneaud, deacons exercise a "pastoral ministry for the good of human beings," to quote the Holy See's *Directory* again.[97] The American bishops stated: "the deacon leads the community to reflect on its communion and mission in Jesus Christ, especially impelling the community of believers to live lives of service."[98] In their ministerial communion, bishops, priests, and deacons serve the broader communion of the church, the people of God, upon whose members Christ through the Spirit has bestowed his threefold office in baptism.

Omnium in Mentem and the Sacramental Representation of Christ

While John Paul II's correlation of the diaconate to the threefold office of Christ opened a theological discourse that

[96] Anthony Barratt, "The Sacrament of Order and the Second Vatican Council: The Presbyter-Bishop Relationship Revisited," *International Journal for the Study of the Christian Church* 2, no. 2 (2002): 21–25.

[97] Congregation for the Clergy, "Directorium," 904, no. 44.

[98] United States Conference of Catholic Bishops, *National Directory* (2005), 18, no. 32; *National Directory* (2021), 25, no. 34.

enhanced reflection on the relationship of deacons to Christ, to their communion with other ordained ministers, and to the wider ecclesial communion, he also authorized a change in the church's teaching with vexing repercussions for the theology of the diaconate. The second edition of the *Catechism of the Catholic Church* (1997) modified a passage in paragraph 875 on the ordained ministry. In the first edition (1992), the passage read: "No one can bestow grace on himself; it must be given and offered. This fact presupposes ministers of grace, authorized and empowered by Christ. From him, they receive the mission and faculty ('the sacred power') to act *in persona Christi Capitis*."[99] Revised in the second edition, the last sentence now reads: "From him, bishops and priests receive the mission and faculty ('the sacred power') to act *in persona Christi Capitis*; deacons receive the strength to serve the people of God in the *diaconia* of liturgy, word, and charity, in communion with the bishop and his presbyterate."[100] The first edition of the *Catechism* implied that all ordained ministers—bishops, priests, and deacons—received from Christ "the mission and faculty ('the sacred power') to act *in persona Christi Capitis*." But the second edition limited the graced commission to act in the person of Christ, the head of the church, to bishops and priests, while leaving unclear whether or how deacons represent Christ in their ministry.

This revision in teaching about the theological quality of the action of ordained ministers gained greater attention owing to the *motu proprio*, *Omnium in Mentem*, issued by Pope Benedict XVI in 2009. The pope explained the purpose of the revision CCC 875 by his predecessor: "that the teaching of the Dogmatic Constitution *Lumen Gentium* (no. 29) of the Second Vatican Council with reference to deacons

[99] *Catechism of the Catholic Church* (Ottawa: Canadian Conference of Catholic Bishops; Vatican City: Libreria Editrice Vaticana, 1994), 192.

[100] *Catechism of the Catholic Church*, 2nd ed. (Washington, DC: United States Catholic Conference; Vatican City: Libreria Editrice Vaticana, 2000), 232.

should be more appropriately restated (*recoleretur*)." Accordingly, Benedict XVI decided to revise cc. 1008 and 1009 in the Code of Canon Law.[101]

The following table provides a comparative reading, in translation, of these canons in their original form from 1983[102] and in the revision of 2009.[103]

1983 Code of Canon Law	Revision of 2009
CAN. 1008 By divine institution, the sacrament of orders establishes some among the Christian faithful as sacred ministers through an indelible character which marks them. They are consecrated and designated, each according to his grade, to nourish (*ut pascant*) the people of God, fulfilling in the person of Christ the Head the functions of teaching, sanctifying, and governing.	CAN. 1008 By divine institution, some of the Christian faithful are marked with an indelible character and constituted as sacred ministers of holy orders. They are thus consecrated and deputed so that, each according to his own grade, they may serve the people of God by a new and specific title.

[101] Benedict XVI, "Omnium in Mentem," *Acta Apostolicae Sedis* 102, no. 1 (January 2010): 8.

[102] *Code of Canon Law: Latin-English Edition*, first printing (Washington, DC: Canon Law Society of America, 1999), 321–22.

[103] *Code of Canon Law: Latin-English Edition*, fourth printing (Washington, DC: Canon Law Society of America, 2023), 327–28.

CAN. 1009 §1. The orders are the episcopate, the presbyterate, and the diaconate. §2. They are conferred by the imposition of hands and the consecratory prayer which the liturgical books prescribe for the individual grades.	CAN. 1009 §1. The orders are the episcopate, the presbyterate, and the diaconate. §2. They are conferred by the imposition of hands and the consecratory prayer which the liturgical books prescribe for the individual grades. §3. Those who are constituted in the order of the episcopate or the presbyterate receive the mission and capacity to act in the person of Christ the Head (*missionem et facultatem agendi in persona Christi Capitis accipiunt*), whereas deacons are empowered to serve the People of God ([*accipiunt*] *vim populo Dei serviendi*) in the ministries (*in diaconia*) of the liturgy, the word and charity.

The revised canons reconfigure and separate the communion of ordained ministers. Martin Kirschner welcomed the paradigm shift in c. 1008 from leadership, expressed by the verb *pascere*, to service, as reflective of the responsibility of ordained ministers to serve the mission of all the baptized, a responsibility that implies a certain subordination to the people of God.[104] Yet, the new legislation abandoned the exercise of the threefold office of Christ, by which all ordained ministers represent Christ, the head of the church,

[104] Martin Kirschner, "Amtlich in der Person Christi handeln – als Diakon?," *Diaconia Christi* 45, nos. 1 and 2 (2010): 233, 234.

in favor of a narrowed focus on the enactment of Christ's headship, reserved for bishops and priests. The limitation imposed in c. 1009 §3 on acting "in the person of Christ the Head" followed the revision of CCC 875. But unlike the revision of CCC 875, the new c. 1009 §3 did not repeat from LG 29 the communion of ordained ministers and thus reformulated the conciliar teaching on the diaconate less appropriately than the revision of the *Catechism* required by John Paul II.

The revisions authorized by John Paul II and Benedict XVI placed bishops and priests on the one hand and deacons on the other in separate theological domains, bestowing a christological preeminence on the former while relating the latter to the people of God without any christological reference. Benedict XVI retained the notion of the "power" of serving the people of God. Yet the significance of restating LG 29 by attributing "power" to serving the people of God remains unclear, unless it endows diaconal ministry with a dignity or prerogative for its loss of acting in the person of Christ the head. The cost of this newly claimed power is unfortunate, since the rewording of CCC 875 and c. 1009 §3 suggests a separation of Christology from ministry, of Christ from his church, and of bishops and priests from deacons that disrupts a communion of ordained ministers in the service of the people of God.

National directories on the diaconate responded to the canonical changes. In the four following examples, episcopal conferences demonstrated a revaluation of the diaconate. They mitigated the deficiencies inherent in the approach of *Ominium in Mentem* towards deacons by reclaiming them for a communion of ordained ministers and by underpinning the sacramentality of the diaconate in its representation of Christ and in its expression of Christ's threefold office.

The German bishops had already quoted cc. 1008 and 1009 §1 in the opening section on "Vocation and Ecclesial Setting" in their *Framework for Permanent Deacons* of 1994, which they republished in 2000 in the wake of the Holy

See's *Basic Norms* and *Directory*.[105] In 2015, in the same section, they quoted the revised cc. 1008, 1009 §1, and 1009 §3 before repeating from the previous *Framework* the position of the deacon "within the one mission of ecclesial office to bear the love of Christ to those in particular need of help" and a reference to the *motu proprio* of Pope Paul VI, *Sacrum Diaconatus Ordinem* (1967), that all the deacon's "tasks must be exercised in perfect communion with the bishop and his presbyterate."[106] Embedding the canonical changes within an existing ecclesiological framework reaffirmed a communion of ordained ministers.

In 2016, the Australian bishops embedded their glancing recognition of *Omnium in Mentem* in a Christology of the diaconate. Two quotations, the first from the Holy See's *Basic Norms* and the second from John Paul II's speech of November 30, 1995, to the plenary assembly of the Congregation for the Clergy, served as the christological gambit in the Australian document: "The diaconate, 'as a participation in the one ecclesiastical ministry, . . . is a specific sacramental sign, in the Church, of Christ the servant,' 'a particular configuration to Christ . . . who for love of the Father made himself the least and the servant of all.'"[107] Strategically, the

[105] German Conference of Bishops, *Rahmenordnung für Ständige Diakone in den Bistümern der Budesrepublik Deutschland / Richtlinien über persönliche Anforderungen an Diakone und Laien im pastoralen Dienst im Hinblick auf Ehe und Familie, 1. February 2000* (Bonn: Sekretariat der Deutschen Bischofskonferenz, 2000), 15, no. 1.2

[106] German Conference of Bishops, *Rahmenordnung für Ständige Diakone* (2016), 9, no. 1.2. Paul VI, "Sacrum Diaconatus Ordinem," *Acta Apostolicae Sedis* 59 (1967): 702, no. 23, specified that the deacon's ministerial communion came "under the authority of the bishop and of the presbyter, who are responsible for the care of the faithful in a given place (*eo loci*)."

[107] Australian Catholic Bishops Conference, "Norms for the Formation of Permanent Deacons and Guidelines for the Ministry and Life of Permanent Deacons," *The Canonist* 8, no. 1 (2017): 28, section 3.3.2. See *Basic Norms*, no. 5 in *Basic Norms/Directory*, 24; John Paul II, "Ad eos qui plenario coetui Congregationis pro Clericis interfuerunt," *Acta Apostolicae Sedis* 88 (1996): 707.

Australian bishops omitted the pope's specification of the deacon's "particular configuration to Christ, head and shepherd (*Capo e Pastore*) of the church" to align themselves with the more recent formulations that reserved acting in the person of Christ the head to bishops and priests.[108] Accepting this limitation, the Australian bishops nevertheless claimed a relationship with Christ for deacons through ordination: "The configuration to Christ that results from ordination by the laying on of hands and the gift of the Holy Spirit is not a participation in the priesthood of Christ as head of the church, but a conformation to Christ so as to be 'empowered to serve the People of God in the ministries of the liturgy, the word and charity.'"[109] The bishops embellished the final phrase of c. 1009 §3 to restore a christological dimension to diaconal ministry that the new canon omitted.

The Canadian *Directory* (2017) quoted c. 1009 §3 after a reference to the threefold office of Christ, in part restoring what had been deleted from c. 1008: "The deacon exercises the three *munera* proper to his ecclesiastical ministry which foster the Church's mission of service and communion."[110] After the canonical quotation, the *Directory* pointed out: "The deacon shares in Christ's threefold mission of teaching, sanctifying and leading the People of God."[111] A "correction" of 2018, however, deleted this specification of the *munera*, leaving intact the following and original reference to the threefold *diaconia*: "While the unifying principle of the

[108] John Paul II, "Ad eos qui plenario coetui Congregationis pro Clericis interfuerunt," 707: "Mediante l'imposizione delle mani del Vescovo e la specifica preghiera di consacrazione, il diacono riceve una peculiare configurazione a Cristo, Capo e Pastore della Chiesa che, per amore del Padre, si è fatto l'ultimo e il servo di tutti."

[109] Australian Catholic Bishops Conference, "Norms," 28, section 3.3.2.

[110] Canadian Conference of Catholic Bishops, *National Directory for the Ministry, Formation and Life of Permanent Deacons in Canada* (Ottawa: Canadian Conference of Catholic Bishops, 2017), 19, no. 8.

[111] Canadian Conference of Catholic Bishops, *National Directory*, 19, no. 9.

deacon's ministry is the service of charity, which shapes his service of the word and of the liturgy, the three duties are inextricably interrelated."[112]

In the second edition of their *Directory* (2021), the American bishops quoted c. 1009 §3 at the end of a paragraph that initiated the section on the "Relationship with the Priesthood." They preceded the quotation with an assertion of the value of the diaconate. They upheld the ministerial communion of deacons with the bishop and priests of their diocese, presenting deacons and priests as "collaborators in ministry" and as "two complementary but subordinate participants in the one apostolic ministry bestowed by Christ upon the Apostles and their successors." Finally, the bishops declared: "The diaconate is not an abridged or substitute form of the priesthood; it is a full order in its own right."[113]

Canonists were less circumspect than episcopal conferences in their assessment of *Omnium in Mentem*. Jean Werckmeister held that the changes in cc. 1008 and 1009 represented "a theological evolution or clarification that scarcely has any practical canonical consequences."[114] Giuliano Brugnotto clearly disagreed. The clarification that deacons do not act in the person of Christ the head and thus have no presbyteral identity corroborated norms that in effect exclude them from celebrating the sacrament of the anointing of the sick (c. 1003 §1) or from serving as chaplains

[112] See the "Link to the corrected page (PDF)" at Canadian Conference of Catholic Bishops, "Correction to page 19 of the National Directory for the Ministry, Formation and Life of Permanent Deacons in Canada," https://www.cccb.ca/announcement/correction-to-page-19-of-the-national-directory-for-the-ministry-formation-and-life-of-permanent-deacons-in-canada/.

[113] United States Conference of Catholic Bishops, *National Directory* (2021), 37, no. 54.

[114] Jean Werckmeister, "Le motu proprio *Omnium in mentem* et le mariage des ex-catholiques," *Revue de droit canonique* 57, no. 1 (2010): 241.

(cc. 564, 566), since these are ministries reserved for priests.[115] Brugnotto singled out passages in the rite of admission of candidates for holy orders in the Roman Pontifical that ought to be revised because they suggested a projected association with priestly ministry that was unsuitable for "candidates destined for the permanent diaconate."[116] Their exclusion from acting in the person of Christ the head meant that deacons could not celebrate the sacraments of the Eucharist or of penance and could not preside over a Christian community, Renato Coronelli concluded. Despite this exclusion, he believed that deacons could still exercise "an albeit limited and subordinate participation in the pastoral *munus* of Christ."[117]

Alphonse Borras expressed misgivings about the original legislation. To associate diaconal ministry with the person of Christ the head ran the risk of confusion. Strictly speaking, acting *in persona Christi* referred in the tradition of Catholic theology, especially as formulated by Thomas Aquinas, to a priest's celebration of the Eucharist. While Borras acknowledged the possibility of a more expansive ministerial context for acting *in persona Christi* than presiding at the Eucharist, he preferred to say that deacons minister *in nomine Christi*, "in the name of Christ," a formula that the Holy See's *Directory* employed.[118]

[115] Giuliano Brugnotto, "Alcune conseguenze pratiche per il diaconato permanente dal *motu proprio Omnium in mentem*," *Quaderni di diritto ecclesiale* 24, no. 2 (April 2011): 169–72.

[116] Brugnotto, "Alcune conseguenze pratiche," 176–77, quotation: 176. For the rite of admission, see *Pontificale Romanum* (1990), 232–37.

[117] Renato Coronelli, "Il diaconato alla luce delle modifiche apportate al Codice dal *motu proprio Omnium in mentem*," *Quaderni di diritto ecclesiale* 24, no. 2 (April 2011): 154.

[118] Borras, *Le diaconat au risque de sa nouveauté*, 135, 141; *Directory*, nos. 28, 37 in *Basic Norms/Directory*, 94, 101. On the development of the concept that, sacramentally, a priest acts in the person of Christ, see Bernard Dominique Marliangeas, *Clés pour une théologie du ministère: In persona Christi, In persona Ecclesiae* (Paris: Éditions Beauchesne, 1978). For the

The difference between ministering *in persona Christi* and ministering (*in*) *nomine Christi* has received scant attention in theology, however. For some theologians, as Michael Seewald has observed, ministering *in persona Christi* is equivalent to ministering *in nomine Christi*, or the latter is a specific instance of the former.[119] Seewald differentiated the expression *in nomine Christi* from the adverbial phrase *Christi nomine* (LG 11) and *nomine Christi* (LG 25, LG 27), employed in *Lumen Gentium*.[120] The latter underlines ministerial action imbued with Christ's presence, while the former draws attention to the ordained minister as the subject of ministry who ministers in Christ's name.[121] Seewald attributed acting *nomine Christi* to all ordained ministers, responsible to ensure that the priestly, prophetic, and royal offices of Christ, which determine the identity of all the baptized, "are actually exercised in the church." Ordained ministers do not receive this responsibility as a delegation from their communities, but its fulfillment signals "an indispensable part of that action that maintains the church in following Jesus."[122]

The offense to legal terminology committed by and in c. 1009 §3 drew Borras's ire as a canonist. Its reference to the *missio* and *facultas* that bishops and priests receive imported theological concepts into a juridical framework that did not understand these words as the pope intended. Furthermore, nowhere in the Code did the phrase *vim accipere*, applied to

---

theological contribution of Thomas Aquinas, see Marliangeas, *Clés*, 89–140.

[119] Michael Seewald, "Wer stellt wen dar? Über drei Formen der Repräsentation und die Stellung des ordinierten Amtes in der katholischen Kirche," in *Christusrepräsentanz: Zur aktuellen Debatte um die Zulassung von Frauen zum priesterlichen Amt*, ed. Margit Eckholt and Johanna Rahner (Freiburg im Breisgau: Herder, 2021), 29.

[120] Tanner, *Decrees*, 2: 857, 869, 871.

[121] Seewald, "Wer stellt wen dar?," 29–30.

[122] Seewald, "Wer stellt wen dar?," 41.

deacons, mean "to receive the power to do something."[123] Although he recognized the "didactic" value of "inserting theology" into canon law, Borras insisted on the separation of Code and *Catechism*. He cited the adage: *Lex iubet, non docet*—"The law commands; it does not teach."[124]

Borras also expressed theological regrets. In *Omnium in Mentem*, Benedict XVI did not repeat from LG 29 that a deacon ministered "in communion with the bishop and his presbyterate."[125] The focus on *in persona Christi* risked, moreover, "sacralizing the separation between priests and the laity," and thus c. 1009 §3 "errs by 'maximalism of the priesthood.'"[126] This same canon, Borras warned, must not turn "the doctrinal distinction" between deacons, who lack a pastorally presidential function, and bishops and priests, for whom that function is inherent, into "an absolute separation."[127] Diaconate and priesthood are inseparable ministries: "these two realities intersect as much in the people of God as in the ministry of the Church."[128]

Ironically, despite *Omnium in Mentem*, it remains unclear whether deacons minister *in persona Christi capitis*. Some paragraphs in the second and current edition of the *Catechism of the Catholic Church* suggest that deacons represent Christ the head because the *Catechism* relates this representation to those who receive the sacrament of order. "In the ecclesial service of the ordained minister," the *Catechism* teaches, "it is Christ himself who is present to his Church as Head of his Body, Shepherd of his flock, high priest of the redemptive sacrifice, Teacher of Truth" (CCC 1548).

[123] Alphonse Borras, "Les diacres d'après les nouveaux canons 1008 et 1009 §3," *Revue théologique de Louvain* 43, no. 1 (2012): 69.

[124] Borras, "Les diacres," 73–74.

[125] Borras, "Les diacres," 67.

[126] Alphonse Borras, "The Diaconate after *Omnium in Mentem* within the Context of the Shortage of Priests," in *Unlocking the Future: Women and the Diaconate*, ed. Hildegard Warnink (Leuven: Peeters, 2020), 98.

[127] Borras, "The Diaconate," 99.

[128] Borras, "The Diaconate," 98.

Furthermore, "by ordination one is enabled to act as a representative of Christ, Head of the Church, in his triple office of priest, prophet, and king" (CCC 1581). To receive "the ministry conferred by the sacrament of Holy Orders" means to assume the responsibility "to serve in the name of and in the person of Christ the Head in the midst of the community" (CCC 1591).[129] CCC 1549 affirms: "Through the ordained ministry, especially that of bishops and priests, the presence of Christ as head of the Church is made visible in the midst of the community of believers."[130] Yet what applies "especially" to bishops and priests does not apply exclusively to them. It can also apply to deacons, and thus, Kirschner argued, the phrasing of CCC 1549 demands "a further theological specification of how deacons make Christ the head visible in the communion of the faithful."[131]

Complications also arise within canon law. If c. 1009 §3 implies that only bishops and priests have the power of governance because they alone represent Christ the head, then c. 129 §1 poses a problem: "Those who have received sacred orders are qualified, according to the norm of the prescripts of the law, for the power of governance which exists in the Church by divine institution and is also called the power of jurisdiction." This canon must include deacons as ordained ministers. Judith Hahn pointed to the "ambiguity" in c. 129 §1 that those in sacred orders do not possess the power of governance but are "qualified" to exercise it. "Thus," she wrote, "the ordinations of bishops and priests have a two-fold effect: they convey upon the ordained the power of orders and the *capacity* to receive the power of governance."[132] What remains legally unclear is if deacons receive the power of governance at ordination. While not

[129] *Catechism of the Catholic Church* (2000), 387, 395, 398.

[130] *Catechism of the Catholic Church* (2000), 387.

[131] Kirschner, "Amtlich in der Person Christi handeln – als Diakon?," 237.

[132] Judith Hahn, "*Potestas incerta*: The Ambiguity of the Ecclesiastical Law on Power with Respect to Lay Leadership," *The Canonist* 13, no. 2 (2022): 185, emphasis in the original.

expressly denying that deacons receive this power, *Omnium in Mentem* suggests that they do not receive it because it separated them from bishops and priests. Confusion reigns, owing to the difficulty in reconciling c. 1009 §3 with c. 129 §1, and thus, according to Hahn, c. 1009 §3 "is another piece of the power puzzle which suggests that the legislator is unconcerned with clearly divulging the actual intended meaning of his norms."[133]

Confusion continues, owing to differences in translating the Final Document of the Synod on Synodality which potentially contravene *Omnium in Mentem*. Article 33 of the Final Document began by quoting article 67 of the ITC's document on *Synodality in the Life and Mission of the Church* (2018) and then drew a conclusion about the sacrament of orders. The English version of article 33 reported:

> The authority of pastors "is a specific gift of the Spirit of Christ the Head for the upbuilding of the entire Body" (ITC 67). This gift is bound to the Sacrament of Orders, which configures pastors to Christ, Head, Shepherd and Servant, and places them at the service of the holy People of God in order to safeguard the apostolicity of the proclamation and to promote ecclesial communion at all levels.[134]

This passage turns on one word: "pastors." In canon law, a pastor is either a bishop (c. 375 §1) or a presbyter who leads a parish (c. 519). The German, like the English, version of the Final Document also affirmed that the gift of the Spirit "is bound to the sacrament of orders, which configures

[133] Hahn, "*Potestas incerta*," 185.

[134] Francis and XVI Ordinary General Assembly of the Synod of Bishops, *For a Synodal Church: Communion, Participation, Mission—Final Document*, 14, no. 33, November 24, 2024, Vatican website, https://www.synod.va/content/dam/synod/news/2024-10-26_final-document/ENG---Documento-finale.pdf.

pastors to Christ, Head, Shepherd, and Servant."[135] The reference to pastors connects the second sentence to the first. In view of *Omnium in Mentem*, the question arises whether the configuration "to Christ, Head, Shepherd and Servant" applies to pastors exclusively. If so, such a configuration would exclude presbyters who are not pastors and would therefore potentially restrict acting in the person of Christ the head more than *Omnium in Mentem* did. The repetition of pastors did not occur, however, in the second sentence of article 33 in the original Italian version of the Final Document, which only described the effect of the sacrament of order without associating it with anyone: *Tale dono è legato al sacramento dell'Ordine che configura a Cristo Capo, Pastore e Servo*. The gift of the Holy Spirit "is bound to the sacrament of order, which configures to Christ, Head, Shepherd, and Servant."[136] A different approach surfaced in the French, Spanish, and Dutch versions. These all indicated that the sacrament "configures those who receive it to Christ, Head, Shepherd, and Servant."[137] The expansive conception of the

[135] Francis and XVI Ordinary General Assembly of the Synod of Bishops, *Für eine synodale Kirche: Gemeinschaft, Teilhabe, Sendung—Schlussdokument* 16, no. 33, November 24, 2024, Vatican website, https://www.synod.va/content/dam/synod/news/2024-10-26_final-document/DEU---Documento-finale.pdf: "Diese Gabe ist an das Sakrament der Weihe gebunden, das die Hirten Christus, dem Haupt, Hirten und Diener, gleichgestaltet."

[136] Francis and XVI Ordinary General Assembly of the Synod of Bishops, *Per una Chiesa sinodale: comunione, partecipazione, missione—Documento finale*, 16, no. 33, November 24, 2024, Vatican website, https://www.synod.va/content/dam/synod/news/2024-10-26_final-document/ITA---Documento-finale.pdf.

[137] Francis and XVI Ordinary General Assembly of the Synod of Bishops, *Pour une Église synodale: communion, participation, mission: Document final*, 16, no. 33, November 24, 2024, Vatican website, https://www.synod.va/content/dam/synod/news/2024-10-26_final-document/FRA---Documento-finale.pdf: "Ce don est lié au sacrement de l'ordre, qui configure ceux qui le reçoivent au Christ Tête, Pasteur et Serviteur." Francis and XVI Ordinary General Assembly of the Synod of Bishops, *Por una Iglesia*

sacrament of order in the Italian, French, Spanish, and Dutch versions of the Final Document allows for a configuration of deacons to Christ the head, which is at odds with *Omnium in Mentem*.

Beyond exacerbating the inconsistency of magisterial teaching in the *Catechism of the Catholic Church* on ordained ministry, *Omnium in Mentem* risks forcing magisterial teaching into an impasse. Magisterial teaching must either retreat from the position that acting *in persona Christi capitis* is a characteristic exclusive to the ministry of bishops and priests, or it must deny the sacramentality of the diaconate. Accordingly, Adolfo Longhitano responded to *Omnium in Mentem* with the observation that reserving "to bishops and presbyters the function of presiding over the community in the name of Christ the head introduces a dangerous division within the sacrament of order, makes it difficult to determine the identity of the deacon, and does not allow rendering a coherent assessment of his ministry."[138] Differentiating the diaconate from the episcopate and the presbyterate in the form of the new legislation "could offer new inspiration to those who deny" the sacramentality of the diaconate and who "propose considering deacons simply as baptized people (*semplici battezzati*), to whom specific ministries are

---

sinodal: comunión, participación y misión: Documento final, 13, no. 33, November 24, 2024, Vatican website, https://www.synod.va/content/dam/synod/news/2024-10-26_final-document/ESP---Documento-finale.pdf: "Este don está vinculado al sacramento del Orden, que configura a quienes lo reciben con Cristo Cabeza, Pastor y Siervo." Francis and XVI Ordinary General Assembly of the Synod of Bishops, *Voor een synodale kerk: gemeenschap, participatie, zending—Slotdocument*, 36–37, no. 33, November 24, 2024, Vatican website, https://www.synod.va/content/dam/synod/news/2024-10-26_final-document/DOCUMENTO-FINALE_FIAMMINGO.pdf: "Deze gave is verbonden met het sacrament van de wijding, dat wie het ontvangt gelijkvormig maakt aan Christus als Hoofd, Herder en Dienaar."

[138] Adolfo Longhitano, "Come leggere il *Motu proprio?*," *Il diaconato in Italia* 42, no. 161 (March/April 2010): 29.

entrusted."[139] The new cc. 1008 and 1009 obstructed a complex theological grasp of ordained ministry in general and of the diaconate in particular, Longhitano concluded.[140]

One way out of the theological impasse into which *Omnium in Mentem* has brought magisterial teaching is to recognize that deacons minister in the person of Christ the head of the church. This solution characterizes Manfred Hauke's response to the *motu proprio*. Hauke appealed to historical precedent: the seven deacons who exercised administrative leadership in ancient Rome. From a theological perspective, the sacrament of order and the threefold *diaconia* expressed in LG 29 justify the claim that deacons minister in the person of Christ the head. Central to Hauke's argument is that presiding at the Eucharist does not exhaust this personification of Christ. Rendering a deacon's representation of Christ in a purely functional way, Hauke held that a deacon acts in the person of Christ the head when he baptizes, witnesses marriage vows, and presides at funerals, burials, and other liturgical services since he acts toward or in the face of the church. Hauke established a gradation in representing Christ the head in the following descending order: a bishop presides over his diocese; a priest celebrates the Eucharist; a deacon exercises functions of leadership consistent with his ministry; laypeople exercise ministries entrusted to them by the hierarchy based on their baptism and confirmation and work for the coming of God's reign; those who are not Christians baptize in urgent situations.[141]

139 Longhitano, "Come leggere il *Motu proprio?*," 29. Here I have deliberately mistranslated *semplice battezzati*, which literally means "simple baptized people," to avoid offending laypeople.

140 Longhitano, "Come leggere il *Motu proprio?*," 30.

141 Manfred Hauke, "Der Diakonat und das Handeln *in persona Christi capitis*: Randbemerkungen zum Motuproprio *Omnium in mentem*," *Forum Katholische Theologie* 26, no. 3 (2010): 196–205. For a similar response to *Omnium in Mentem*, see Manfred Hauke, "Die spezifische Christusrepräsentation des Presbyters und des Diakons," in *Der Diakonat:*

Resisting the separate designations for priests as acting in the person of Christ the head and for deacons as acting in the person of Christ the servant,[142] Hauke would oppose another conception of the diaconate. Identifying deacons exclusively with Christ the servant would remedy the christological neglect that they encounter in c. 1009 §3 and thus revalue their ministry while leaving intact an exclusive attribution of acting in the person of Christ the head to priests and bishops. Such a remedy, however, does not adequately address the link between the sacrament of order and ministry in the person of Christ the head. Nor does it assert, from the perspective of this link, the sacramentality of the diaconate, even though the *Catechism* teaches that the "character" that deacons receive in the sacrament of order "configures them to Christ, who made himself the 'deacon' or servant of all" (CCC 1570).[143]

The identification with Christ the servant has become a commonplace in the theology of the diaconate. By repeating this diaconal identity, the Holy See's *Basic Norms* and *Directory* have contributed to its diffusion. Perhaps owing to the repetition, the official English translation of the *Directory* changed the manifestation of Christ as savior (*Salvator*) in the deacon's assistance of a bishop or a priest at the celebration of the Eucharist into a manifestation of "Christ, the Servant."[144] The *Basic Norms* and *Directory* principally expressed the relationship with Christ the servant in

---

Geschichte und Theologie, ed. Manfred Hauke and Helmut Hoping (Regensburg: Verlag Friedrich Pustet, 2019), 341–60, esp. 357–58 for the gradation in representing Christ the head; and Manfred Hauke, "Cristologia e diaconato," *Il diaconato in Italia* 52, nos. 224–25 (September/December 2020): 42–46.

[142] Hauke, "Der Diakonat," 200; Hauke, "Die spezifische Christusrepräsentation des Presbyters und des Diakons," 353–57; Hauke, "Cristologia e diaconato," 44.

[143] *Catechism of the Catholic Church* (2000), 392.

[144] Congregation for the Clergy, "Directorium," 895, no. 32; *Directory*, no. 32 in *Basic Norms/Directory*, 97.

sacramental and spiritual dimensions. In the sacrament of order, deacons receive a conformity with or configuration to Christ the servant.[145] That conformity underpins ministerial action in accordance with this identity of and with Christ.[146] Ordination makes the deacon "a living icon of Christ the servant within the Church."[147] This representation of Christ is the spiritual model of deacons.[148] He is the organizing principle of their spirituality and orients them spiritually to the church and to the Blessed Virgin Mary.[149]

Tim O'Donnell has developed the iconic value of Christ the servant for deacons in two ways. First, they exemplify Christ's "humble service" as manifested in the washing of his disciples' feet and his association "with sinners and outcasts."[150] As a Christ-like "humble servant," a deacon "occupies the 'lower level'" of the clergy "with the most limited powers in both the sacramental and pastoral realms."[151] In relation to bishops and priests, "the deacon serves with a completeness of subordination, of servanthood, that is unique among three grades of ordained ministry."[152] Second, the model of Christ the servant gives the deacon an exclusive identity, offering "a distinctive key to the deacon's ecclesial identity, one qualitatively different from that of bishops and priests on the one hand and of all the baptized on the other."[153]

An exclusive sacramental identity with Christ the servant for deacons makes no sense, however, because Christ-like

[145] *Basic Norms*, nos. 5, 85; *Directory*, nos. 46, 47, 67 in *Basic Norms/Directory*, 24, 67, 112, 113, 132.

[146] *Directory*, no. 47 in *Basic Norms/Directory*, 113.

[147] *Basic Norms*, no. 11 in *Basic Norms/Directory*, 28.

[148] *Basic Norms*, no. 11 in *Basic Norms/Directory*, 28; *Directory*, nos. 43, 45 in *Basic Norms/Directory*, 110, 111.

[149] *Directory*, nos. 50, 57 in *Basic Norms/Directory*, 116, 120.

[150] O'Donnell, *The Deacon*, 89.

[151] O'Donnell, *The Deacon*, 93.

[152] O'Donnell, *The Deacon*, 92.

[153] O'Donnell, *The Deacon*, 93.

service is the vocation of all the baptized and of all ministers. Yves Congar, a pioneer of the *diaconia* of Christ as a theological construct, claimed:

> Christian ministries are nothing but a participation in the service, in the total *diaconia* that Jesus Christ accomplished for God and for the world. In exercising them, each according to her or his vocation, we take our place in the plan of universal salvation, of which Christ is the absolute principle."[154]

These ministries of *diaconia* are not exclusively ordained ministries, as Alain Grau correctly observed. Congar's concept of ministry went beyond the ordained to encompass the mission of all the baptized "for the church and for the world."[155]

Yet what applies to all the baptized certainly applies to all the ordained. The Holy Spirit in the sacrament of order configures ordained ministers as servant-leaders to Christ the servant. Borras appropriately contended: "The representation of Christ the servant cannot be a differentiating criterion in the sense of a quality exclusively attributable to deacons among ordained ministers."[156]

For Pope John Paul II, in his apostolic exhortation on priestly formation, *Pàstores Dabo Vobis* (1992), the sacramental configuration of presbyters to Christ the head of the church was equivalent to the sacramental configuration to Christ the servant, who expressed his authority as head of the church in his mission of service in giving his life "as a ransom for many" (Mark 10:45). Christ fulfilled this "service or ministry" by accepting "death on the cross." His authority

[154] Congar, "Le diaconat," 137. Alain Grau, "'Diaconie du Christ': De l'analogie pratique à la catégorie théologique," *Communio: revue catholique internationale* 26, no. 2 (March/April 2001): 32, claimed that Congar was the first to mention, at least in French, "the theme of Christ the servant."

[155] Grau, "'Diaconie du Christ,'" 33.

[156] Borras, *Le diaconat au risque de sa nouveauté*, 143.

as head of the church corresponds to his "service, gift, total dedication, replete, moreover, with humble love for the church." Thus, the pope maintained: "Especially by this form of authority, namely in the service offered to the church, does the entire spiritual existence of each presbyter find inspiration and life, and it attains perfection in his demanding configuration to Christ Jesus, head and servant of the church."[157] Since sacramental configuration to Christ the head and sacramental configuration to Christ the servant necessarily cohere for presbyters because Christ is both head and servant of the church, then these two ways of conceptualizing a sacramental configuration to Christ should also apply to bishops and deacons. Configuration to Christ the head demands configuration to Christ the servant and vice versa.

John Paul II's theology of the priesthood ought to encourage a holistic Christology for ministers, a Christology that integrates the various characteristics of Christ instead of isolating or separating them. When Jesus washed the feet of his disciples at the Last Supper—a commonplace for asserting a deacon's configuration to Christ the servant and even for the institution of the diaconate[158]—he applied his example of service, intended for all his disciples, to his identity as "Lord and Teacher" (John 13:14, NRSV). The footwashing startlingly expressed the love and respect of Jesus for his disciples, who in their culture would have expected disciples to wash their teacher's feet. The magisterial authority of Jesus, the washer of feet, remained intact, especially as he commissioned his disciples to be a communion of love in imitation of his example, obliging them as his "blessed" emissaries to extend the communion of love that he founded

[157] John Paul II, "Pastores Dabo Vobis," *Acta Apostolicae Sedis* 84 (1992): 689, no. 21.

[158] Kasper, "Der Diakon," 154; Glover, "The Permanent Diaconate," 194.

(John 13:14-17).[159] The washer of feet is also Christ, the Lord and teacher, and Christ the head of the church. Just as the hypostatic union does not allow a dichotomy between Christ the Son of God and Christ the servant,[160] so too must what the Council of Chalcedon called "the confession of one and the same Son, our Lord Jesus Christ" not permit disjunctions or divisions in the one Jesus Christ.[161] Consequently, as Grau argued, Christ's *diaconia* or service is salvific because Christ orients his *diaconia* to redemption, to the ransoming of the many with his life. "Thus," Grau wrote, "Christ's *diaconia* is first of all and essentially the paschal mystery."[162] Jesus's act of washing the feet of his disciples constituted "the indispensable prelude to the Last Supper," to "the paschal banquet," to the sacramental offering of his Body and Blood.[163] His redemptive death on the cross, configured as his filial service to God, expressed his "authority" and "sovereignty" as Son of God.[164]

In view of his integration of Christ's *diaconia* with his redemptive and sovereign sonship, Grau drew a surprising conclusion about deacons. They exercised their *diaconia* in "its natural state" (*à l'état brut*) in their inability to do anything. The deacon "can do nothing" because, as Grau explained, he, unlike bishops and priests, lacked "sacred powers," and thus could not act in the person of Christ the head.[165] Grau elaborated: "The excessive character of the unique and definitive 'diaconia' of Christ defines the very person of the deacon, who can only 'serve,' inasmuch as this

[159] Anni Hentschel, *Die Fußwaschungserzählung im Johannesevangelium: Ein Beitrag zur johanneischen Ekklesiologie* (Tübingen: Mohr Siebeck, 2022), 297–304.

[160] Grau, "'Diaconie du Christ,'" 40.

[161] I quoted from the English translation of the Chalcedonian definition of faith in Tanner, *Decrees*, 1: *86.

[162] Grau, "'Diaconie du Christ,'" 41.

[163] Grau, "'Diaconie du Christ,'" 43.

[164] Grau, "'Diaconie du Christ,'" 45.

[165] Grau, "'Diaconie du Christ,'" 50.

service has become radical and only when it is rendered perfectly radical."[166] By apparently divorcing Christ's *diaconia* from his redemptive and sovereign sonship with respect to deacons, Grau's conclusion betrayed the very Christology that he espoused, namely a Christology free of dichotomy. In such a Christology, deacons should, by virtue of the sacrament of order, represent and act in the person of Christ the servant who is also Christ the head of the church.

Since these and other titles or offices of Christ figure in the economy of salvation that he accomplished, Gerhard Müller's concept of ordained ministries merits attention. He called for avoiding the danger of apportioning the various offices of Christ among the offices of ordained ministry in its various grades. Müller agreed that "the one messianic salvific ministry of Christ to the church and the world" may be expressed through "the different titles of Jesus (shepherd, priest, prophet, servant, apostle, bishop, Lord, head, etc.)." Yet each ordained ministry "represents the entirety of the one salvific ministry of Christ, although in differentiated participation."[167] However a synodal church assesses that participation, all ordained ministers have a communion in making present in the church and in the world the one saving Christ.

Perhaps under the influence of the thinking of Müller, who contributed to the ITC's document on the diaconate, the ITC asked of ordained ministers: "Could 'headship' and 'service' in the representation of Christ be separated so as to make each of the two a principle of specific differentiation?" This rhetorical question intended a negative response. The ITC proposed three principles to steer theologians away from "disproportionate theological exchanges" on the representation of Christ in ordained ministry: "the unity of the person of Christ, the unity of the sacrament of order, and

[166] Grau, "'Diaconie du Christ,'" 50–51.

[167] Gerhard Ludwig Müller, "Theologische Überlegungen zur Weiterentwicklung des Diakonats," *Münchener Theologische Zeitschrift* 40, no. 2 (June 1989): 137.

the symbolic character of the terms used to represent Christ ('head,' 'servant,' 'shepherd,' 'spouse')."[168] Clearly, the ITC's theological advice did not inform the crafting of c. 1009 §3.

The best doctrinal solution for conceptualizing the sacramental and ministerial representation of Christ that deacons express is to abandon Christological specifications or precisions for deacons and for all ministers. This solution serves the communion of ordained ministers and the broader ecclesial communion. In this communion, all the baptized have clothed themselves with the one Jesus Christ (Gal 3:27), whose Spirit God sent into their hearts to be God's children in freedom, not in slavery (Gal 4:6-7). Christ has set them free for freedom (Gal 5:1), for a freedom of equality enacted in the charisms bestowed by the Spirit, in mutual service, and in a synodal church through a "mutual recognition of participation as peers."[169]

Assigning, in a theology of ministry, Christ the head exclusively to bishops and priests, and Christ the servant exclusively or preeminently to deacons, divides the one Jesus Christ and thus the communion, effected by his Spirit, that Christ's disciples have with him and with each other. Introducing christological distinctions to guarantee the distinctiveness, and thus the worthiness and dignity, of ministerial identities contravenes the teaching of Jesus. The rites of ordination of bishops, priests, and deacons all may use Matthew 20:25-28 for the gospel reading at Mass.[170] This pericope makes it clear that Jesus did not want his disciples to erect systems of subordination, to "lord it over" each other. "It will not be so among you," he insisted. Their greatness consisted in serving each other "just as the Son of Man came not to be served but to serve, and to give his life a ransom

[168] ITC, *From the Diakonia of Christ to the Diakonia of the Apostles*, chapter VII, section II.4.

[169] Thomas O'Laughlin, "Equality as a Theological Principle within Roman Catholic Ecclesiology," *Ecclesiology* 18, no. 1 (2022): 49–50, 51, 55, quotation: 55.

[170] *Pontificale Romanum* (1990), 223, no. 351/4.

for many." With Jesus all Christians are servants of each other and of all human beings. To claim, as O'Donnell did, that deacons distinctively represent Christ the servant in a way that is "qualitatively different" from bishops, priests, and laypeople establishes a privileged relation between deacons and Christ and a privileged place for deacons in the church and risks exalting deacons while humbling them.[171]

A Christology of ordained ministry can begin, as Jesus's ministry began, with the Holy Spirit. Empowered by the Spirit, Jesus taught in synagogues (Luke 4:14-15). At home in the synagogue of Nazareth, he affirmed his being anointed by the Spirit "to bring good news to the poor" and liberation to those deprived of freedom (Luke 4:18, 21). Jesus's service to the liberative reign of God constitutes the ministry of bishops, priests, and deacons, who, in different ways, represent Christ, the anointed one, in their servant-leadership of the people of God, "in whose hearts the Holy Spirit dwells as in a temple" (LG 8).[172] Christ, certainly, is the head of his "messianic people" (LG 8).[173] But he is and remains in his ordained ministers "as one who serves" (Luke 22:27) among his disciples, not elevated above them.

When, in his encyclical *Mediator Dei* (1947), Pope Pius XII developed the idea, if not the exact formula, that a priest, by virtue of celebrating the Eucharist, acts in the person of Christ the head, he gave a priest a privileged status in the church. According to the pope, at the altar "as a minister of Christ" a priest "acts as (*gerit*) the person of Our Lord Jesus Christ, inasmuch as he is head of all the members," while offering Christ for the people and for himself. Thus, a priest is "inferior to Christ but superior to the people."[174] The canonical reform decreed by *Omnium in Mentem* has a similar effect in sacralizing bishops and priests into a relationship

[171] O'Donnell, *The Deacon*, 93.

[172] Tanner, *Decrees*, 2: 856.

[173] Tanner, *Decrees*, 2: 856.

[174] Pius XII, "Mediator Dei," *Acta Apostolicae Sedis* 39 (1947): 553.

with Christ the head, setting them apart from deacons and the people of God.

In their analysis of the diaconate, the bishops of Quebec offered a characterization of diaconal ministry helpful for a communion of ministers. While they adhered to the traditional formula of the deacon as the representation of Christ the servant,[175] and while they even went so far as to state that "together" all ordained ministers "sacramentally represent Christ the shepherd and servant in the midst of the ecclesial community,"[176] they were also able to relate deacons to Christ without rank or title, as it were. After disagreeing with making general the practice of having deacons assume "the pastoral direction of a Christian community because this would harm the diaconal identity and the presbyteral identity," the bishops wrote: "The practice of diaconal ministry should not therefore be assessed or evaluated starting from the abilities to accomplish certain tasks or functions, but first from a consideration of the significance of his sacramental participation in the ministry of Christ in the world and in the Christian community."[177] Through deacons, Christ ministers in the church and in the world that he has redeemed. The same can and must be said of all ordained and lay ministers. The teaching, sanctifying, and liberating Christ acts through his ministers, serving in communion the people of God, by the power of the Spirit whom they received in the sacrament of baptism and, in the case of some ministers, in the sacrament of order to exercise the ministry of Christ.

A principle stated by Pius XII can justify the retreat from the application of acting in the person of Christ the head to bishops and priests only. The phrase *in persona Christi capitis*

[175] Comité des ministères de l'Assemblée des évêques catholiques du Québec, *Le diaconat permanent au Québec: Avancées, hésitations, prospectives* ([Montreal]: Fides, 2006), 17, no. 15; 19, no. 23; 29, no. 44; 31, no. 48.

[176] Comité des ministères, *Le diaconat*, 17, no. 14.

[177] Comité des ministères, *Le diaconat*, 28, nos. 40, 41.

agere first appeared in 1965 in *Presbyterorum Ordinis* (PO 2).[178] Since then, the magisterium and theologians have frequently invoked this "recent innovation."[179] In 1947, the same year in which he issued *Mediator Dei*, Pius XII redefined the matter and form of the sacrament of order in *Sacramentum Ordinis*, as chapter 1 pointed out. The pope taught that the matter of the sacrament of order consisted of the laying on of hands, while the form of the sacrament consisted of the designated words spoken by the ordaining bishop at the laying on of his hands.[180] He thus revoked the teaching of the Council of Florence in 1439 that the *traditio instrumentorum*, the handing over of the instruments (the chalice and paten for ordination to the priesthood and the gospel book for ordination to the diaconate) constituted the matter of the sacrament and that the words spoken by the ordaining bishop at the *traditio instrumentorum* constituted the form of the sacrament.[181] To justify his decision, the pope declared: "But, if in the past, the church decided and decreed that something was actually necessary for validity, everyone knows that the church also has the power to change and to abrogate what it has established."[182] According to Seewald, this declaration justified "a serious intervention" in the

[178] Tanner, *Decrees*, 2: 1044.

[179] Seewald, "Wer stellt wen dar?," 36.

[180] Pius XII, "Sacramentum Ordinis," *Acta Apostolicae Sedis* 40 (1948): 6, no. 4.

[181] Tanner, *Decrees*, 1: 549–550; Michael Seewald, *Reform—Dieselbe Kirche anders denken* (Freiburg im Breisgau: Herder, 2018), 82.

[182] Pius XII, "Sacramentum Ordinis," 6, no. 3: "Quod si ex Ecclesiae voluntate et praescripto eadem aliquando fuerit necessaria ad valorem quoque, omnes norunt Ecclesiam quod statuit etiam mutare et abrogare valere." On the controversy within the Holy Office about the church's ability to reform doctrine that marked the redaction of *Sacremntum Ordinis*, see Matthias Daufratshofer, "Did Pius XII Change a Dogma in 1947? The Apostolic Constitution *Sacramentum ordinis* and its Underestimated Potential," *Journal of Modern and Contemporary Christianity* 3, no. 1 (April 2024): 247–90.

church's teaching on the sacrament of order.[183] Furthermore, it signaled a doctrinal development that showed that the church could correct its own teaching on a subject as important as the sacrament of order.[184] The church can again apply Pius XII's principle of ecclesial self-correction to its teaching on the sacrament of order by abandoning the specification of acting in the person of Christ the head of the church for (some) ordained ministers.

Two considerations support such a self-correction. First, under the guidance of the Holy Spirit, the church always undertakes the duty "of carefully investigating the signs of the times and of interpreting them in the light of the gospel" (GS 2).[185] In 1965, before the development of a post-conciliar theology of the diaconate and of lay ministry, the Second Vatican Council taught that the character bestowed by the sacrament of order in the configuration to Christ the priest enables a presbyter "to act in the person of Christ the head" (PO 2).[186] Now, the church, guided by the Spirit "into all the truth" of and about Christ (John 16:13-14), has the power to abandon this formula as a doctrinal statement owing to its incoherence with a communion of ordained ministers and a co-responsibility of all the baptized in the evangelizing mission of the church. Second, as Serena Noceti has argued, the post-conciliar magisterial and theological development of the formula *in persona Christi* with its various specifications, including that of Christ the head, has proceeded in a defective direction. The development has emphasized a priest's individual symbolic representative relationship to Christ, especially in the celebration of the Eucharist, a mediator between God and the church without adequate reflection on the difference between Christ and a priest. This emphasis comes at the cost of the pneumatological and ecclesiological dimensions of priestly ministry. In

[183] Seewald, *Reform*, 84.
[184] Seewald, *Reform*, 84–85.
[185] Tanner, *Decrees*, 2: 1070.
[186] Tanner, *Decrees*, 2: 1044.

other words, the emphasis on a priest's acting in the person of Christ the head has muted a substantive recognition of the Holy Spirit's agency in the priest's ministry and the positioning of that ministry within the people of God.[187] Noceti's qualification of *in persona Christi* in its post-conciliar development as an *espressione abusata* applies also to the specification *in persona Christi capitis*: "an expression that has become overused and misused and, consequently, is no longer capable of clarity and precision."[188]

Diaconal Communion

The laborious discussion provoked by *Omnium in Mentem* shows the theological precarity of deacons as ordained ministers in the church. In its failure to recognize the communion of ordained ministers in service of the people of God and in its silence about the sacramental representation of Christ by deacons, c. 1009 §3 aids and abets an auxiliary and ancillary identity of deacons. Communion, owing to the revision in canon law, easily yields to *suppléance*. Reflecting on c. 1009 §3, Glover, a deacon and a canonist, arrived at a startling conclusion: "deacons are, almost by definition, expendable." He explained:

> We deacons are not truly needed, at least not in the same sense as the priests or laity. But far from being a cry for defeatism, this spirituality of expendability should be a means by which deacons are able to identify with and minister to those who feel most abandoned, most ostracized, most forgotten—in short, those in most need of unrecognized, unrewarded service.[189]

[187] Serena Noceti, "*In persona Christi:* Limits and Potential of an *Espressione abusata*," *Studia Canonica* 56, no. 2 (2022): 462–64.

[188] Noceti, "*In persona Christi*," 444.

[189] Glover, "The Permanent Diaconate," 212.

The unacceptability of Glover's conclusion reflects the unacceptability of c. 1009 §3. At issue is something much more fundamental than the gradation and value of ministries. The essential diaconal character of the church is in danger of being forgotten. Christ's service to "those who feel most abandoned, most ostracized, most forgotten" belongs inherently, not peripherally, to his church's mission of proclaiming God's reign. That service and mission must be manifest, not "unrecognized." By ministering to the poor, deacons sacramentally represent what Christ wishes his church to be: a serving and saving church, the "universal sacrament of salvation," upon which his guiding Spirit rests (LG 48).[190] To think of deacons as expendable substitutes in the church's mission and ministries undermines the place of the poor "at the heart of the Church,"[191] since they would be as peripheral and as forgotten as the supposedly expendable deacons who identify with them.

The warning about the devaluing of the diaconate that Ottmar Fuchs issued nine years before *Omnium in Mentem* remains relevant because of the revision of canon law:

> Every form of downgrading (*Abstufung*), even the exclusion of the diaconate from the sacrament of order, is justifiable neither in ecclesiology nor in the theology of ministry. On the contrary, this demands the declaration of massive resistance because the value of the *diaconia* of the church as a whole is at risk.[192]

Downgrading the diaconate not only marginalizes the exercise of *diaconia* by deacons but damages another fundamental reality of the church: communion. Deacons minister

[190] Tanner, *Decrees*, 2: 887.

[191] Francis and XVI Ordinary General Assembly of the Synod of Bishops, *For a Synodal Church*, 10, no. 19.

[192] Ottmar Fuchs, "Wer ist der Diakon? Seine Berufung, seine lokalen, überregionalen und globalen Aufgaben," *Diaconia Christi* 35, nos. 3 and 4 (2000): 120.

in communion with the bishop and his presbyterate within the larger communion of the church, in which all the baptized contribute to the church's *diaconia*.

The assertion of the graced communion of deacons with bishops and priests requires structures and theological models of ministerial communion. A structural reform in favor of such a communion requires changes in canon law. Theological models will help the universal and especially the local church reconceptualize the ministry of deacons as ministers among other ministers.

Canonical revision must happen at the level of ecclesial governance so that deacons contribute to decision-making processes that affect the ways in which a local church expresses itself through ministries required by its historical circumstances. Glover pointed out that in its identification of ecclesial subjects, whom a bishop must invite to a diocesan synod, c. 463 does not explicitly mention deacons.[193] The explanation for this omission most likely stems from the church's limited experience of the diaconate in the period of revising the Code of Canon Law before 1983. A relatively easy correction of c. 463 would indicate the necessary presence of deacons at a diocesan synod, provided that a diocese has deacons.

Replacing the presbyteral council (cc. 495–501) with a ministerial council, through which a bishop takes advice from priests *and* deacons, represents a more pronounced structural reform than the specification of whom a bishop must consult at a diocesan synod. The Second Vatican Council called for the establishment of "a council or senate of priests, representing the presbyterate" to assist the bishop in governing a diocese "for the needs of pastoral work and for the good of the diocese" (PO 7).[194] More than sixty years after the council, deacons increasingly exercise roles of servant-leadership in various pastoral ministries, often with

[193] Glover, "The Permanent Diaconate," 204–5.
[194] Tanner, *Decrees*, 2: 1052.

expertise gained from ministerial experience. A bishop should formally take advice from deacons as well as from priests in a diocesan synodal structure, given the one sacrament of order by which a bishop serves the people of God in communion with priests and deacons. A bishop's college of consultors (c. 502) should therefore also include deacons.

The legislating of a synodal communion of a bishop, priests, and deacons would parallel the way in which one ancient church order reversed the prescription of a predecessor. While the *Apostolic Tradition* denied that deacons were advisers of the clergy,[195] the *Testamentum Domini*, probably composed in the fifth century,[196] asserted the opposite. It insisted that the deacon should be "an advisor of the entire clergy and, as it were, a mystery (or symbol) of the universal church."[197]

Alternatively, a synodal church could revise its law by supporting the diocesan bishop's decisions in pastoral matters with a single synodal structure. This revision would dissolve the presbyteral council in favor of the diocesan pastoral council (cc. 511–514), which would thus become in law a required, not simply recommended, synodal structure, as proposed by the Synod on Synodality.[198] Members of the laity, diaconate, and presbyterate would serve on such

[195] Hippolytus of Rome, *La tradition apostolique d'après les anciennes versions*, 2nd ed., rev., trans. and ed. Bernard Botte, Sources Chrétiennes vol. 11/2 (Paris: Les Éditions du Cerf, 1984), 60.

[196] Paul F. Bradshaw, *The Search for the Origins of Christian Worship: Sources and Methods for the Study of Early Liturgy*, 2nd ed. (Oxford: Oxford University Press, 2002), 87.

[197] Ignatius Ephraem II Rahmani, ed., *Testamentum Domini Nostri Jesu Christi* (Mainz: Franz Kirchheim, 1899), 81. I translated from Rahmani's Latin translation of the Syriac text that he established, which was a translation of the original Greek version, which has not survived. On the *Testamentum Domini*, see Bradshaw, *The Search for the Origins of Christian Worship*, 86–87.

[198] Francis and XVI Ordinary General Assembly of the Synod of Bishops, *For a Synodal Church*, 37, no. 104.

a reconstituted diocesan pastoral council, which would serve as a synodal structure of the local church, representing an ecclesial communion.

Bernd Jochen Hilberath proposed a model of the diaconate as an autonomous ministry within an ecclesial and ordained communion. With their bishop, deacons and priests lead a local church in the three interrelated expressions of the church, in which all the baptized share: *martyria* (witness), *leiturgia* (worship), and *diaconia* (service). Their leadership in these three manifestations of the church operates within a two-fold "dimension" of a church that lives not of itself (i.e., a church that lives by grace) and that lives not for itself. A priest and a deacon provide a complementary and interdependent leadership of a parish community. The emphasis in a priest's leadership is a *martyria* that proclaims dependence on God's salvific action in Christ and that functions most prominently in *leiturgia*. *Diaconia* constitutes the focus of a deacon's leadership, which in witness and worship represents God's salvific work in Christ through the church for all human beings.[199] A bishop has the fullness of order insofar as priests and deacons assist him by exercising their interrelated ministries to make their Christian community a concrete social reality.[200]

According to the model of Fuchs, the communion of leadership of a priest and deacon is so intertwined that their ministries intersect in their sacramental representation of the inseparability of God's salvific love for human beings and the love of neighbors for each other. A priest's *martyria* of the proclamation of God's love implies a deacon's *diaconia* of neighborly love, and vice versa. Thus, since the celebration of the sacraments expresses both the church's witness and service, Fuchs conceived of a diaconal priesthood and

[199] Bernd Jochen Hilberath, "Thesen zur Theologie des Diakonats," in *Ständige Diakone—Stellvertreter der Armen? Projekt Pro Diakonia: Prozess—Positionen—Perspectiven*, ed. Klaus Kießling (Berlin: LIT Verlag, 2006), 95–104.

[200] Hilberath, "Thesen zur Theologie des Diakonats," 102.

a priestly diaconate, in which deacons, ordained for leadership, could celebrate the sacraments.[201] Their spiritual leadership justified their presiding at the Eucharist within the specific diaconal environment in which they exercise leadership.[202]

A saying of Jesus in John's gospel offers an alternative approach to ministerial communion and the relationship with Christ. John 12:26 figures negligibly in the philological and exegetical analysis of *diakonia* because its use of *diakonos* points to a servant, possibly a disciple, but not to someone with a divine or ecclesial commission for ministry.[203] Jesus says: "Whoever serves [*diakonē*] me must follow me, and where I am, there will my servant [*ho diakonos ho emos*] be also. Whoever serves me, the Father will honor." Service to Christ here means being present to him, not making him present, not representing him. Where is Christ so that his disciples must turn to him? He is present in the "crucified people" of the world, to borrow Ignacio Ellacuría's term,[204] and they are the hungry, the thirsty, the stranger, the naked, the sick, and the prisoners (Matt 25:35-36). Those who minister to "one of these of my brothers who are the least (*heni*

[201] Fuchs, "Wer ist der Diakon?," 118–20; Ottmar Fuchs, "Das diakonale Amt als Sacrament der Kirche für die Welt," in *Ständige Diakone*, 69–72.

[202] Fuchs, "Das diakonale Amt," 88.

[203] John N. Collins, *Diakonia: Re-interpreting the Ancient Sources* (New York: Oxford University Press, 1990), 248.

[204] Ignacio Ellacuría, "The Crucified People: An Essay in Historical Soteriology," trans. Phillip Berryman and Robert R. Barr, in Ignacio Ellacuría, *Essays on History, Liberation, and Salvation*, ed. Michael E. Lee (Maryknoll, NY: Orbis Books, 2013), 195–224. Referring to the suffering people identified in Jesus's parable in Matthew 25:34-40, the ITC recently affirmed: "But let us make no mistake: these crucified people of history *are Christ among us*, in the strongest possible sense: 'you did it to *me*' (Mt 25:40)." See ITC, *Jesus Christ, Son of God, Saviour: 1700th Anniversary of the Ecumenical Council of Nicaea, 325-2025*, April 3, 2025, Vatican website, https://www.vatican.va/roman_curia/congregations/cfaith/cti_documents/rc_cti_doc_20250403_1700-nicea_en.html, no. 123, emphasis in the original.

toutōn tōn adelphōn mou tōn elaxistōn)" (Matt 25:40), Jesus says, serve him, and he calls his servants "blessed by my Father" (Matt 25:34). His communion is with his brothers and sisters, the poor and the suffering, in whom "the church recognizes the image of its founder, poor and suffering" (LG 8).[205] In embracing "with love all people afflicted by human frailty" (LG 8),[206] the church realizes itself as a communion of service, a diaconal communion, ministering to the crucified people and to Christ.

Another name for this graced diaconal communion is the people of God. Deacons belong to this people equally with all the baptized in a common mission to proclaim Christ's good news of God's reign. All members of the people of God carry out, or ought to carry out, this mission without a literally degrading *suppléance*. What in synod the Amazonian bishops desired in 2019 for the church in their region should be the synodal objective of all local churches: "a concurrence of communion and participation, of the co-responsibility and ministeriality (*ministerialidad*) of all, paying special attention to the effective participation of laypeople in the discernment and the taking of decisions, [and] promoting the participation of women."[207] How deacons serve among the synodal people of God, suffused with the gifts of the Spirit for ministry, forms the subject of the next chapter.

[205] Tanner, *Decrees*, 2: 855.

[206] Tanner, *Decrees*, 2: 855.

[207] Synod of Bishops, "Coetus specialis pro regione amazonica documentum finale," *Acta Apostolicae Sedis* 111, no. 11 (November 2019): 1775, no. 92.

Chapter 3: Service to the People of God

Sacrament of the Spirit

Thomas O'Meara rightly equated a theology of ministry with "a theology of the Holy Spirit."[1] Such a theology overcomes the division of the church into a ministering, active clergy and a passive laity, replacing it with O'Meara's model of concentric circles of ministry that encompass all the baptized.[2] The 1917 Code of Canon Law understood laypeople as passive recipients of pastoral care, having "the right to receive from the clergy, in accordance with the norm of ecclesiastical discipline, spiritual goods and, especially, assistance necessary for salvation" (c. 682).[3] A pneumatic theology of ministry, however, begins with the premise that all the baptized receive charisms from the Spirit to act in the church's service of God's reign,[4] to serve in the church's mission to be the sacrament of salvation for all human beings. O'Meara affirmed: "Charism is diaconal."[5] Since the Spirit bestows gifts on all the baptized, O'Meara concluded: "Every Christian has a vocation to ministry, to serving the

[1] Thomas F. O'Meara, *Theology of Ministry*, rev. ed. (New York: Paulist Press, 1999), 38.

[2] O'Meara, *Theology of Ministry*, 179–80.

[3] *Codex iuris canonici Pii X Pontificis Maximi iussu digestus, Benedicti Papae XV auctoritate promulgatus* (Roma: Typis Polyglottis Vaticanis, 1917), 204.

[4] O'Meara, *Theology of Ministry*, 205.

[5] O'Meara, *Theology of Ministry*, 206.

kingdom of God."[6] Such a universal claim for ministry is too expansive, however, since it confuses the general concept of service, carried out occasionally and spontaneously, with ministry, instituted or ordained, as the exercise of a stable servant-leadership with a defined and authorized purpose.[7] Of course, the gifts of the Spirit enable both service and ministry. Deacons serving the people of God minister within a servant church among diverse ministers empowered for *diaconia* by the Spirit, who is Lord (2 Cor 3:17)[8] as well as servant, mediating Christ's truth to his disciples (John 16:14-15).

In O'Meara's model of ministry, bishops and presbyters occupy the inner circle from which emanate other circles of ministry. These ordained ministers serve "to facilitate and coordinate ministries," a responsibility that "involves attracting, educating, and directing an ensemble of ministries and not just hiring or controlling people."[9] Ministries expanding from the center "could be established as forms of the diaconate, a diaconate for women as well as men," benefiting deacons with "clear ministerial activities."[10] In a future synodal church, in which women and men minister as deacons, these ministers should participate in a diocesan coordination of ministries by virtue of the sacrament of

[6] O'Meara, *Theology of Ministry*, 210.

[7] On the distinction of service and ministry, see Yves Congar, "Le diaconat dans la théologie des ministères," in *Le diacre dans l'Église et le monde d'aujourd'hui*, ed. Paul Winninger and Yves Congar (Paris: Les Éditions du Cerf, 1966), 124–25; Yves Congar, "Ministères et structuration de l'Église," in Congar, *Ministères et communion ecclésiale* (Paris: Les Éditions du Cerf, 1971), 43–46; Francis and XVI Ordinary General Assembly of the Synod of Bishops, *For a Synodal Church: Communion, Participation, Mission—Final Document*, 27–28, nos. 75–76, November 24, 2024, Vatican website, https://www.synod.va/content/dam/synod/news/2024-10-26_final-document/ENG---Documento-finale.pdf.

[8] Emily Wong, "The Lord Is the Spirit (2 Cor 3,17a)," *Ephemerides Theologicae Lovanienses* 61, no. 1 (April 1985): 48–72.

[9] O'Meara, *Theology of Ministry*, 182.

[10] O'Meara, *Theology of Ministry*, 183.

order, which brings them into a graced communion with their bishop and presbyters. The circles of ministry ought not only to expand outwards but also to settle inwards so that, in a local synodal church, ministerial planning is the co-responsible service of the graced communion of the baptized.

The coordination of ministries will take place among the people of God thanks to the ferment of the Spirit through dialogue, debate, and discernment. For Pope Francis, the "dynamism" of synodal "reciprocal listening, conducted at all levels, engaging all the people of God," enables the attentive to have "ears for catching the wind of the Spirit, which causes disruptions, prepares (*riserva*) surprises, thrusts open doors and windows, demolishes walls, opens up borders."[11] The pope, of course, alluded to the Spirit who surprised the disciples, gathered in Jerusalem, with a heavenly "sound like the rush of a violent wind" (Acts 2:2). A predictable business as usual is not the métier of the Holy Spirit, the divine improviser in what Elizabeth Johnson called "the infinite creativity of God," which "is much more closely allied to the outbreak of novelty than our older order-oriented theology ever imagined." Johnson explained: "The indwelling Creator Spirit grounds not only life's regularities but also the novel occurrences that open up the *status quo*, igniting what is unexpected, interruptive, genuinely uncontrolled, and unimaginably possible."[12] Víctor Codina, the eminent pneumatologist among liberation theologians, asserted: "The Spirit is vivifying, is Lord and giver of life, is innovation, always reaches beyond known boundaries, disrupts plans, surprises, never abandons us, never goes on strike."[13] Karl Rahner, Codina's teacher, agreed: "God does

[11] Pope Francis with Carlo Musso, *Spera: L'autobiografia* (Milan: Mondadori, 2025), 269.

[12] Elizabeth A. Johnson, *Ask the Beasts: Darwin and the God of Love* (London: Bloomsbury Continuum, 2014), 173.

[13] Víctor Codina, *El Espíritu sopla desde abajo* (Barcelona: Cristianisme i Justícia, 2023), 9.

not abdicate in the church in favor of the church and its smoothly functioning administration. [God's] Holy Spirit still works directly in the church today, and [the Spirit] still blows in historically new, unique situations in such a way that the direction of this work could not be predetermined by the church's law."[14] Appealing for support from "the encyclical of Pope Pius XII"—presumably *Mystici Corporis Christi* (1943)—Rahner maintained that "the charismatic" (*das Charismatische*), which he described as "an element of dynamic unrest—if not also of revolutionary upheaval," belongs inherently to the church.[15] The Second Vatican Council attributed that unrest to all of humanity, which, the church knew, could never regard "the problems of religion" with indifference since the human person is "incessantly impelled by God's Spirit" (GS 41).[16]

After centuries during which the church equated ministry with the priesthood, the Second Vatican Council made the revolutionary recognition that the Holy Spirit "sanctifies the people of God with sacraments and ministries," bestowing charisms among all believers so that they could exercise "various works or offices beneficial for the renewal and more ample building up of the church" (LG 12).[17] Pastors should recognize "the ministries (*ministrationes*) and charisms" of laypeople for "the common work" of the church

[14] Karl Rahner, "Der Einzelne in der Kirche," *Stimmen der Zeit* 139, no. 4 (January 1947): 274.

[15] Rahner, "Der Einzelne in der Kirche," 274. In *Mystici Corporis Christi*, Pius XII rejected the opposed claims that that the church consisted only of "the ranks of the hierarchy" or exclusively of "the charismatic, who, equipped with lavish gifts, to be sure, will never be absent in the church." See Pius XII, "Mystici Corporis Christi," *Acta Apostolicae Sedis* 35 (1943): 200: "Minime autem reputandum est hanc ordine digestam, seu 'organicam,' ut aiunt, Ecclesiae Corporis structuram solis hierarchiae gradibus absolvi ac definiri; vel, ut opposita sententia tenet, unice ex *charismaticis* constare; qui quidem donis prodigialibus instructi, numquam sunt in Ecclesia defuturi" (emphasis in the original).

[16] Tanner, *Decrees*, 2: 1094.

[17] Tanner, *Decrees*, 2: 858.

(LG 30).[18] Ministry was no longer singularly sacerdotal. The Spirit enriches the people of God with an abundant plurality of ministries to make the church "the universal sacrament of salvation" (LG 48).[19]

On August 15, 1972, Pope Paul VI published two documents that represented the evolution of the church's ministries in ways that would have been unimaginable before the council. Each document was a *motu proprio: Ministeria Quaedam* and *Ad Pascendum*. In *Ministeria Quaedam*, the pope established the instituted, not ordained, ministries of lector and acolyte to be conferred on laymen "by the ordinary (the bishop and, in institutes of clerical perfection, the major superior) in a liturgical rite" that required approval by the Holy See.[20] Furthermore, he allowed for episcopal conferences to petition the Holy See to establish lay ministries germane to their own regions, such as "the offices (*munera*) of porter, exorcist and catechist, and also other offices (*munera*) to be entrusted to those who are devoted to the works of charity, where this ministry (*ministerium*) has not been conferred on deacons."[21] Five years after *Sacrum Diaconatus Ordinem* (1967), the pope continued the articulation of norms governing the diaconate in *Ad Pascendum*.

Paul VI interpreted the Second Vatican Council's wish to restore a stable diaconate by defining its position in the church. He claimed that the council aimed at the establishment of

> an intermediary order (*medius ordo*) between the higher grades of the ecclesiastical hierarchy and the rest of the people of God, an agent (*interpres*), as it were, of the needs

[18] Tanner, *Decrees*, 2: 875.

[19] Tanner, *Decrees*, 2: 887.

[20] Paul VI, "Ministeria Quaedam," *Acta Apostolicae Sedis* 64 (1972): 531 (the differentiation of ordained and instituted ministries), 533, no. VII (the reservation of the two ministries for laymen), 533, no. IX (the liturgical conferral of the two ministries).

[21] Paul VI, "Ministeria Quaedam," 531.

> and also wishes of Christian communities, a catalyst (*in-stimulator*) of the service or the *diaconia* of the church among local Christian communities, a sign or sacrament of Christ the Lord himself, who *came not to be served, but to serve.*[22]

As a catalyst of the local ecclesial *diaconia*, of services and ministries exercised by the baptized, the diaconate could justify the claim of Alphonse Borras: "Pluriministeriality is without doubt one of the major gains of the restoration of the diaconate."[23]

Yet the deliberate pairing of *Ministeria Quaedam* and *Ad Pascendum* warrants another conclusion. In concert, the two papal rescripts breached the mentality of ministry as a sacral, sacerdotal monolith in favor of a variety of ministries, instituted and ordained, that evince the Holy Spirit's bestowal of charisms on all the baptized to fashion the entire church into a Spirit-empowered sacrament of, and communion in, the *diaconia* of Jesus Christ. The overdue recognition of lay ministries manifests the sacramentality of the church's ministry as much as the restoration of the diaconate.

In both *Ministeria Quaedam* and *Ad Pascendum*, the pope legislated that candidates for the diaconate and the priesthood "must receive . . . and for an appropriate time exercise" the ministries of lector and acolyte.[24] This requirement resulted in the paradoxical degrading of the two ministries for laypeople. Seminarians and candidates for the diaconate receive liturgical institution in ministries that they only briefly exercise, while laypeople, who exercise these ministries regularly and more prominently than candidates for

[22] Paul VI, "Ad Pascendum," *Acta Apostolicae Sedis* 64 (1972): 536, emphasis in the original.

[23] Alphonse Borras, *Le diaconat au risque de sa nouveauté* (Brussels: Éditions Lessius, 2007), 205.

[24] Paul VI, "Ministeria Quaedam," 533, no. XI; "Ad Pascendum," 539, no. II.

ordination, do so usually without the liturgical commissioning of their bishop.[25]

Despite the distortion of *Ministeria Quaedam*, its original pairing with *Ad Pascendum* allows for the principle of the co-responsibility of lay and diaconal ministries, both formally re-created after the Second Vatican Council. Paul VI began *Ministeria Quaedam* by recalling: "Certain ministries were already in the earliest times instituted by the church for offering fitting worship to God and for providing service to the people of God according to needs. And in those times, to the faithful were entrusted the exercise of offices of the sacred liturgy and of charity adapted to various circumstances."[26] In the post-conciliar church, laypeople and deacons again exercise ministry in the liturgy and in charity. Deacons have no monopoly on the *diaconia* of charity. Together, *diaconia*, the proclamation of God's word, and liturgical worship express, as Pope Benedict XVI wrote, "the intimate nature of the church."[27] All the baptized, including lay ministers and deacons, are responsible, in accordance with their charisms, for making the church what it is: a diaconal communion that serves Christ in the poor and the marginalized and that serves them in Christ.

Marking in 2022 the fiftieth anniversary of *Ministeria Quaedam*, Pope Francis wrote that it "unlocked the door for the renewal of ministry in the experience of the faithful, reborn out of the water of baptism, confirmed with the seal of the Spirit, and filled with the living Bread come down from heaven."[28] He interpreted two decrees of 2021—his formal inclusion of women in the ministries of lector and acolyte and his establishment of the ministry of lay

[25] John M. Grondelski, "Lay Ministries? A Quarter Century of *Ministeria Quaedam*," *Irish Theological Quarterly* 63, no. 3 (September 1998): 279.

[26] Paul VI, "Ministeria Quaedam," 529.

[27] Benedict XVI, "Deus Caritas Est," *Acta Apostolicae Sedis* 98, no. 3 (March 2006): 236, no. 25a.

[28] Francis, "Quinquagesimo Interveniente Anniversario," *Acta Apostolicae Sedis* 114, no. 9 (September 2022): 1148, no. 9.

catechist—as developments of *Ministeria Quaedam*. The anniversary afforded an opportunity for continuing the search for "the meaning of ministries" begun by Paul VI.[29]

A pneumatology of ministry figures conspicuously in Francis's retrospective. Francis formulated two principles of ministry: (1) with the Holy Spirit, God accomplishes "all things in all people" and (2) "the goal of all ministries is always the common good (cf. 1 Cor 12:7), the building up of the community (cf. 1 Cor 14:12)."[30] The Spirit enables the differentiated and complementary participation of all members of the church in Christ's priesthood, for the Spirit "renders all of human nature ministerial (*omnem humanitatem facit ministerialem*) for the building up of his ecclesial body." Structurally, ministry "is dynamic, vigorous (*vivax*), flexible, like the action of the Spirit."[31]

The Spirit's dynamic presence in and leadership of the church makes possible the equation of the people of God, whom deacons serve in their ministry, with the sacrament of the Spirit, an ecclesiological expression first formulated by Walter Kasper and Medard Kehl in the 1970s.[32] Undoubtedly, this concept of the church is indebted to the sacramentality of the church asserted at Second Vatican Council and proposed before the council by Otto Semmelroth, Karl Rahner, Edward Schillebeeckx, and Henri de Lubac, among

[29] Francis, "Quinquagesimo Interveniente Anniversario," 1145, no. 2. On the inclusion of women in the ministries of lector and acolyte, see Francis, "Spiritus Domini," *Acta Apostolicae Sedis* 113, no. 2 (February 2021): 169–70. On the establishment of the ministry of lay catechist, see Francis, "Antiquum Ministerium," *Acta Apostolicae Sedis* 113, no. 6 (June 2021): 527–33.

[30] Francis, "Quinquagesimo Interveniente Anniversario," 1146, no. 3.

[31] Francis, "Quinquagesimo Interveniente Anniversario," 1146, no. 4.

[32] Walter Kasper, "Kirche als Sakarament des Geistes," in *Kirche—Ort des Geistes*, ed. Walter Kasper and Gerhard Sauter (Freiburg im Breisgau: Herder, 1976), 13–55; Medard Kehl, "Kirche – Sakrament des Geistes," in *Gegenwart des Geistes: Aspekte der Pneumatologie*, ed. Walter Kasper (Freiburg im Breisgau: Herder, 1979), 155–80.

other theologians.[33] The people of God is an eschatological, pilgrim people, a people with the mission of anticipating God's reign by proclaiming and actualizing Christ's gospel in all the times and places along its pilgrim journey. As an historical entity, this people, the church, necessarily manifests itself as a "social organization" (*socialis compago*), which seeks not to sustain its own structures and institutions, as if they were monolithic and immutable, but to serve the Spirit of Christ, who fills the church with life (LG 8).[34] Drawing its life from the Spirit, the people of God journeys through history as a sacrament or sign of the Spirit, revealing the dynamic Spirit, whose own free choice determines where the Spirit blows (John 3:8) and how the Spirit distributes gifts among the members of the body of Christ (1 Cor 12:11).

As the sacrament of the dynamic, vigorous, and flexible Spirit, the church is, according to Kasper, "an improvisation of the Spirit,"[35] a sacrament of the improvising Spirit. It submits itself to "the unforeseeable, the new, the unpredictable, and the impracticable."[36] The sacrament of the Spirit is an "open system,"[37] a concept that Kasper and Kehl probably borrowed from Rahner. In an article published in 1969, Rahner insisted upon the church as an "open system," a system that embraced an "openness to the future" owing to the presence within the church of "the charismatic," which constituted an essential "characteristic of the system

[33] Matthäus Bernards, "Zur Lehre von der Kirche als Sakrament: Beobachtungen aus der Theologie des 19. und 20. Jahrhunderts," *Münchener Theologische Zeitschrift* 20 (1969): 29, 35–40. Bernards traced a sacramental ecclesiology in modern theology to the first half of the nineteenth century. See Bernards, "Zur Lehre von der Kirche als Sakrament," 40–51.

[34] Tanner, *Decrees*, 2: 854.

[35] Kasper, "Kirche als Sakarament des Geistes," 150.

[36] Kasper, "Kirche als Sakarament des Geistes," 150.

[37] Kasper, "Kirche als Sakarament des Geistes," 153; Kehl, "Kirche – Sakrament des Geistes," 172.

as a whole."[38] For Kehl the church as an open system serves "as the free, constantly contentious leeway of charism and institution, as the venue of dialogue (and of debate too!) and of criticism, as the pilgrim people of God on the path to the consummate form of communion."[39] This dynamic, vigorous, and flexible people ministers as a church for others in "missionary self-transcendence" for "the complete reconciliation and unification of all people" and for the healing of creation.[40] In its sacramental representation of the Holy Spirit, the church signifies the all-unifying Spirit, who effects "the universal communion of the reign of God."[41]

Thanks to the impulse and support of the "Spirit of truth," the people of God possesses a *sensus fidei* (LG 12),[42] which Pope Francis called "a certain connaturality with divine realities, and a wisdom which enables" Christians "to grasp those realities intuitively, even when they lack the wherewithal to give them precise expression."[43] The intuitive and unerring grasp of what the people of God believes allows it, under the leadership of the magisterium, to accept the word of God, embracing and deepening the faith of tradition for its application in life (LG 12, LG 25).[44] Applying the *sensus fidei* involves a constitutive act of the church: discernment. Pope Francis reminded the church that discernment is grace, a divine gift.[45] It represents "a true departure from ourselves towards the mystery of God, who helps us fulfill the mission to which [God] has called us for

[38] Karl Rahner, "Bemerkungen über das Charismatische in der Kirche," *Geist und Leben* 42, no. 4 (July-August 1969): 260.

[39] Kehl, "Kirche – Sakrament des Geistes," 172.

[40] Kehl, "Kirche – Sakrament des Geistes," 163.

[41] Kehl, "Kirche – Sakrament des Geistes," 160.

[42] Tanner, *Decrees*, 2: 858.

[43] Francis, *The Joy of the Gospel: Evangelii Gaudium* (Washington, DC: United States Conference of Catholic Bishops; Vatican City: Libreria Editrice Vaticana, 2013), 60, no. 119.

[44] Tanner, *Decrees*, 2: 858, 870.

[45] Francis, "Gaudete et Exsultate," *Acta Apostolicae Sedis* 110, no. 8 (August 2018): 1159, no. 170.

the good of our brothers [and sisters]."[46] Discernment, Borras wrote "*makes* the church, to the extent that it is together, in the diversity of vocations, charisms, and ministries, that the baptized listen to God's word, investigate the signs of the times, and act in history under the influence of the Holy Spirit."[47] To investigate the signs of the times means for the people of God, guided by the Spirit, "to discern the true signs of God's presence or plan in the events, pressing needs, and also desires" that affect all contemporary human beings. This discernment aims at developing "completely human solutions" to contemporary problems, solutions informed by faith and God's will (GS 11).[48]

The synodal church is a manifestation of the discerning people of God that is the sacrament of the Spirit. In its document on synodality (2018), the International Theological Commission (ITC) explained:

> The whole People of God is an agent of the proclamation of the Gospel. Every baptised person is called to be a protagonist of mission since we are all missionary disciples. The Church is called, in synodal synergy, to activate the ministries and charisms present in her life and to listen to the voice of the Spirit, in order to discern the ways of evangelisation.[49]

As Rafael Luciani insisted, in a synodal church, the people of God possesses an "ontological normativity" since it is the communion of the baptized, who are "all coresponsible

[46] Francis, "Gaudete et Exsultate," 1160, no. 175.

[47] Alphonse Borras, "*Votum tantum consultivum:* les limites ecclésiologiques d'une formule canonique," *Didaskalia* 45, no. 1 (2015): 161, emphasis in the original.

[48] Tanner, *Decrees*, 2: 1075.

[49] International Theological Commission (ITC), *Synodality in the Life and Mission of the Church*, no. 53, March 2, 2018, Vatican website, https://www.vatican.va/roman_curia/congregations/cfaith/cti_documents/rc_cti_20180302_sinodalita_en.html.

members with equal dignity in the mission."[50] Concomitant with the normativity of the people of God is the priority and permanence of the common priesthood of the baptized, whom the ministerial priesthood serves.[51] Synodality requires of the episcopate "a coresponsible interaction and integration with all in the ecclesial body."[52] The same must be said of the presbyterate and diaconate. Of course, the ecclesial interaction and integration of ordained ministers must include their servant-leadership of the people of God, for which the Spirit in the sacrament of order empowers them. Ecclesial co-responsibility makes the *diaconia* of the synodal church a matter of all the baptized as they, in their local contexts, discern how to fulfill what the ITC has identified the diaconal duty of the people of God "to hear the cry of the poor and the cry of the earth, and to draw attention urgently, in determining society's choices and plans, to the place and the privileged role of the poor, the universal destination of goods, the primacy of solidarity and care for our common home."[53] The graced decisions and actions of the people of God in their promotion of the gospel witness to the gifting and the guidance of the Holy Spirit.

How does the diaconate figure in the people of God? Borras did not offer a decisive answer in his chapter on "the diaconate among other ministries." But the chapter yields juxtapositions. Deacons collaborate with the bishop and his presbyterate, but they are also "auxiliaries of the sacerdotal ministry of supervision (*présidence*) of the bishop and of priests."[54] Borras understood deacons as leading "the baptized in becoming a people of servants."[55] Yet he also wished to integrate the diaconate within "the baptismal

[50] Rafael Luciani, *Synodality: A New Way of Proceeding in the Church*, trans. Joseph Owens (New York: Paulist Press, 2022), 53.

[51] Luciani, *Synodality*, 61.

[52] Luciani, *Synodality*, 95.

[53] ITC, *Synodality in the Life and Mission of the Church*, no. 119.

[54] Borras, *Le diaconat*, 207, 210, quotation: 210.

[55] Borras, *Le diaconat*, 210.

co-responsibility of all the faithful according to their individual charisms" and within "the synodality of the church, namely the convergence of each and every person in the witness to the gospel *in this place*."[56] Integrating the diaconate with priestly and lay ministries is "often difficult," Borras maintained, without elaborating on the difficulty.[57] Surely, confusion affects the ministerial identity of deacons in the local church if they are collaborators, auxiliaries, leaders, and co-responsible evangelizers. In his analysis of the French practice of specifying the nature and venue of a ministry in a *lettre de mission*, Borras contended: "If the diocesan bishop and his collaborators cannot say what *from now onwards* differentiates the presence of a deacon from a baptismal witness and what qualifies that presence as ministerial, then it is preferable that they refrain from 'sending him' to those places."[58] A deacon should not appear as a "superior layperson."[59] To impose the differentiating condition that Borras stipulated, especially in the various ministries of charity, would render diaconal ministry impossible, however. Integrating the diaconate and lay ministries by way of differentiation when deacons and laypeople exercise the same or similar ministries would likely lead not to co-responsibility, but to conflict, generated by clericalism and opposition to clericalism.

A configuration of the diaconate as a threshold ministry may or may not help integrate it into the ecclesial sacrament of the Spirit as co-responsible service to and among the people of God. Everything depends on the conceptualization and location of the threshold. The diaconate itself could be an intra-ecclesial threshold, mediating between priest and bishops on the one hand and laypeople on the other. This notion found expression in a late nineteenth-century apology for the rehabilitation of the diaconate as a stable

[56] Borras, *Le diaconat*, 211, emphasis in the original.
[57] Borras, *Le diaconat*, 213.
[58] Borras, *Le diaconat*, 224, emphasis in the original.
[59] Borras, *Le diaconat*, 224.

order in the church. According to Johann Nepomuk Seidl, deacons are "the mediating body (*das Vermittlungsorgan*) between the priest or bishop, who leads the community and offers the sacrifice of the Mass (*opfert*) for it, and between [*sic*] the Christian people that forms the community."[60] Such a diaconal threshold, resuscitated as the *medius ordo* by Paul VI in *Ad Pascendum*, invites ecclesiological mayhem, however, by unhelpfully separating clergy and laity and by stranding deacons in an impossible interstice.

Alternatively, as a conceptual debt to O'Meara's geometry of ministry, the threshold of ministry for deacons and other ministers could surround the church as a circle of ministry to the poor and the marginalized. Borras held that deacons "play an interfacial role, by being 'at the threshold,' at the intersection between the church and history—between the community and its environment."[61] The church's "environment" is the site of its evangelizing mission. Deacons minister at the evangelizing threshold that encircles the church by virtue of the self-gift of the Spirit in the sacrament of order, empowering them for ministry. At this threshold, they minister co-responsibly with all Christians, gifted by the Spirit in baptism. Pope Francis wrote: "Each Christian and every community must discern the path that the Lord points out, but all of us are asked to obey his call to go forth from our own comfort zone in order to reach all the 'peripheries' in need of the light of the Gospel."[62] Ministry to the marginalized at the church's peripheries is a matter for all the people of God. In its openness to the Spirit, the church can summon the courage to devise startlingly new ways for deacons and other ministers to engage in threshold ministry.

[60] Johann Nepomuk Seidl, *Der Diakonat in der katholischen Kirche, dessen hieratische Würde und geschichtliche Entwicklung: Eine kirchenrechtsgeschichtliche Abhandlung* (Regensburg: Georg Joseph Manz, 1884), 237–38.

[61] Borras, *Le diaconat*, 213.

[62] Francis, *The Joy of the Gospel: Evangelii Gaudium*, 11, no. 20.

A pneumatic theology of ministry, therefore, expresses a fundamental characteristic of the church. The Creator Spirit constantly gives life to the people of God, a life overflowing in a rich variety of charisms bestowed sacramentally among all members of the church. All receive the gifts of the Spirit in baptism and thus are co-responsible for discerning the Spirit's guidance for the mission of the church, in the times and places and cultures of its pilgrim journey, to proclaim Christ and his gospel of God's reign. The Spirit empowers some—bishops, priests, and deacons—in the sacrament of order for servant-leadership of the people of God, acting as catalysts for all the baptized to bring Christ to and find him at the threshold of the church.

The Threshold Ministry of the People of God

Paul VI's claim in *Ad Pascendum* that the Second Vatican Council regarded the diaconate as an "intermediate order"[63] between the higher clergy and laity rested not on conciliar documents, but on the opinions expressed by some bishops. Speaking on behalf of forty Asian bishops on October 10, 1963, Archbishop Paul Yu Pin of Nanking said: "deacons best exercise the office of bridge or mediation between the hierarchy and the Christian faithful, for, even though they are classified (*cooptati*) as clerics, they nevertheless make their way into society more easily."[64] Distributed to the conciliar bishops in September 1964, an analysis of the debates on the diaconate in October 1963 included a summary of "the more subtle argument" for married deacons as "a sort of bridge between the 'high' clergy and the people."[65] The report continued: "For while theologically and also canonically they will belong to the clergy, on the other hand, psychologically and also culturally they will belong more to

[63] Paul VI, "Ad Pascendum," 536.

[64] AS 2/2: 431.

[65] AS 3/1: 267.

the people."[66] Perhaps in the sphere of pastoral ministry, the report conjectured, married deacons could mediate the inconvenient distance between celibate priests and the people, a distance caused by seminary formation and the social necessity to safeguard celibacy.[67]

More than forty years after *Ad Pascendum*, W. Shawn McKnight emphatically revived the notion of the diaconate as a *medius ordo*, hailing Paul VI's formulation of the term as prophetic.[68] For McKnight, the diaconate is an "intermediate structure," mediating a bishop's power within the local church along with his care for the laity.[69] As an intermediate structure, the diaconate serves as "an instrument of the Spirit for the growth of the church in the service of the Gospel."[70] While McKnight usually considered deacons as intermediaries of the bishop, he at times extended their mediating function to include priests. Thus, he wrote: "The diaconate order could be socially structured to mediate the power and authority of the bishop and his priests, but only if the deacon were to enjoy immediate contact with the pastoral authority and the people."[71] Active at the diocesan and parochial level, deacons are "intermediaries between the bishop or pastor and the laity."[72] Their unique role as social intermediaries not only ought to distinguish deacons from priests but also positions deacons as intermediaries between the bishop and the poor[73] and between the people of God

[66] AS 3/1: 267.

[67] AS 3/1: 267.

[68] W. Shawn McKnight, *Understanding the Diaconate: Historical, Theological, and Sociological Foundations* (Washington, DC: The Catholic University of America Press, 2018), 257.

[69] McKnight, *Understanding the Diaconate*, 94–95, quotation: 95.

[70] McKnight, *Understanding the Diaconate*, 88.

[71] McKnight, *Understanding the Diaconate*, 104.

[72] McKnight, *Understanding the Diaconate*, 205.

[73] McKnight, *Understanding the Diaconate*, 43, 175.

and the poor.[74] Paul VI's connection between a diaconal *medius ordo* and the stimulus by the diaconate of a local church's *diaconia* underpins ecclesial communion. McKnight explained: "Fulfilling these tasks, the deacon brings about a greater communion among the people of God, rather than being an additional rank-figure in the structure of power and authority between the bishop and priests on the one hand, and the laity on the other."[75] Such a deacon "would function more like a bridge or glue, binding everyone together more closely."[76] As "a symbol of *communitas*" and as "a social intermediary," a deacon ministers as "a bridge-builder drawing church leaders, ordinary believers, and people on the margins of society closer together."[77] Any alternative to the diaconate as an intermediate structure by which the deacon assists "the bishop and his priest [*sic*] in service to the people" ought to be "treated with skepticism," McKnight insisted.[78]

On the contrary, the theology and practice of ministry ought to view with skepticism a theology of a mediating diaconate. Such a diaconate frustrates ecclesial communion. Interposing the diaconate as a ministerial structure between a bishop and priests on the one hand and the laity on the other reinforces the "hierarchization of the church" by adding, unnecessarily and unhelpfully, a layer of separation between clergy and laity.[79] Such a separation is a disservice to all in the people of God because it renders communion less harmonious through degrees of superiority. Furthermore, as long as the church ordains only men to the diaconate, a mediating diaconate would sustain what Serena

[74] McKnight, *Understanding the Diaconate*, 86, 103, 104, 105, 106, 109, 258.

[75] McKnight, *Understanding the Diaconate*, 60.

[76] McKnight, *Understanding the Diaconate*, 59.

[77] McKnight, *Understanding the Diaconate*, 254.

[78] McKnight, *Understanding the Diaconate*, 106.

[79] Stefan Sander, *Das Amt des Diakons: Eine Handreichung*, rev. ed. (Freiburg im Breisgau: Herder, 2013), 145.

Noceti has called the "hierarchical logic" of a "clerical-masculine culture" that wounds women by ignoring or devaluing their voices and contributions to ministry and ecclesial decision-making.[80] The last thing that Catholic women need is for another (ordained) man to exhort them to use their charisms for the ministry of charity and ecclesial communion. For women and for all the people of God, the prompting of the Holy Spirit is sufficiently fundamental.

Bishops, priests, and deacons all belong equally to the people of God. Their ordination does not transcend their baptism. The self-gift of the same Spirit is at work in all sacraments. A diaconal "'bridge' between the hierarchy and the laity" qualifies as an expression that is "scarcely satisfactory" because it supposes that bishops and priests are "somewhere else."[81] The separation of bishops and priests from the laity was not a certainty and ought to be avoided, Francis Deniau maintained before he became bishop of Nevers.[82] As a bishop, he warned against the notion of the diaconate as a bridge, for it belonged to "language that undervalues the ministry of priests."[83] Closeness to people and to their way of life was fundamental, Deniau insisted, to the life and commitment of priests.[84] They are, as the Second Vatican Council taught, disciples with all Christian disciples and brothers in baptism with their sisters and brothers in Christ (PO 9).[85] According to Pope John Paul II,

[80] Serena Noceti, *Reforming the Church: A Synodal Way of Proceeding*, trans. Joseph Owens (New York: Paulist Press, 2023), 50–51.

[81] Francis Deniau, "Le diaconat à la lumière des trois 'fonctions' du Christ et de l'Église, selon Vatican II," in *Diaconat, XXIe siècle: Actes du Colloque de Louvain-la-Neuve (13–15 septembre 1994)*, ed. André Haquin and Philippe Weber (Brussels: Éditions Lumen Vitae, 1997), 106.

[82] Deniau, "Le diaconat," 106.

[83] Francis Deniau, "Diacres et prêtres en France: des années 1970 aux transformations actuelles," in *Le diaconat permanent: Relecture et perspectives*, ed. Bruno Dumons and Daniel Moulinet (Paris: Les Éditions du Cerf, 2007), 302.

[84] Deniau, "Diacres et prêtres en France," 302.

[85] Tanner, *Decrees*, 2: 1054.

priests must advocate "the preferential option for the poor (*pro tenuioribus*)."[86] Priests do not require deacons to mediate their ministry as priests to and on behalf of the poor. Without a deacon's mediation, canon law authorizes and obliges a parish priest to care pastorally for his parishioners, including the *diaconia* of fostering "works through which the spirit of the gospel is promoted, even in what pertains to social justice" (c. 528 §1), of "sharing especially in the cares, anxieties, and griefs of the faithful," of caring for the sick and the dying, and of seeking out "the poor, the afflicted, the lonely, those exiled from their country, and similarly those weighed down by special difficulties" (c. 529 §1).

The Holy See's *Directory for the Pastoral Ministry of Bishops* (2004) offered an example of a ministry of charity oriented towards co-responsible, not mediated, ministry. It directed the attention of bishops to the increasing movement and presence of migrants. Bishops could manifest the church's pastoral care for migrants by sending "priests, deacons and other faithful to accompany the emigrants, founding special centres to train them for their work."[87] A commission from their diocesan bishop suffices for ministers to address pastoral needs identified synodally by the local church. Restricting bridge-building to deacons undermines the synodal principle of immediacy "between the community and its Pastors" in the local articulation and exercise of the church's evangelizing mission.[88]

Being a bridge-builder, a pontifical title, bestows no privileges on a deacon in McKnight's theology. Deacons for McKnight do not seem to have their own Spirit-empowered ministry; they are "ordained to the ministry of the bishop."[89]

86 John Paul II, "Pastores Dabo Vobis," *Acta Apostolicae Sedis* 84 (1992): 707, no. 30.

87 Congregation for Bishops, *Directory for the Pastoral Ministry of Bishops: "Apostolorum Successores"* (Vatican City: Libreria Editrice Vaticana, 2004), 227–28, no. 206a, quotation: 228.

88 ITC, *Synodality in the Life and Mission of the Church*, no. 69.

89 McKnight, *Understanding the Diaconate*, 104.

Consequently, he preferred to restrict a deacon's ministry of liturgical preaching and sacramental ministry.[90] McKnight's rejection of the attribution of Christ's threefold *munera* to deacons is at odds with the position of *Basic Norms* and the *Directory* for the diaconate published by the Holy See in 1998.[91]

While recognizing the authority of the Holy See's *Directory*, McKnight conceded that it did "not fully enflesh the unique social quality of the diaconate as an intermediate order."[92] Only the *Basic Norms* (*Ratio fundamentalis*), not the *Directory*, used the bridge metaphor, applying it to all "sacred ministers" with a passage taken out of context from *Pastores Dabo Vobis* by Pope John Paul II, who understood a priest's humanity as a bridge to Christ.[93] The *Ratio fundamentalis* stated: "The goal of human formation is to fashion the person of sacred ministers in such a way that in it 'human beings may find not an obstacle but a bridge by which with fewer steps (*brevius*) they can reach Jesus Christ, the Redeemer of human beings.'"[94] Thus, all ordained ministers, not only deacons, serve as personal connections to Christ.

A synodal church requires more than the evangelizing outreach of ordained ministers. The charisms bestowed by the Spirit on all the baptized empower them for the church's evangelizing mission. To determine how it evangelizes, the local church needs intermediate structures, such as the existing synodal structures of the parish and diocesan pastoral councils.[95] The diaconate cannot be one of these structures

[90] McKnight, *Understanding the Diaconate*, 224–26.

[91] McKnight, *Understanding the Diaconate*, 44, 49, 52, 265.

[92] McKnight, *Understanding the Diaconate*, 205, 261, quotation: 261.

[93] John Paul II, "Pastores Dabo Vobis," 732, no. 43.

[94] Congregation for Catholic Education, "Ratio fundamentalis institutionis diaconorum permanentium," *Acta Apostolicae Sedis* 90 (1998): 869, no. 66.

[95] Noceti, *Reforming the Church*, 17.

because it encompasses only deacons, not other members of the people of God.

If deacons are "ministers of the threshold," as McKnight claims,[96] it is crucial to identify the threshold of ministry. This threshold should not run through the liturgy of the Eucharist. With their limited functionality in the Roman Rite, deacons, *pace* McKnight, are hardly "the ones who assist the assembly to enter the profundity of the mystery being celebrated and thereafter to go back to the world to which the assembly is sent."[97] Apart from the Spirit who makes Christ present among them, worshippers do not require a mediator to enter into communion with the crucified and risen Lord, with each other in the celebration of the Eucharist, and with the world.

The church's connection to the world serves as a more appropriate threshold for ministry. When Yves Congar pioneered the notion of the diaconate as a threshold ministry, he wondered whether it could be "a new instrument of encounter (*contact*) and of passage between the church and the world." The church itself could have a liminal extension as "a sort of catechumenal church, a church of the threshold and of frontiers," to which deacons could minister in "communities of welcome," in which people attracted to the church could find "possibilities for prayer, for faith, for the exercise of brotherly and sisterly love (*l'amour fraternel*), and for charity."[98] The ITC too correlated the deacon's ministry of charity with "the frontier Church," proposing "work in surroundings where the priest is not present, and also with one-parent families, couples, prisoners, young people, drug addicts, AIDS victims, the elderly, disadvantaged groups, etc."[99]

[96] McKnight, *Understanding the Diaconate*, 192.
[97] McKnight, *Understanding the Diaconate*, 192.
[98] Congar, "Le diaconat," 139.
[99] ITC, *From the Diakonia of Christ to the Diakonia of the Apostles*, chapter VI, 2002, Vatican website, https://www.vatican.va/roman_curia/

As a "ministry of the threshold," the diaconate, according to Erio Castellucci, "preserves its character of *bridge* between the church and the world, of *connection* between the demands of communion and those of mission."[100] Deacons have the charge of serving as the church's egress into the world and of the world's entrance into the church, as a "wake-up call" (*sveglia*) for the church to abandon self-maintenance for mission in the proclamation of the gospel and the exercise of charity, "especially in its provocative and uncomfortable dimension, but essential for the refuge of the least."[101] Deacons symbolize a church that does not merely wait for "the faithful at the threshold of entrance" but goes out, enabled by "the sacrament of order, into the heart of the world: into homes, the factory, the school, the family, the office, the neighborhood, the hospital." And thus "the diaconate is a provocative sign of Christ the servant not only for other ordained ministers and for other baptized people, but for *society as a whole*."[102]

Tim O'Donnell suggested that deacons are the unique and chief ministers to the ecclesial threshold. Their threshold ministry is "clearly recognizable as different from the ministry of priests and bishops," who preside over the eucharistic assembly and exercise "pastoral oversight."[103] O'Donnell differentiated diaconal ministry with its roots in the liturgy and its "permanent and public commitment" from the ministry of laypeople. He concluded: "Only the

congregations/cfaith/cti_documents/rc_con_cfaith_pro_05072004_diaconate_en.html.

[100] Erio Castellucci, "Il 'ministero della soglia.' Una lettura teologica del diaconato a partire dal Nuovo Testamento," *Seminarium* 48 (2008): 641, emphasis in the original.

[101] Castellucci, "Il 'ministero della soglia,'" 641–42.

[102] Castellucci, "Il 'ministero della soglia,'" 644, emphasis in the original.

[103] Tim O'Donnell, *The Deacon: Icon of Christ the Servant, Minister of the Threshold* (New York: Paulist Press, 2020), 125.

diaconate is modeled on a ministry of the threshold in all its dimensions."[104]

Ministering to those on and beyond the peripheries of ecclesial communion, as O'Donnell appropriately located the threshold,[105] involves all ecclesial subjects, however. What did Castellucci have in mind when he considered the paths traversed by a deacon at the threshold that are "normally closed to the presbyter and to the bishop"?[106] Bishops and priests inhabit and minister to the world beyond the sanctuary. For bishops and priests, hospitals, prisons, and shelters for the homeless are as compelling and as accessible venues to serve Christ in the afflicted as they are for deacons. Indeed, the obligation to complete the liturgy of the Eucharist with an evangelization of the world beyond the vestibule falls on all the baptized. With its emphasis on the apostolate of the laity to transform the "temporal" world with the gospel for God's reign (e.g., LG 31, 35; AA 2, 4, 7),[107] the Second Vatican Council arguably made a threshold ministry the special mission of laypeople. The Holy See's *Directory* for bishops warned them:

> [I]t is important that the laity should not become unduly absorbed in ecclesial tasks and services other than those required by a particular vocation, because it would distance them from the secular realm, whether it be professional, social, economic, cultural or political. These are the areas in which they have a clear responsibility, and in which their apostolic action is irreplaceable.[108]

This warning risked sharply dividing the church and the world and invalidating lay ecclesial ministry. But its location

[104] O'Donnell, *The Deacon*, 125.

[105] O'Donnell, *The Deacon*, 124.

[106] Castellucci, "Il 'ministero della soglia,'" 638–39.

[107] Tanner, *Decrees*, 2: 875, 878, 982, 984, 986.

[108] Congregation for Bishops, *Directory for the Pastoral Ministry of Bishops*, 124–25, no. 111.

of laypeople in the "secular realm" translates as a recognition of their importance in the ministry to the church's threshold. In that secular space, laypeople, deacons, priests, and bishops, by virtue of their baptismal charisms, take on Christ's priestly, prophetic, and royal mission to all of God's children in whatever periphery they inhabit.

In Christ and empowered by his Spirit, all the baptized cooperate in ministering at the church's threshold. The threshold is not the exclusive ministerial domain of deacons, "for," as Alphonse Borras and Bernard Pottier insisted, "all the baptized are called to take position at the threshold of the church." Borras and Pottier thus affirmed: "The entire church is at the threshold. It is by nature turned outwards."[109] Prominent among those whom it encounters at its threshold are the sick and the suffering. In the anointing of the sick, Christ has equipped the church with a sacrament for its threshold ministry.

Anointing the Sick: A Threshold Ministry

The people of God journey to the threshold as a privileged place to encounter Christ. The Second Vatican Council taught: "The church lovingly embraces all people afflicted with human frailty. Even more, it recognizes in the poor and in the suffering the image of its poor and suffering founder. In its preoccupation to relieve their poverty, it aims at serving Christ in them" (LG 8).[110] Jesus pointed out in whom he could be loved and served: in the hungry, the thirsty, the stranger, the naked, the sick, and the prisoner (Matt 25:35-36).

The church's *diaconia* has long cared for the suffering. *The Passion of Perpetua and Felicity* points to a prison ministry in Carthage at the beginning of the third century. Two deacons,

[109] Alphonse Borras and Bernard Pottier, *La grâce du diaconat: Questions actuelles autour du diaconat latin* (Brussels: Éditions Lessius, 1998), 138.

[110] Tanner, *Decrees*, 2: 855.

Tertius and Pomponius, resorted to bribery to allow neophytes to spend "a few hours" away from the heat and darkness of their crowded confinement "in a better part of the prison."[111] In a vision, Perpetua saw Pomponius, a Christ figure, take her by the hand and lead her to the amphitheater, the place of her martyrdom, promising: "I am here with you, and I will struggle with you."[112] The Epistle of James refers to a ministry to the sick, in which "elders of the church" prayed over and anointed them (Jas 5:14).

Care for the sick in their homes as well as in hospitals and hospices remains a prominent and stable threshold ministry for laypeople, deacons, and priests. This ministry includes companionship, prayer, and the administration of sacraments. By the sacrament of the anointing of the sick, *Lumen Gentium* explained,

> and also by the prayer of presbyters, the entire church entrusts the sick to the suffering and glorified Lord so that he might relieve and heal them (cf. Jas 5:14-16); indeed, it encourages them, as they freely unite themselves to the suffering and death of Christ (cf. Rom 8:17, Col 1:24, 2 Tim 2:11-12, 1 Pet 4:13), to devote themselves to the good of the people of God (LG 11).[113]

The anointing of the sick assumes the prayerful participation of the entire church for Christ's healing of the sick, whose ministers are presbyters.

Presbyters or priests have not always been the sole ministers to anoint the sick. In the West, laypeople too anointed the sick—themselves and others—with oil blessed by the

[111] Thomas J. Heffernan, *The Passion of Perpetua and Felicity* (Oxford: Oxford University Press, 2012), 126 (quotation from Heffernan's English translation of the *Passion*).

[112] Heffernan, *The Passion of Perpetua and Felicity*, 129 (quotation from Heffernan's English translation of the *Passion*), 251 (Pomponius as "a type of Christ").

[113] Tanner, *Decrees*, 2: 857.

bishop until the Carolingian liturgical reforms in the eighth and ninth centuries. When at that time the sacrament became intended for the dying and associated with the Viaticum and the sacramental absolution of sins, priests became the sole ministers of the sacrament.[114] In 1439, the Council of Florence identified the priest (*sacerdos*) as the minister.[115] On November 25, 1551, at its fourteenth session, the Council of Trent taught that "either bishops or priests (*sacerdotes*)" were "the proper ministers of this sacrament," equating them with the anointing presbyters of James 5:14.[116] The 1983 Code of Canon Law stipulates: "Every priest and a priest alone (*omnis et solus sacerdos*) validly administers the anointing of the sick" (c. 1003 §1).

In a section on "the pastoral care of the sick," the Holy See's *Directory* (1998) on the diaconate pointed out that reserving the administration of the sacrament of the anointing of the sick to bishops and presbyters was "defined doctrine" owing to the sacrament's connection with "the forgiveness of sins and the worthy reception of the Eucharist." If assigned to the pastoral care of the sick, deacons could fulfill three functions: "active service in alleviating their suffering, catechesis that prepares them to receive the sacrament of anointing, substitution for the priest in the preparation of Christ's faithful for death, and the administration of Viaticum with the proper rite."[117] Unfortunately, the *Directory* conceived of an important part of ministry to the dying—surely, an obvious diaconal ministry of charity—as substitutionary when exercised by deacons, even though it later insisted on a complete exercise of "their own ministry in preaching, in liturgy, and in charity" without relegation "to secondary offices, to substitutionary services (*munera*), or

[114] Herbert Vorgrimler, *Buße und Krankensalbung*, 2nd ed. (Freiburg im Breisgau: Herder, 1978), 218–21.

[115] Tanner, *Decrees*, 1: 549.

[116] Tanner, *Decrees*, 2: 711.

[117] Congregation for the Clergy, "Directorium pro ministerio et vita diaconorum permanentium," *Acta Apostolicae Sedis* 90 (1998): 897, no. 34.

to works that can usually be carried out by the Christian faithful who are not ordained."[118]

Tridentine teaching on the minster of the sacrament of the anointing of the sick did not deter Jean-Charles Didier from arguing in 1964 for deacons as extraordinary ministers of the sacrament. His argument rested on two premises. First, the Council of Trent's identification of priests and bishops as "the proper ministers" of the sacrament was not restrictive.[119] Trent did not exclude the possibility of other ministers. Second, and more important, the church retains considerable power over the sacraments, *salva illorum substantia*—provided that its power does not affect their substance.[120] This second premise evoked a principle declared by Trent on July 16, 1562, at its twenty-first session: "this power has always been in the church, that, in the administration of the sacraments, except for their substance (*salva illorum substantia*), it may establish or change whatever it deems more useful for the benefit of those receiving them or for the veneration of the sacraments themselves, given the variety of circumstances, times, and places."[121]

Owing to this discretionary power asserted by the church at Trent, Didier could claim that it was of little importance whether Trent's "doctrine of the minister of extreme unction" was a defined matter of faith. Every decision that the church took about the sacraments had a relevance that was "practical and theoretical, disciplinary and doctrinal." Once it had taken a decision, however, it was "never inviolable, if the church, aware of its power, intends to alter it."[122] Didier invoked as a significant precedent the redefinition by Pius XII of the matter and form of the sacrament of order in *Sacramentum Ordinis* (1947). Indeed, the pope declared

[118] Congregation for the Clergy, "Directorium," 900, no. 40.

[119] Jean-Charles Didier, "Sur le ministre de l'Onction des Malades," *L'ami du clergé* 74, no. 31 (July 30, 1964): 491.

[120] Didier, "Sur le ministre de l'Onction des Malades," 488.

[121] Tanner, *Decrees*, 2: 726.

[122] Didier, "Sur le ministre de l'Onction des Malades," 491.

that neither he nor the church had power over "the substance of the sacraments, namely in those things, as testified by the sources of divine revelation, which Christ the Lord himself established for the observance of a sacramental sign."[123] Furthermore, the way in which the Council of Florence called for the handing over the instruments as the matter of the sacrament of order clearly did not reflect Christ's will "for the substance and validity of this sacrament," the pope wrote.[124] In the "bright light" of the papal precedent, Didier contended that the church "has the right not to feel bound by" Trent's decision to subject "the validity of the anointing of the sick to the administration of a priest" as if this were an "irreformable" decision, inasmuch as it remains within the purview of the church to determine that the question of the minister of the sacrament does not affect its "substance." Thus, Didier concluded: "the church could authorize deacons, as extraordinary ministers, to administer the anointing of the sick."[125]

Considerations of the church's discretionary power over the sacraments, as outlined by Didier, were undoubtedly far from the crafting of the *Note* by the Congregation for the Doctrine of the Faith (CDF) that Cardinal Joseph Ratzinger signed on February 11, 2005. The *Note* restated the limiting determination of c. 1003 §1 to reinforce the traditional teaching about the minister of the sacrament of the anointing of the sick.[126] Ratzinger went further by declaring in his preface that the teaching that "only priests (bishops and presbyters) are ministers of the sacrament of the anointing of the sick" must be "held definitively."[127] The binding nature of this

[123] Pius XII, "Sacramentum Ordinis," *Acta Apostolicae Sedis* 40 (1948): 5, no. 1.

[124] Pius XII, "Sacramentum Ordinis," 6, no. 3.

[125] Didier, "Sur le ministre de l'Onction des Malades," 492.

[126] Congregation for the Doctrine of the Faith, "Nota circa il ministro del sacramento dell'unzione degli infermi," *Notitiae* 41, nos. 9–10 (September/October 2005): 480, 483.

[127] Congregation for the Doctrine of the Faith, "Nota," 479.

declaration is doubtful, however, given the lack of explicit papal approval *in forma specifica*.[128] After the doctrinal declaration, Ratzinger continued: "Neither deacons nor laypeople, therefore, can exercise the said sacrament, and any action in this sense constitutes a simulation of the sacrament."[129] In its reference to c. 1379, the *Note* recalled the legal provision for the penalty of simulation if a deacon or a layperson attempted to administer the sacrament.[130] To simulate a sacrament incurs "a *latae sententiae* penalty of interdict" (c. 1379 §1, §5)—in effect, automatic excommunication.

In offering historical evidence for its position, the CDF's *Note* began with an error. It cited a letter that Pope Innocent I wrote to Bishop Decentius of Gubbio in 416. The *Note* correctly reported the pope's statement that bishops could administer the sacrament as well as presbyters. But it incorrectly claimed that the papal rescript, "like other attestations too from the first millennium (Caesarius of Arles, the Venerable Bede), do not supply, therefore, any proof of the possibility of introducing ministers who are not priests for the sacrament of the anointing the sick."[131] All three sources—Innocent I, Caesarius of Arles, and Bede—did not consider priests as the exclusive ministers of the sacrament. With reference to James 5:14, which he quoted, Innocent explained: "And there is no doubt that this should be accepted and understood concerning the faithful who are sick, who can be anointed by the holy oil of chrism, which, confected by the bishop, may be used for anointing not only by priests (*sacerdotibus*) but also by all Christians in their own need or

[128] On this form of papal approval for instructions by dicasteries of the Holy See, see John M. Huels, "Interpreting an Instruction Approved *in forma specifica*," *Studia Canonica* 32, no. 1 (1998): 8–12.

[129] Congregation for the Doctrine of the Faith, "Nota," 479.

[130] Congregation for the Doctrine of the Faith, "Nota," 483.

[131] Congregation for the Doctrine of the Faith, "Nota," 479.

in the need of their relatives (*in suorum necessitate*)."[132] Owing to the inclusion of Innocent's letter in most Western compilations of canons before the ninth century, the pope's instruction about the anointing of the sick became "universally known in the West."[133] In his sermons, Caesarius, the sixth-century bishop of Arles, urged the sick to anoint themselves with blessed oil.[134] Twice he specified that the oil was "blessed by presbyters,"[135] and twice he justified his command to the sick with James 5:14.[136] In the early eighth century, while interpreting James 5:14 in his *Commentary on the Seven Catholic Epistles*, Bede, the English monastic exegete and historian, noted the contemporary "custom of the church," by which presbyters anointed the sick with "consecrated oil." But on the strength of the letter of Pope Innocent, he claimed that all Christians could anoint the sick.[137]

For the CDF, history (albeit partially misconstrued), doctrine, and theology outweighed pastoral exigency. Its *Note* acknowledged that the scarcity of priests in some regions made it difficult to administer the sacrament. This difficulty suggested the solution that "permanent deacons and also qualified laypeople could be appointed (*deputati*) as ministers of the sacrament." The CDF, however, aimed at thwarting the implementation of what it interpreted as this dangerous solution "to the detriment of the faith and with

[132] Robert Cabié, ed. and trans., *La lettre du Pape Innocent Ier à Décentius de Gubbio (19 mars 416): texte critique, traduction et commentaire* (Louvain: Publications universitaires de Louvain / Bureau de la *Revue d'Histoire ecclésiastique*, 1973), 30.

[133] Antoine Chavasse, "L'onction des infirmes dans l'Église latine du IIIe siècle à la réforme carolingienne: les textes," *Revue des Sciences Religieuses* 20, nos. 3–4 (1940): 301–2.

[134] CCSL 103: 66, 225, 232; CCSL 104: 751.

[135] CCSL 103: 66, 232.

[136] CCSL 103: 66; CCSL 104: 751.

[137] CCSL 121: 221. On the *Commentary*, see Arthur G. Holder, "Bede and the New Testament," in *The Cambridge Companion to Bede*, ed. Scott Degregorio (Cambridge: Cambridge University Press, 2010), 145–46.

grave spiritual harm of the sick, who want help."[138] After a chronological review of Catholic teaching, the CDF invoked the sacramental authority of the priest, who "acts *in the person of Christ the head* and *in the person of the church*." The priest is "the living and visible instrument of Christ" and the priest's prayer, gathering up the church's prayer, will be heard.[139]

Magisterial teaching has not prevented statements and arguments in favor of deacons as ministers of anointing. Since laypeople had administered the sacrament in the church's medieval past, Congar saw no reason why contemporary deacons could not anoint the sick.[140] Ecclesiology shaped Philippe Rouillard's reasoning that deacons can act as ministers of the sacrament of the anointing of the sick. Caring for the sick belonged to "the permanent *diaconia* of the church." Deacons were "the regular and instituted representatives" of the church's service to the sick. "It would seem logical and lawful," Rouillard concluded, "that deacons be entrusted by the church with the sacramental ministry of the Spirit for people whose suffering appeals with loud cries to the presence and the power of the Spirit of God."[141] Even though Gisbert Greshake attributed to deacons "the sacramental representation of the serving Christ *and* of the serving church,"[142] and not the representation of Christ the head, he proposed for a diocesan bishop's pastoral planning that deacons anoint the sick and, given ancient precedent, hear their confessions as well as those of

[138] Congregation for the Doctrine of the Faith, "Nota," 480.

[139] Congregation for the Doctrine of the Faith, "Nota," 483, emphasis in the original.

[140] Congar, "Le diaconat," 134.

[141] Philippe Rouillard, "Le ministre du sacrement des malades," *Nouvelle revue théologique* 101, no. 3 (1979): 402.

[142] Gisbert Greshake, *Priester sein in dieser Zeit: Theologie, Pastorale Praxis, Spiritualität* ([Würzburg:] Echter Verlag, 2005), 173–74.

prisoners.[143] Susan Wood argued that the anointing of the sick was primarily a sacrament of healing, whose "by-product" was the forgiveness of sins. Without prejudice to priests as ministers of the sacrament of reconciliation, deacons, representing the church by virtue of their ordination, could anoint the sick in accordance with "the very concept of diaconal service."[144]

William Ditewig pointed out that the CDF's *Note* did not propose a remedy for the pastoral problem that it identified. Increasing the number of priests or delegating deacons as ministers of the sacrament represented two remedies for "the great frustration and anger" that families feel when a priest cannot come to anoint a loved one.[145] Ditewig called for a solution as creative as that of the church's renewal of the diaconate at the Second Vatican Council. That solution must confront three evident facts about the sacrament of the anointing of the sick: "(1) the pastoral need for the sacrament persists; (2) the current practice of the Church cannot adequately meet that need; and (3) the people of God have a right to the sacrament."[146]

A synodal church can devise a creative solution. The people of God must discern the Spirit's guidance for a ministry to the sick that is "the common responsibility of all Christians."[147] In his apostolic constitution *Sacrum Unctionem Infirmorum* (1972), which approved a revised rite for the anointing of the sick, Pope Paul VI established a helpful

[143] Greshake, *Priester sein in dieser Zeit*, 174–75. For the precedent of deacons hearing confessions in the absence of a priest, see Cyprian of Carthage (d. 258), epistle 18, CCSL 3B: 101.

[144] Susan K. Wood, "The Paschal Mystery: The Intersection of Ecclesiology and Sacramental Theology in the Care of the Sick," in *Recovering the Riches of Anointing: A Study of the Sacrament of the Sick*, ed. Genevieve Glen (Collegeville, MN: Liturgical Press, 2002), 16.

[145] William T. Ditewig, *Courageous Humility: Reflections on the Church, Diakonia, and Deacons* (New York: Paulist Press, 2022), 203.

[146] Ditewig, *Courageous Humility*, 204.

[147] Wood, "The Paschal Mystery," 13.

principle for revision and discernment, namely that "whatever is subject to change should be better accommodated to the conditions of our time."[148] This principle aligned with the Tridentine declaration that the church could introduce changes to the administration of the sacraments "given the variety of circumstances, times, and places."[149] A decline in the number of priests in many local churches affects their present circumstances. These churches rely increasingly on laypeople, women and men religious, and deacons for threshold and other ministries. Some of these laypeople, religious, and deacons already exercise a stable ministry to the sick in parishes or in institutions of health care. They stand ready to serve the sick as ministers of Christ's gracious healing in the sacrament of the anointing of the sick to meet the need that the revised rite for anointing the sick expressed: "Those who are seriously ill need the special help of God's grace in this time of anxiety, lest they be broken in spirit and, under the pressure of temptation, perhaps weakened in their faith."[150] Deacons can anoint the sick by virtue of the self-gift of the Spirit whom they receive in the sacrament of order "for the faithful exercise of the work of ministry," in the words of the epiclesis of the consecratory prayer of ordination.[151] Furthermore, in exercising their ministry at the church's threshold, they carry out, Peter Hünermann affirmed, "the mission of Jesus Christ" to the poorest people on the margins of society, including "the

[148] Paul VI, "Sacrum Unctionem Infirmorum," *Acta Apostolicae Sedis* 65 (1973): 8.

[149] Tanner, *Decrees*, 2: 726.

[150] International Commission on English in the Liturgy, *The Rites of the Catholic Church: Study Edition*, 2 vols. (Collegeville, MN: Liturgical Press, 1990), 1: 779, no. 5.

[151] *Pontificale Romanum ex decreto sacrosancti oecumenici Concilii Vaticani II renovatum auctoritate Pauli PP. VI editum Ioannis Pauli PP. II cura recognitum: De ordinatione episcopi, presbyterorum et diaconorum*, 2nd ed. (1990; repr., Vatican City: Libreria Editrice Vaticana, 2011), 122, no. 207 (ordination of more than one deacon); 138, no. 235 (ordination of one deacon).

sick, the ailing, the dying." In his advisory opinion on deacons as ordinary (not extraordinary) ministers of the sacrament of the anointing of the sick submitted to the synod of West Germany's Catholic dioceses, Hünermann argued that, in view of Christ's "saving ministry" to the sick, it would be "absurd" not to make deacons ministers of "that sacrament, in which God's grace has known its symbolic concentration precisely for this group of people."[152] Laypeople and members of religious institutes can administer this sacrament by virtue of their baptism and through a liturgical commissioning in which their bishop invokes the Spirit to empower them to be ministers of Christ's healing. Surely, the need of the sick outweighs theological intransigence about priests as the exclusive ministers of the sacrament of anointing. A synodal church can take inspiration from Jesus, who healed the sick out of love for them in the teeth of theological intransigence (Matt 12:9-14; Mark 3: 1-6; Luke 13:10-17, 14:1-16).

While the CDF's *Note* suggested that the sick would suffer "grave spiritual harm"[153] if anyone other than a priest sacramentally anointed them, the real spiritual harm consists in denying the sacrament to the sick owing to a shortage of priests. By clinging to the proximate past and invoking the priest's representation of Christ the head in favor of an exclusively priestly sacramental ministry, the *Note* limits the access of the sick and dying to sacramental grace. The rigid preservation of ecclesial structures risks impeding the Spirit of Christ. Current dominant formulations of canon law and of the sacramental ministry to the sick represent obstructive structures that frustrate ministry to the sick and risk making the church into what Rahner called a "closed system," in

[152] Peter Hünermann, "Gutachten zur Bestellung des Diakons (der Diakonin) zum ordentlichen Spender der Krankensalbung," *Diaconia Christi* 9, no. 3 (August 1974): 28.

[153] Congregation for the Doctrine of the Faith, "Nota," 480.

which one hierarchical reference point determines the church's great variety.[154]

Thanks to the improvising Spirit, the church is an open system. Under the improvisation of the Spirit, an ongoing "pastoral conversion" of the church embraces what Pope Francis called "the renewal of structures."[155] Although he did not refer to sacramental ministry, the reform of the celebration of the sacrament of the anointing of the sick may belong to a renewal of structures that represents "an effort to make them more mission-oriented, to make ordinary pastoral activity on every level more inclusive and open, to inspire in pastoral workers a constant desire to go forth and in this way to elicit a positive response from all those whom Jesus summons to friendship with himself."[156] An inclusivity and openness of ministry to the marginalized reflects for the entire church "the co-responsibility and ministeriality (*ministerialidad*) of all" that the Amazonian bishops intended for the church in their region.[157] The inclusion of laypeople, deacons, and priests in the church's common mission to comfort the sick and dying with the presence of Christ in the sacrament of anointing overcomes the restrictive ministerial self-referentiality implied by the CDF's *Note*.

In a communion of ministers at the church's threshold, deacons exercise their own form of leadership, their own *munus regendi*. Their role in a Christian community is not to function as a bridge between clergy and laity for a bishop's direction of ecclesial *diaconia*. Direction or leadership from a deacon certainly expresses itself in inspiring Christian service. But it also builds community by motivating

[154] Rahner, "Bemerkungen über das Charismatische in der Kirche," 256.

[155] Francis, *The Joy of the Gospel: Evangelii Gaudium*, 15, no. 27.

[156] Francis, *The Joy of the Gospel: Evangelii Gaudium*, 15, no. 27.

[157] Synod of Bishops, "Coetus specialis pro regione amazonica documentum finale," *Acta Apostolicae Sedis* 111, no. 11 (November 2019): 1775, no. 92.

service to the threshold and service by members of a threshold community.

Diaconal Leadership in Threshold Ministry

During a pastoral visit to Milan in 2017, Pope Francis rejected "the image of the deacon as a kind of intermediary between the faithful and the pastors." In opposition to the mediating image, Francis proposed "the characteristic charism of the diaconate," which he understood in terms of service.[158] As "*the guardian of service in the church*," a deacon reminds "all of us," the pope said, "that faith in its various expressions—the communitarian liturgy, personal prayer, the various forms of charity—and in its various states of life—lay, clerical, familial—possesses an essential dimension of service."[159] At a time when in "our culture" people want to know how prayer, community, and charity benefit them, deacons take a contrarian position. In his closing words to the deacons of Milan, the pope affirmed: "You are the gift that the Spirit gives us to see that the correct way leads in the opposite direction: in prayer I serve, in the community I serve, with solidarity I serve God and neighbor."[160]

[158] Francis, "In visitatione pastorali in Archidioecesi Mediolanensi. Occursus cum sacerdotibus et viris mulieribusque consecratis in templo Cathedrali," *Acta Apostolicae Sedis* 109, no. 4 (April 2017): 376. Oddly, the official title for the pope's statements in Milan's cathedral failed to mention that he also met with deacons, or at least with one deacon. Pope Francis responded to a question posed by a deacon, Roberto Crespi, who asked what role deacons should play in presenting the humble, unselfish, and blessed face of the church. See Francis, "In visitatione pastorali in Archidioecesi Mediolanensi," 375.

[159] Francis, "In visitatione pastorali in Archidioecesi Mediolanensi," 377, emphasis in the original.

[160] Francis, "In visitatione pastorali in Archidioecesi Mediolanensi," 377.

In proposing concrete manifestations of the "stature of the diaconate,"[161] Walter Kasper elaborated on diaconal leadership. As a minister who raises up people from their brokenness, the deacon serves as the "advocate of the small and the weak as well as of all those who lack a voice and a lobby."[162] That advocacy finds an outlet in diaconal preaching and liturgical ministry at a community's celebration of the Eucharist and motivates its solidarity with those in need. Deacons seek, form, and accompany co-workers in the ministry of charity.[163] Owing to their participation in the church's one sacrament of order, deacons share in "the leadership of the community" by emphasizing the place of the ministry of charity in pastoral care and by coordinating that ministry among parish communities.[164]

Threshold ministries, such as to patients in hospitals, hospices, and residents of care facilities; prisoners; seafarers; ground staff, crews, and passengers in airports; migrant workers; Indigenous communities; members of sexual minorities; students on a university campus; and people seeking spiritual discernment and renewal in retreat centers, take deacons beyond parish structures. They witness to a reality that Rahner identified in 1948: the parish priest is not the exclusive pastoral minister, and the parish is not the sole venue for pastoral care. Thus, the human person who, in her or his various social groupings and settings, receives pastoral care constitutes the measure of ministry, not the parish.[165] In a lecture that he gave twenty years later in 1968, Rahner proposed the incorporation of marginalized persons

[161] Walter Kasper, "Der Diakon in ekklesiologischer Sicht angesichts der gegenwärtigen Herausforderungen in Kirche und Gesellschaft," in Walter Kasper, *Theologie und Kirche*, vol. 2 (Mainz: Matthias-Grünewald-Verlag, 1999), 159.

[162] Kasper, "Der Diakon," 160.

[163] Kasper, "Der Diakon," 160.

[164] Kasper, "Der Diakon," 161.

[165] Karl Rahner, "Friedliche Erwägungen über das Pfarrprinzip," *Zeitschrift für katholische Theologie* 70, no. 2 (1948): 178.

into civil and ecclesial society as "a special unfolding of the one office" of the church, which it must undertake and for which the diaconate was ideally suited.[166] In other words, deacons should take responsibility for "the formation of the Christian community in a human and Christian integration of the person who today is to a great extent religiously and socially disintegrated in the civil and ecclesial community."[167] This specification of diaconal ministry, equivalent today to a threshold ministry and presumably not limited to parish ministry, represented "a creative concept of the diaconate of the future," unfettered by the ancient model of the diaconate.[168] For Rahner, community formation expressed positively a distinctive characteristic of diaconal ministry, apart from several negatively formulated distinguishing features, such as the incapacity for "a function of leadership as such." This function was "the unique feature of the episcopal and priestly office."[169]

In 1977, Rahner doubted this limitation of the function of leadership, given the leadership of deacons in "priestless communities." Owing to this pastoral situation, he wondered why deacons were not allowed to celebrate the Eucharist, a "partial function" of a priest's leadership of a community.[170] By "priestless communities" Rahner presumably meant parishes without priests. Yet his question applies also to a deacon who, by episcopal appointment, serves as the stable and sole minister of a threshold community. Should not such a deacon, empowered by the Holy Spirit for the faithful exercise of ministry, form such a community by celebrating the Eucharist and the sacrament of reconciliation, through which Christ graciously establishes the

[166] Karl Rahner, "Über den Diakonat," in Rahner, *Schriften zur Theologie*, vol. 9 (Einsiedeln: Benziger Verlag, 1970), 408–9, quotation: 409.

[167] Rahner, "Über den Diakonat," 409.

[168] Rahner, "Über den Diakonat," 401.

[169] Rahner, "Über den Diakonat," 405–6.

[170] Karl Rahner, "Pastorale Dienste und Gemeindeleitung," *Stimmen der Zeit* 195, no. 11 (November 1977): 735.

communion of the marginalized with each other and with God? Could a local church—and the universal church too—decide to interpret the ministry for which the Spirit empowers deacons to include the celebration of these two sacraments owing to the *munus regendi* that they received in the sacrament of order?

These questions sound a disturbing tocsin in the traditional theology of ministry. They challenge the vexing ancient distinction between priesthood and ministry: deacons were ordained for the latter, but not for the former. The Second Vatican Council resuscitated this distinction at the same time as it proposed for deacons in LG 29 liturgical ministries previously exercised by priests. In the wake of the council, Paul Winninger warned of positioning the deacon as "the head of a community." He predicted: "Such a diaconate, by the nature of things, will aspire almost irresistibly to the fullness of the exercised function, that is, to the priesthood."[171] Diaconal leadership of a community would run the risk of schismatic or sectarian "insubordination," a "usurpation of the powers of consecration and absolution," and a distortion of the meaning of the priesthood and of the Mass.[172] A deacon, Winninger explained, "is not ordained for the sacraments (*sacerdotium*), but to the Levitical ministry (*ministerium*), that is, to the service of the priesthood."[173] McKnight believed that the exercise of the liturgical functions attributed by the council to deacons would turn them into "mini-priests."[174] The proper alternative requires, he believed, a consideration of "what is unique and necessary

[171] Paul Winninger, "Les ministères des diacres dans l'Église d'aujourd'hui," in *L'Église de Vatican II: Études autour de la Constitution conciliarie sur l'Église*, ed. Guilherme Baraúna and Y. M.-J. Congar, vol. 3 (Paris: Les Éditions du Cerf, 1966), 1005.

[172] Winninger, "Les ministères des diacres," 1006.

[173] Winninger, "Les ministères des diacres," 1007.

[174] McKnight, *Understanding the Diaconate*, 54, 175.

to the charisms of deacons as 'ordained to the ministry, not the priesthood.'"[175]

The defense of the shibboleth *non ad sacerdotium, sed ad ministerium*, often invoked but rarely explained theologically, raises several questions. What was the rationale for this ancient axiom as it applied to deacons? Does that rationale remain valid in today's church, especially if deacons belong, by virtue of the sacrament of order, to "the ministerial or hierarchical priesthood" (LG 10) and in view of the recognition that they participate in "the mission and grace" of Christ's priesthood "in their own way" (LG 41)?[176] How has the meaning of *sacerdotium* and *ministerium* evolved from the *Apostolic Tradition* to the Second Vatican Council and to the current discernment of pastoral and synodal conversion in the church? Does recourse to the distinction between *sacerdotium* and *ministerium* express a theology of ministry that upholds a sacramental communion of ordained ministers dedicated to the service of the people of God, or does it primarily function as a principle of hierarchical order in the church, an order in which deacons minister as subservient substitutes or auxiliaries? What do priesthood and ministry mean in the concrete situations of today's church for bishops, priests, and deacons?

Furthermore, does "the precise content" of the episcopate, presbyterate, and diaconate lack clarity so that the church can modify them?[177] In a lecture that he gave on the priesthood in 1969, Rahner claimed that the church could modify these three ministries and went on to refer to a priest's ability to administer the sacrament of confirmation and to ordain other priests, functions usually associated with bishops.[178] In his 1968 lecture on the diaconate, Rahner recognized the unavoidable blurring of the distinction

[175] McKnight, *Understanding the Diaconate*, 253.

[176] Tanner, *Decrees*, 2: 857, 882.

[177] Karl Rahner, "Zum Selbstverständnis des Amtspriesters," in Rahner, *Schriften zur Theologie*, vol. 10 (Zurich: Benziger Verlag, 1972), 456.

[178] Rahner, "Zum Selbstverständnis des Amtspriesters," 456.

between the ministry of deacons and priests owing to "an adaptable division of the one office in the church" and to the uncertainty whether an unprecedented division of office corresponded to the essence of the diaconate.[179] Could deacons, relatively without precedent but consistent with their office in the church, exercise Christ's priesthood "in their own way" by, among other things, celebrating the Eucharist in the threshold communities that they lead?[180]

The probing questions about diaconal ministry will take time for theology and the church to answer. Above all, they require the grace of discernment evident in an ecclesial attentiveness to the Holy Spirit. Posing and wrestling with these questions is a sign of taking seriously the relationships among ordained minsters and between ordained and lay ministers, and of rethinking the meaning and place of the diaconate in today's church through a deepening of the conciliar teaching on the diaconate, as called for by the Synod on Synodality.[181]

If a synodal church decides with the Spirit (cf. Acts 15:28) to mandate deacons to celebrate the sacraments of communion in a threshold community that they lead, these deacons will not usurp the priesthood, especially of priests who lead a parish. Instead, empowered by the Spirit, they will make Christ's unique priesthood present in the celebration of the Eucharist and of the sacrament of reconciliation for those who by physical necessity or by unjust

[179] Rahner, "Über den Diakonat," 404–5, quotation: 405.

[180] In 314, the Synod of Arles legislated in one of its canons against the widespread practice of the celebration of the Eucharist by deacons: "De diaconibus quos cognouimus multis locis offere, placuit minime fieri debere." See CCSL 148: 12. Carl Joseph von Hefele argued that *offere* here meant celebrating the Eucharist, not distributing Communion. Hefele assumed that deacons celebrated the Eucharist, especially in the absence of a bishop or priest during the Diocletian persecution of Christians. See Carl Joseph von Hefele, *Conciliengeschichte. Nach den Quellen bearbeitet*, vol. 1, 2nd ed. (Freiburg im Breisgau: Herder, 1873), 213–14.

[181] Francis and XVI Ordinary General Assembly of the Synod of Bishops, *For a Synodal Church*, 26, no. 73.

discrimination find themselves removed or alienated from parish life. Of course, by the current standards of ecclesial life and the theology of ministry, these deacons would function as priests. But their celebration of the Eucharist and the sacrament of reconciliation would flow from their ordination as deacons and from their bishop, who, by virtue of what the Second Vatican Council recognized as "the fullness of the sacrament of order" (LG 21)[182] that he received at his ordination, can commission them to provide diaconal leadership of a threshold community that includes the celebration of the sacraments for that community. The celebration of the sacraments by deacons will not affect the substance of the sacraments but will reflect the church's power over their administration, in accordance with the principle articulated at the Council of Trent. The Eucharist and the sacramental absolution of sins will remain what they must be, but in deacons, owing to the sacrament of order, they will have new ministers.

Two more magisterial voices, beyond the synodal voices of the Council of Trent and the Second Vatican Council, can assist in integrating a sacramental ministry for deacons. These are the voices of Pius XII, describing the sacrament of order in his encyclical *Mystici Corporis Christi* (1943), and the Australian bishops, locating deacons within the saving mystery of Christ's death and resurrection in their directory for the diaconate (2016). As it contemplates the novelty of a sacramental ministry for deacons, the church can listen to these voices within the development of Catholic tradition and in accordance with "the nature of true reform," which Benedict XVI described as a discontinuity within abiding principles, or "a process of innovation within continuity."[183] This idea of reform emerged in the pope's famous speech to the Roman Curia on December 22, 2005, a speech in

[182] Tanner, *Decrees*, 2: 865.

[183] Benedict XVI, "Ad Romanam Curiam ob omina natalicia," *Acta Apostolicae Sedis* 98 (January 2006): 49.

which he proposed "the hermeneutic of reform" as a principle by which to interpret the Second Vatican Council: the hermeneutic "of renewal within continuity of the one subject-church, which the Lord has given to us." The pope continued: "it is a subject that grows over time and develops, remaining, however, always the same, the unique subject of the people of God *en route*."[184]

In *Mystici Corporis Christi*, Pius XII taught that Christ especially established two sacraments for "the social needs of the church." Marriage, in which the spouses are for each other "ministers of grace," increases "Christian community" and assures "the correct and religious education of children," without which the church, the Mystical Body of Christ, would face a "most serious danger." The pope proceeded to the second sacrament: "By sacred order, they are given over (*mancipantur*) and consecrated to God who offer up the eucharistic sacrifice, who nourish the flock of the faithful with the bread of angels and the food of doctrine, who guide it with divine commandments and counsel, who, finally, strengthen it with other gifts from above."[185]

The pope's language about the sacrament of order is both unappealing to modern ecclesial sensibilities and theologically instructive. The verb *mancipare* refers in the first instance to a commercial transaction: the sale or transfer of slaves or other property. Presumably, the pope's objective was to emphasize the dedication to the service of God among the ordained, but the lexical implication of the clergy as God's chattel undermines the graced freedom by which the ordained respond to sacramental grace. A contemporary theology of ministry, furthermore, would wish for an explicit formulation of the functions of the ordained as service to the people of God, among whom laypeople are more than recipients of pastoral care. These functions, as theologians today would recognize, correspond to the threefold office

[184] Benedict XVI, "Ad Romanam Curiam ob omina natalicia," 46.
[185] Pius XII, "Mystici Corporis Christi," 202.

of Christ: sanctification, teaching, and governance. The encyclical obviously paired sanctification with the celebration of the Eucharist. While he may have thought of "sacred order" only in terms of the presbyterate, the pope used wording that could be read expansively to apply to all who receive and minister by virtue of the sacrament of order, including bishops and deacons. Four years after the encyclical, in *Sacramentum Ordinis*, the pope laid an authoritative foundation for the sacramentality for all three ordained ministries. Since the self-gift of the Spirit empowers deacons for ministry within the threefold office of Christ, as the development in the theology of the diaconate and magisterial teaching has shown, the celebration of the Eucharist could or should belong to Christ's sanctifying office as exercised by deacons in view of the statement about the sacrament of order by Pius XII in *Mystici Corporis Christi*.

For their part, the Australian bishops in their directory for the diaconate (2016) associated diaconal ministry with "the specific service given by the Lord in fulfilling the paschal mystery."[186] They reiterated: "The central mystery that the deacon serves is the Paschal Mystery." While the Australian bishops went on to relate a deacon's service of "the mysteries of Christ" to a commitment "to evangelization in the Church and in the world" without reference to the sacraments,[187] serving the paschal mystery could also include the celebration of the Eucharist in threshold communities.

In his 1969 lecture on the priesthood, Rahner considered ordaining priests for the leadership of similar communities that did not conform to the territorial parish. He called this proposal "relative ordination."[188] But much of what he said about the priesthood in that lecture could also apply to the

[186] Australian Catholic Bishops Conference, "Norms for the Formation of Permanent Deacons and Guidelines for the Ministry and Life of Permanent Deacons," *The Canonist* 8, no. 1 (2017): 26, section 3.2.

[187] Australian Catholic Bishops Conference, "Norms," 31, section 3.4.

[188] Rahner, "Zum Selbstverständnis des Amtspriesters," 460.

diaconate in a threshold ministry. If the needs of the future and the needs arising "from below," as distinct from hierarchical decrees "from above," should determine the exercise of the priesthood in today's church,[189] the same determinants can contribute to the discernment about the diaconate that a local church requires. Such needs have already put deacons in the position of leading threshold communities and even parishes. If the leadership of a Christian community, as Rahner contended, was the point of departure of priestly ministry and the prerequisite for a ministry of the word and a sacramental ministry,[190] would these ministries follow too from a diaconal leadership of a Christian community? A similar question probably informed Rahner's query in 1977 why deacons who lead "priestless communities" could not celebrate the Eucharist.[191]

A threshold ministry corresponds to the *munus regendi* of deacons, as identified by the Holy See's *Basic Norms* (*Ratio fundamentalis*) for the diaconate: "the development of religious life in a community or in its individual associations with special consideration retained for charity."[192] In that development or formation, the ministry of charity could include a sacramental ministry, if a deacon is the sole, stable ordained minister in the threshold community on the principle that the minister who leads the community celebrates the sacraments for it. A community's religious life consists of a synergy of worship, of the proclamation of God's word, and of charity. In the Eucharist, Christ enables this synergy for the community, and as the ordained minister of Christ and of his church, a deacon-leader of a threshold community could preside over its celebration of the Eucharist.

[189] Rahner, "Zum Selbstverständnis des Amtspriesters," 458.

[190] Rahner, "Zum Selbstverständnis des Amtspriesters," 454–55.

[191] Rahner, "Pastorale Dienste und Gemeindeleitung," 735.

[192] Congregation for Catholic Education, "Ratio fundamentalis institutionis diaconorum permanentium," *Acta Apostolicae Sedis* 90 (1998): 848, no. 9.

A ministry of charity in a threshold or any community is a ministry of co-responsibility. Just as pastors cannot by themselves take on the "entire salvific mission of the church" and must therefore cooperate with laypeople, owing to their "ministries and charisms" (LG 30),[193] so too deacons cannot develop or form a community on their own. With their charisms all members contribute to the formation of their Christian community, for their communion is ultimately the work of the Spirit, who "joins together everyone so intimately in Christ that [the Spirit] is the principle of the church's unity" (UR 2).[194] What applies to the universal church applies also to its local manifestations, including threshold communities, which too may be considered altar communities "under the sacred ministry of a bishop," expressing the charity and unity of the church and revealing the presence of Christ, no matter how "small and poor or dispersed" these communities might be (LG 26).[195] As the sole and stable ordained minister in a threshold community, a deacon is a fellow builder, not the architect, of communion. There the deacon's *munus regendi* is a leadership of service to and with fellow community members in "the *diakonia* of the Spirit" (2 Cor 3:8), who makes Christ present among the marginalized.

Of course, many deacons minister in parish communities led by priests. Should a bishop allow these deacons to celebrate the Eucharist and the sacrament of reconciliation in their parishes? Surely, it would be more appropriate for a deacon, a resident ordained minister known in the parish community, to celebrate these sacraments in the service of fellow parishioners when the pastor is absent on vacation or for some other reason than for the pastor to struggle to find a retired or visiting or monastic priest to replace him temporarily. The church could change canon law to consider deacons as parochial vicars (cc. 546–51) with the expectation

[193] Tanner, *Decrees*, 2: 875.
[194] Tanner, *Decrees*, 2: 909.
[195] Tanner, *Decrees*, 2: 870.

that deacons, by appointment of the diocesan bishop, would exercise co-responsible leadership with the pastor and laypeople in parish ministries of charity to the poor and marginalized. A bishop could grant these parish deacons the faculties to celebrate the sacraments in circumstances relevant to their co-responsible leadership and in view of self-gift of the Spirit that they received for ministry in the sacrament of order. Parish deacons could revitalize the missionary impetus of parishes, which began as outposts or thresholds of evangelization as Christianity spread from cities to the countryside in the Roman empire.[196] In parishes reconfigured at the church's evangelizing threshold, deacons, as co-responsible servant-leaders and not as substitutionary auxiliaries, "could demonstrate a church that is missionary through and through."[197]

The Reconfiguration of the Threshold

A pneumatic theology of ministry requires deacons and other ministers in the servant church to engage its periphery in a radically new way. The Spirit impels the church not only from within but breaks in from the periphery, as when the Spirit, with a heavenly "rush of violent wind" (Acts 2:1), surprised cosmopolitan residents of Jerusalem with provincial Galileans speaking in an astonishing variety of languages (Acts 2:5-12). As globalization, climate change, social polarization, and armed conflict exacerbate poverty today, the Spirit groans with the cry of the poor: the Spirit of freedom who expresses "the longing for liberation of oppressed peoples."[198] Codina insisted: "In the clamor of the poor, therefore, the action of the Spirit becomes discernible, who

[196] James A. Coriden, *The Parish in Catholic Tradition: History, Theology and Canon Law* (New York: Paulist Press, 1997), 22–25.

[197] Gerard Kelly and Richard Lennan, "The Diaconate: Possibilities and Challenges," *Australian Catholic Record* 74, no. 2 (April 1997): 140.

[198] Víctor Codina, *Creo en el Espíritu Santo: Pneumatología narrativa* (Santander: Editorial Sal Terrae, 1994), 79.

cries out through them, demanding justice and liberation."[199] The poor evangelize the church, the periphery the center, answering the desire of Pope Francis for a "Church which is poor and for the poor."[200]

Since Christ "became poor" (2 Cor 8:9) and preferentially identifies with those deprived of the necessities of life, and with strangers, the sick, and prisoners (Matt 25:35-36), the poor preferentially represent him and his message of the liberating reign of God. They "keep alive," Jon Sobrino wrote, "the question of God, of his kingdom, of Christ, justice, and sin."[201] Just as "the Spirit of Jesus is in the poor," so too "the Spirit is in the Church of the poor."[202] Sobrino proposed a destination for the church of the poor: it "should migrate to the periphery and share the powerlessness of the poor, at the feet of a crucified God, so that it might there cultivate Christian hope and develop effective (and, in this sense, powerful) activity."[203] But this periphery is also the ecclesial center, recreated by the Spirit, where the poor reconstitute the principle of the church's "structure, organization, and mission."[204]

The reconfiguration of the church's periphery as its center requires a profound pastoral and synodal conversion of the church's *diaconia*. Listening to the Spirit's clamor in the poor, the people of God constantly and co-responsibly recalibrates its "social organization" (LG 8)[205] for its mission in service of Christ's inauguration of God's reign, which is "righteousness and peace and joy in the Holy Spirit" (Rom 14:17). In communion with their bishop and with priests, deacons serve the people of God in a co-responsible *diaconia*,

[199] Codina, *Creo en el Espíritu Santo*, 84.

[200] Francis, *The Joy of the Gospel: Evangelii Gaudium*, 100, no. 198.

[201] Jon Sobrino, *The True Church and the Poor*, trans. Matthew J. O'Connell (Maryknoll, NY: Orbis Books, 1984), 97.

[202] Sobrino, *The True Church and the Poor*, 93, 96.

[203] Sobrino, *The True Church and the Poor*, 98.

[204] Sobrino, *The True Church and the Poor*, 93.

[205] Tanner, *Decrees*, 2: 854.

evangelized by the poor for solidarity with them in bringing Christ's liberating gospel to those for whom he has made his preferential option. The church's diaconal "love for the poor" must manifest itself as "a love that becomes justice and renews the structure of society."[206] As ordained ministers at the church's reconfigured threshold, deacons exercise their *munus regendi* in announcing and making tangible God's justice for the poor.

[206] Sobrino, *The True Church and the Poor*, 107–8.

Conclusion: The Perturbation of the Diaconate

In the first edition of their *Directory* for the diaconate, published in 2005, the American bishops associated the diaconal *munus regendi* with the promotion of justice. A deacon, the *Directory* stated,

> articulates the Church's concern for justice by being a driving force in addressing the injustices among God's people. He thus symbolizes in his roles the grounding of the Church's life in the Eucharist and the mission of the Church in her loving service of the needy. In the deacon, in a unique way, is represented the integral relationship between the worship of God in the liturgy that recalls Jesus Christ's redemptive sacrifice sacramentally and the worship of God in everyday life where Jesus Christ is encountered in the needy.[1]

Although the *Directory*'s connection of justice to the Eucharist and to the service of the poor is more oblique than forceful, the quoted statement suggests that worship and *diaconia* in combination underpin a commitment to justice that informs ecclesial leadership in diaconal ministry. The American bishops entitled their section on the deacon's

[1] United States Conference of Catholic Bishops, *National Directory for the Formation, Ministry, and Life of Permanent Deacons in the United States* (Washington, DC: United States Conference of Catholic Bishops, 2005), 20–21, no. 37.

munus regendi "The Church's Ministry of Charity and Justice: The Deacon as Witness and Guide."[2]

In 2021, in the second edition of the American *Directory*, justice no longer figured in the deacon's *munus regendi*, presented in the section with the revised title: "The Church's Ministry of Charity: The Deacon as Witness and Guide."[3] Ministry in charity "to both the spiritual and physical needs of others" formed the premise for the conclusion that the American bishops drew:

> The deacon thus symbolizes in his roles the grounding of the Church's life in the Eucharist and the mission of the Church in her loving service. The deacon's service begins at the altar and returns there. The sacrificial love of Christ celebrated in the Eucharist nourishes him and motivates him to lay down his life on behalf of God's People.[4]

Ministry to the poor vanished from the modern deacon's *munus regendi*. It figured only in a reference to the ancient practice of the diaconate and as a rationale for liturgical ministry: "The ancient tradition appears to indicate that, because the deacon was the servant at the table of the poor, he had his distinctive liturgical roles at the Table of the Lord."[5] In referring to the deacon as "a driving force for service, or *diakonia*," the American bishops decided to quote the Holy See's *Basic Norms for the Formation of Permanent*

[2] United States Conference of Catholic Bishops, *National Directory* (2005), 20.

[3] United States Conference of Catholic Bishops, *The National Directory for the Formation, Ministry, and Life of Permanent Deacons in the United States of America*, 2nd ed. (Washington, DC: United States Conference of Catholic Bishops, 2021), 27.

[4] United States Conference of Catholic Bishops, *National Directory* (2021), 28–29, no. 39.

[5] United States Conference of Catholic Bishops, *National Directory* (2021), 28, no. 39.

Deacons, instead of repeating their own and earlier characterization of the deacon as "a driving force in addressing the injustices among God's people."[6]

Deletion does not necessarily mean denial, however. Whatever a directory may say about diaconal ministry, the resolute pursuit of justice is indispensable for its exercise. A commitment to justice corresponds to a blending of the figure of the Samaritan and of the prophet in Paul Zulehner's typology of deacons. The Samaritan-deacon cares for suffering individuals, while the prophetic deacon identifies social and ecclesial structures in need of reform to prevent the human suffering that these structures cause.[7] In their ministry to marginalized people, deacons contribute to the church's indispensable mission to denounce injustice "publicly, incessantly, and forthrightly," as Ignacio Ellacuría insisted,[8] and to bring about the liberation of human beings from oppressive structures that entrench poverty. Ellacuría presented this liberation as profoundly theological. Human liberation does not merely stand as a "sign of credibility" that the church is the sacrament of salvation for all people, but it belongs to "the very essence" of the church's mission "because it is an inescapable obligation in its service to the

[6] United States Conference of Catholic Bishops, *National Directory* (2021), 28, no. 39; *Basic Norms*, no. 5 in *Basic Norms/Directory*, 25. The *Basic Norms* quoted Paul VI, who in *Ad Pascendum* called the diaconate "instimulator famulatus seu *diaconiae* Ecclesiae." See Paul VI, "Ad Pascendum," *Acta Apostolicae Sedis* 64 (1972): 536.

[7] Paul M. Zulehner, *Dienende Männer – Anstifter zur Solidarität: Diakone in Westeuropa* (Ostfildern: Schwabenverlag, 2003), 65–67. Zulehner completed his typology of deacons with a third type: the Levite. "Levites," Zulehner explained, "are cryptopriests, that is, deacons in presbyteral standby." These deacons would like to minister as priests. They suffer when they cannot meet the expectations of "some members of the church" to exercise "priestly functions, such as hearing confessions or celebrating the anointing of the sick in the pastoral care of the sick." See Zulehner, *Dienende Männer*, 68.

[8] Ignacio Ellacuría, *Freedom Made Flesh: The Mission of Christ and His Church*, trans. John Drury (Maryknoll, NY: Orbis Books, 1976), 115.

world."[9] The church owes its liberative mission to the God of justice and of freedom for the familial fellowship of all human beings, the God whom the sin of injustice denies.[10] Ellacuría argued: "To become an effective sign of the gospel message, the Church must first recognize its contribution to the unjust oppression of human beings."[11] Faithful to their *munus regendi* in the synergy of charity and justice, deacons must confess the church's faults of commission or omission in human suffering to be credible ministers of a credible church. In this way, deacons sacramentally represent the local church in its own sacramental mission to signify and effect God's love for human beings and their unifying love for each other, since, as Gerard Kelly and Richard Lennan contended, "the diaconate cannot thrive unless it relates to a local church where the spirit of service and a commitment to justice also thrive." Kelly and Lennan concluded: "A local church which wants a healthy diaconate must, therefore, be prepared to be self-critical regarding its own mode of presence in the world."[12]

In drawing the church out of itself for its mission, deacons, according to Alphonse Borras, serve as "troublemakers" (*perturbateurs*).[13] But the perturbation of the diaconate is as much an objective as it is a subjective genitive. The diaconate can and should unsettle the church for its liberating mission of proclaiming Christ's gospel, but the diaconate itself is certainly theologically unsettled. In 2012, after publishing two books on the diaconate, Borras conceded: "Today the diaconate still remains an ecclesial reality with scarcely any elaboration in theology." Its "relatively recent" emergence within Catholicism explained the inadequate

[9] Ellacuría, *Freedom Made Flesh*, 110.

[10] Ellacuría, *Freedom Made Flesh*, 112.

[11] Ellacuría, *Freedom Made Flesh*, 113.

[12] Gerard Kelly and Richard Lennan, "The Diaconate: Possibilities and Challenges," *Australian Catholic Record* 74, no. 2 (April 1997): 140.

[13] Alphonse Borras, *Le diaconat au risque de sa nouveauté* (Brussels: Éditions Lessius, 2007), 234.

theological attention, he believed.[14] Inadequate theology can contribute to inequitable conditions for the exercise of diaconal ministry. After hearing a presentation on the diaconate by Deacon William Ditewig, a priest from an American diocese, in which deacons had ministered for more than twenty-five years, approached Ditewig in an "agitated" state. The priest remorsefully admitted to having treated deacons as menial laborers, "like dirt on my shoes."[15]

How can the diaconate move beyond subservience to become "a full and equal order" in the church? James Barnett famously asserted this designation as the title of his book on the diaconate.[16] Similarly, the American bishops taught: "The diaconate is not an abridged or substitute form of the priesthood; it is a full order in its own right."[17] Its equality, according to Ditewig, is not a matter of pastoral governance, the remit of bishops and priests. But the diaconate is equal to the episcopate and presbyterate "in the communion of holy orders and its mature exercise of *diakonia*."[18] Barnett believed that the preservation of a "transitional diaconate" constituted an obstacle to the recognition and functioning of a stable diaconate as "the full and equal order

[14] Alphonse Borras, "Les diacres d'après les nouveaux canons 1008 et 1009 §3," *Revue théologique de Louvain* 43, no. 1 (2012): 52.

[15] William T. Ditewig, *Courageous Humility: Reflections on the Church, Diakonia, and Deacons* (New York: Paulist Press, 2022), 211.

[16] James Monroe Barnett, *The Diaconate: A Full and Equal Order*, rev. ed. (Valley Forge, PA: Trinity Press International, 1995).

[17] United States Conference of Catholic Bishops, *National Directory* (2021), 37, no. 54. An endnote in support of this claim directs readers to the Holy See's *Directory for the Ministry and Life of Permanent Deacons*, nos. 1 and 41. See United States Conference of Catholic Bishops, *National Directory* (2021), 61, n. 26. The two sections of the Holy See's *Directory* do not explicitly refer to the diaconate as a full order. Section 1 identifies the deacon as "a sacred minister," a condition that "determines his theological and juridical status in the Church." Section 41 stipulates that deacons "have the right to be accepted and fully recognized by all." See *Directory*, nos. 1, 41 in *Basic Norms/Directory*, 75, 106.

[18] Ditewig, *Courageous Humility*, 216.

that will hold the image of the servant-Christ before the Church and the world as the model for all ministry."[19] Ditewig emphatically agreed, advocating the end of the practice of ordaining candidates for the priesthood to the diaconate for a brief transitional experience of pastoral ministry. A transitional diaconate is both "unnecessary" and "harmful and detrimental to the organic development of the order of deacons" since it "distorts and minimizes the sign that the diaconate is supposed to be in service to the Church."[20]

Fullness and equality evoke the relationship between gender and ministry. The Synod on Synodality announced that "the question of women's access to diaconal ministry remains open. This discernment needs to continue."[21] Discernment is certainly necessary, but it should be truly synodal with the widest participation possible in attentiveness to the Holy Spirit's guidance for the church's ministry. Left to a small committee of experts meeting privately, the discernment about ordaining women to the diaconate perturbs diaconal ministry. Severely limiting discernment raises questions not only about women as deacons, but also about the validity of the diaconate itself, when women, without benefit of the grace of the sacrament of order, assume roles of ministerial leadership commensurate to those of male deacons.

The root of the theological perturbation of the diaconate lies in *Geistvergessenheit*. Diaconal ministry will flourish through the dismantling of this neglect of the Spirit in the theology and the praxis of the diaconate. To assert with Ditewig an equality of ordained ministries "in the com-

[19] Barnett, *The Diaconate*, 211.

[20] Ditewig, *Courageous Humility*, 223.

[21] Francis and XVI Ordinary General Assembly of the Synod of Bishops, *For a Synodal Church: Communion, Participation, Mission—Final Document*, 22, no. 60, November 24, 2024, Vatican website, https://www.synod.va/content/dam/synod/news/2024-10-26_final-document/ENG---Documento-finale.pdf.

munion of holy orders"[22] means an appreciation that bishops, priests, and deacons receive the self-gift of the Spirit in the sacrament of order. Ordained ministry represents a gracious gift for and in the church that ordained ministers ought to recognize in each other for the sake of their graced ministerial communion exercised in co-responsible service to the people of God. Hervé Legrand wrote: "the ministries of priest and deacon have their own proper foundation. They are not a derivation of that of the bishop and their meaning may not be reduced to reinforce the bishop. On the other hand, they are his natural collaborators (*collaborateurs-nés*) and can only exercise their ministry in communion with him."[23] The communion of ordained ministers is as vertical as it is horizontal, as divinely given as humanly received and expressed.

However a local church configures the diaconate for the mission of Christ's gospel, it must do justice to the primacy of sacramental grace. The Spirit empowers deacons for ministry, co-responsibly exercised with their bishop and the priests of the local church. Their co-responsible ministry is incompatible with *suppléance*. Deacons are not subservient substitutes or auxiliaries. They receive the self-gift of the Spirit to exercise sacramentally Christ's threefold office. In Christ and for his people, they sanctify, teach, and lead those whom they serve in a manner that corresponds to the specific mission that they receive from their bishop.

Diaconal ministry, and all ordained ministry, ought to recognize the gifts of the Spirit among the people of God. As Klemens Ambrunster and Mathias Mühl observed: "The image of the body of Christ with its members appears only in the consecratory prayer (*Ordinationsgebet*) of the

[22] Ditewig, *Courageous Humility*, 216.

[23] Hervé Legrand, "Le diaconat dans sa relation à la théologie de l'Église et des ministères: Réception et devenir du diaconat depuis Vatican II," in *Diaconat, XXIe siècle: Actes du Colloque de Louvain-la-Neuve (13–15 septembre 1994)*, ed. André Haquin and Philippe Weber (Brussels: Éditions Lumen Vitae, 1997), 35.

ordination of deacons, not in the other two," i.e., not in the consecratory prayers for priests and bishops.[24] On behalf of the church, the ordaining bishop addresses God: "You generously grant Christ's body, your church, adorned with a variety of heavenly graces and joined together with a diversity of its members, united by a wondrous bond through the Holy Spirit, to grow and to expand into the increase of the new temple."[25] The mutual service of the members of Christ's body is the necessary prerequisite for diaconal ministry, and for this service, Ambrunster and Mühl contended, "the deacon is gifted with the Holy Spirit at ordination."[26]

A pneumatic theology of ministry in a synodal church calls for a revision of the consecratory prayers for bishops, priests, and deacons. They should all expressly mention the church as the people of God and conceive of all the baptized as co-responsible for the church's mission, thanks to their charisms. The current prayer for a bishop limits his relationship to the church to his caring for God's flock and his offering of the church's gifts as he manifests to God his "high priesthood."[27] The ordaining bishop prays for priests who will cooperate with him in preaching, administering sacraments, and praying for the people entrusted to them.[28] Apart from the reference to gifted members of the body of Christ, the consecratory prayer for deacons mentions only their "care for the sick and also the poor" and the way in

[24] Klemens Ambrunster and Matthias Mühl, "Geweiht für was? – Die Weihe des Bischofs, der Priester und der Diakone. Ein Vergleich," in *Bereit wozu? Geweiht für was? Zur Diskussion um den ständigen Diakonat*, ed. Klemens Ambrunster and Matthias Mühl (Freiburg im Breisgau: Herder, 2009), 153.

[25] *Pontificale Romanum ex decreto sacrosancti oecumenici Concilii Vaticani II renovatum auctoritate Pauli PP. VI editum Ioannis Pauli PP. II cura recognitum: De ordinatione episcopi, presbyterorum et diaconorum*, 2nd ed. (1990; repr., Vatican City: Libreria Editrice Vaticana, 2011), 121, no. 207 (ordination of more than one deacon); 137, no. 235 (ordination of one deacon).

[26] Ambrunster and Mühl, "Geweiht für was?," 153.

[27] *Pontificale Romanum* (1990), 25, no. 47.

[28] *Pontificale Romanum* (1990), 75, no. 131.

which God's "holy people" should imitate deacons.[29] The baptized appear only as objects of ministry. The consecratory prayers do not envision the baptized as the missionary people of God. This people is "an agent of the proclamation of the Gospel" among whom "every baptized person is called to be a protagonist of mission since we are all missionary disciples," as the Synod of Synodality quoted the International Theological Commission's document on synodality.[30] Of course, the most recent ordination rites date from a period in which the magisterium did not robustly recognize lay ministry in its own right.

The three consecratory prayers should, furthermore, consistently witness to a ministerial communion in co-responsible service to the synodal communion of mission. Such a theology of ministry is absent from these prayers. A bishop seemingly ministers on his own in the consecratory prayer for bishops, although, in the promises that he makes, he resolves to support and lead "God's holy people" with his "fellow ministers the presbyters and deacons."[31] Priests, according to the consecratory prayer for them, are the "co-workers" (*cooperatores*) with bishops in ministry.[32] But the prayer says nothing of their ministerial cooperation with deacons. Deacons promise "to exercise the office of the diaconate with humble charity in aid of the priestly order and for the benefit of the Christian people."[33] Neither the promises nor the consecratory prayer present deacons in communion with their bishop and the priests ministering in their diocese.

[29] *Pontificale Romanum* (1990), 122, no. 207.

[30] Francis and XVI Ordinary General Assembly of the Synod of Bishops, *For a Synodal Church*, 6, no. 4; cf. International Theological Commission, *Synodality in the Life and Mission of the Church*, no. 53, March 2, 2018, Vatican website, https://www.vatican.va/roman_curia/congregations/cfaith/cti_documents/rc_cti_20180302_sinodalita_en.html.

[31] *Pontificale Romanum* (1990), 13, no. 40.

[32] *Pontificale Romanum* (1990), 75, no. 131.

[33] *Pontificale Romanum* (1990), 108, no. 200.

An exploration of the teaching of the Second Vatican Council on the diaconate, advocated by the Synod on Synodality,[34] will give the diaconate a theological stature appropriate for a synodal church. Of deacons, the council taught: "Empowered, in fact, by sacramental grace, they serve the people of God in the *diaconia* of the liturgy, of the word, and of charity in communion with the bishop and his presbyterate" (LG 29).[35] In securing the sacramentality of the diaconate, conciliar teaching laid the foundation for a co-responsible ministry of deacons in a graced communion of ordained ministers, empowered by the Spirit to serve the people of God in Christ's mission to "make disciples of all nations" (Matt 28:19) for God's reign of justice, peace, and love. As a graced ministry of communion, the diaconate disturbs entrenched notions of ministry that make deacons junior ministers of supply in service to bishops and priests, who represent Christ the head of the church, while deacons represent Christ the servant. Even as they exercise Christ's *munus regendi* in a threshold ministry, deacons, by virtue of the self-gift of the one Spirit to ordained ministers in the one sacrament of order, remain in communion with the bishop, who sends them to a threshold ministry, and with priests, who in their own way make sacramentally effective Christ's office of leadership in the church.

Paul's words to the theologically unsettled Galatians apply to the theology and praxis of ministry in today's church: "If we live by the Spirit, let us also be guided by the Spirit. Let us not become conceited, competing against one another, envying one another" (Gal 5:25). The conceit of clericalism and the competition and envy born of the forgetfulness of the Spirit frustrate the self-realization of the church as a diaconal communion ministering at its threshold to the poor and marginalized. But the fruit of the Spirit, who

[34] Francis and XVI Ordinary General Assembly of the Synod of Bishops, *For a Synodal Church*, 26, no. 73.

[35] Tanner, *Decrees*, 2: 874.

unites the church "in communion and ministry" (LG 4),[36] is the antidote for the frictions in ministry, the fruit that is "love, joy, peace, patience, kindness, gentleness, and self-control" (Gal 5:22-23). The fruit of the Spirit is the fruit of the synodal church, which takes its guidance from the Spirit. Synodality reinforces communion, for, as the Synod on Synodality professed: "We can live the communion that saves by walking in a synodal way, in the intertwining of our vocations, charisms and ministries, by going forth to meet everyone in order to bring the joy of thc Gospel: communion with God, with the entire humanity and all of creation."[37] Deacons, unperturbed as the heralds of Christ's gospel,[38] live by the Spirit among the people of God, whom they inspire and, when necessary, disturb to serve the salvific communion at the church's threshold.

[36] Tanner, *Decrees*, 2: 850.

[37] Francis and XVI Ordinary General Assembly of the Synod of Bishops, *For a Synodal Church*, 53–54, no. 154.

[38] *Pontificale Romanum* (1990), 125, no. 210.

Bibliography

Primary Sources: Ecclesiastical Documents

Acta Synodalia Sacrosancti Concilii Oecumenici Vaticani II. 6 vols., 31 tomes. Vatican City: Typis Polyglottis Vaticanis, 1970–1991.

Australian Catholic Bishops Conference. "Norms for the Formation of Permanent Deacons and Guidelines for the Ministry and Life of Permanent Deacons." *The Canonist* 8, no. 1 (2017): 13–73.

Benedict XVI. "Ad Romanam Curiam ob omina natalicia." *Acta Apostolicae Sedis* 98, no. 1 (January 2006): 40–53.

Benedict XVI. "Deus Caritas Est." *Acta Apostolicae Sedis* 98, no. 3 (March 2006): 217–52.

Benedict XVI. "Omnium in Mentem." *Acta Apostolicae Sedis* 102, no. 1 (January 2010): 8–10.

Bertsch, L., Ph. Boonen, R. Hammerschmidt, J. Homeyer, F. Kronenberg, and K. Lehmann, eds. *Gemeinsame Synode der Bistümer der Bundesrepublik Deutschland: Offizielle Gesamtausgabe*. New ed. Freiburg im Breisgau: Herder, 2012.

Bradshaw, Paul. ed. *The Canons of Hippolytus*. Translated by Carol Bebawi. Piscataway, NJ: Gorgias Press, 2010.

Cabié, Robert, ed. and trans. *La lettre du Pape Innocent Ier à Décentius de Gubbio (19 mars 416): texte critique, traduction et commentaire*. Louvain: Publications universitaires de Louvain / Bureau de la *Revue d'Histoire ecclésiastique*, 1973.

Canadian Conference of Catholic Bishops. *National Directory for the Ministry, Formation and Life of Permanent Deacons in Canada*. Ottawa: Canadian Conference of Catholic Bishops, 2017.

Canadian Conference of Catholic Bishops. "Correction to page 19 of the National Directory for the Ministry, Formation and Life of Permanent Deacons in Canada." https://www.cccb.ca/announcement/correction-to-page-19-of-the-national-directory-for-the-ministry-formation-and-life-of-permanent-deacons-in-canada/.

Catechism of the Catholic Church. Ottawa: Canadian Conference of Catholic Bishops; Vatican City: Libreria Editrice Vaticana, 1994.

Catechism of the Catholic Church. 2nd ed. Washington, DC: United States Catholic Conference; Vatican City: Libreria Editrice Vaticana, 2000.

Code of Canon Law: Latin-English Edition. First printing. Washington, DC: Canon Law Society of America, 1999.

Code of Canon Law: Latin-English Edition. Fourth printing. Washington, DC: Canon Law Society of America, 2023.

Codex iuris canonici Pii X Pontificis Maximi iussu digestus, Benedicti Papae XV auctoritate promulgatus. Roma: Typis Polyglottis Vaticanis, 1917.

Comité des ministères de l'Assemblée des évêques catholiques du Québec. *Le diaconat permanent au Québec: Avancées, hésitations, prospectives*. [Montreal]: Fides, 2006.

Conference of the Bishops of France. "Diaconat: Points d'attention votés en Assemblée." *Documentation Catholique* 93, no. 2149 (December 1, 1996): 1012–13.

Congregation for Bishops. *Directory for the Pastoral Ministry of Bishops: "Apostolorum Successores."* Vatican City: Libreria Editrice Vaticana, 2004.

Congregation for Catholic Education. Congregation for the Clergy. *Basic Norms for the Formation of Permanent Deacons. Directory for the Ministry and Life of Permanent Deacons*. Vatican City: Libreria Editrice Vaticana, 1998.

Congregation for Catholic Education. "Ratio fundamentalis institutionis diaconorum permanentium." *Acta Apostolicae Sedis* 90 (1998): 843–79.

Congregation for the Clergy. "Directorium pro ministerio et vita diaconorum permanentium." *Acta Apostolicae Sedis* 90 (1998): 879–927.

Congregation for the Doctrine of the Faith. "Nota circa il ministro del sacramento dell'unzione degli infermi." *Notitiae* 41, nos. 9–10 (September / October 2005): 479–83.

Dix, Gregory, ed. *The Treatise on the Apostolic Tradition of St. Hippolytus of Rome, Bishop and Martyr*. Rev. ed. London: S.P.C.K., 1968.

Francis. *The Joy of the Gospel: Evangelii Gaudium*. Washington, DC: United States Conference of Catholic Bishops; Vatican City: Libreria Editrice Vaticana, 2013.

Francis. "In visitatione pastorali in Archidioecesi Mediolanensi. Occursus cum sacerdotibus et viris mulieribusque consecratis in templo Cathedrali." *Acta Apostolicae Sedis* 109, no. 4 (April 2017): 371–82.

Francis. "Gaudete et Exsultate." *Acta Apostolicae Sedis* 110, no. 8 (August 2018): 1111–61.

Francis. "Spiritus Domini." *Acta Apostolicae Sedis* 113, no. 2 (February 2021): 169–170.

Francis. "Antiquum Ministerium." *Acta Apostolicae Sedis* 113, no. 6 (June 2021): 527–33.

Francis. "Ad Episcopos orbis terrarum in praesentatione Litterarum Apostolicarum Motu Proprio datarum 'Traditionis custodes' de usu Liturgiae Romanae instaurationem anni MCMLXX antecedentis." *Acta Apostolicae Sedis* 113, no. 8 (August 2021): 802–8.

Francis. "Quinquagesimo Interveniente Anniversario." *Acta Apostolicae Sedis* 114, no. 9 (September 2022): 1145–48.

Francis and XVI Ordinary General Assembly of the Synod of Bishops. *For a Synodal Church: Communion, Participation, Mission—Final Document*. November 24, 2024. Vatican website. https://www.synod.va/content/dam/synod/news/2024-10-26_final-document/ENG---Documento-finale.pdf.

Francis and XVI Ordinary General Assembly of the Synod of Bishops. *Für eine synodale Kirche: Gemeinschaft, Teilhabe, Sendung—Schlussdokument*. November 24, 2024. Vatican website. https://www.synod.va/content/dam/synod/news/2024-10-26_final-document/DEU---Documento-finale.pdf.

Francis and XVI Ordinary General Assembly of the Synod of Bishops. *Per una Chiesa sinodale: comunione, partecipazione, missione—Documento finale*. November 24, 2024. Vatican website, https://www.synod.va/content/dam/synod/news/2024-10-26_final-document/ITA---Documento-finale.pdf.

Francis and XVI Ordinary General Assembly of the Synod of Bishops. *Por una Iglesia sinodal: comunión, participación y misión: Documento final*. November 24, 2024. Vatican website, https://www.synod.va/content/dam/synod/news/2024-10-26_final-document/ESP---Documento-finale.pdf.

Francis and XVI Ordinary General Assembly of the Synod of Bishops. *Pour une Église synodale: communion, participation, mission: Document final*. November 24, 2024. Vatican website. https://www.synod.va/content/dam/synod/news/2024-10-26_final-document/FRA---Documento-finale.pdf.

Francis and XVI Ordinary General Assembly of the Synod of Bishops. *Voor een synodale kerk: gemeenschap, participatie, zending—Slotdocument*. November 24, 2024. Vatican website. https://www.synod.va/content/dam/synod/news/2024-10-26_final-document/DOCUMENTO-FINALE_FIAMMINGO.pdf.

Funk, Franz Xaver, ed. *Didascalia et constitutiones apostolorum*. Vol. 2, *Testimonia et scripturae propinquae*. Paderborn: Ferdinand Schoeningh, 1905.

German Conference of Bishops. "Grundsätze der Deutschen Bischofskonferenz vom 2. März 1977 zur Ordnung der Pastoralen Dienste." *Archiv für katholisches Kirchenrecht* 147, no. 2 (November 1978): 486–98.

German Conference of Bishops. "Rahmenordung der Deutschen Bischofskonferenz vom 22. Januar 1979 für Ständige Diakone." *Archiv für katholisches Kirchenrecht* 148, no. 1 (September 1979): 160–71.

German Conference of Bishops. *Rahmenordnung für Ständige Diakone in den Bistümern der Budesrepublik Deutschland / Richtlinien über persönliche Anforderungen an Diakone und Laien im pastoralen Dienst im Hinblick auf Ehe und Familie, 1. Februar 2000*. Bonn: Sekretariat der Deutschen Bischofskonferenz, 2000.

German Conference of Bishops. *Rahmenordnung für Stänidge Diakone in den Bistümern der Budesrepublik Deutschland, 19. Mai 2015*. Bonn: Sekretariat der Deutschen Bischofskonferenz, 2016.

Hippolytus of Rome. *La tradition apostolique d'après les anciennes versions*. 2nd ed., rev. Translated and edited by Bernard Botte. Sources Chrétiennes, vol. 11/2. Paris: Les Éditions du Cerf, 1984.

International Commission on English in the Liturgy. *The Rites of the Catholic Church: Study Edition*. 2 vols. Collegeville, MN: Liturgical Press, 1990.

International Theological Commission. *From the Diakonia of Christ to the Diakonia of the Apostles*. 2002. Vatican website. https://www.vatican.va/roman_curia/congregations/cfaith/cti_documents/rc_con_cfaith_pro_05072004_diaconate_en.html.

International Theological Commission. *Synodality in the Life and Mission of the Church*. March 2, 2018. Vatican website. https://www.vatican.va/roman_curia/congregations/cfaith/cti_documents/rc_cti_20180302_sinodalita_en.html.

International Theological Commission. *Jesus Christ, Son of God, Saviour: 1700th Anniversary of the Ecumenical Council of Nicaea, 325-2025*, April 3, 2025. Vatican website. https://www.vatican.va/roman_curia/congregations/cfaith/cti_documents/rc_cti_doc_20250403_1700-nicea_en.html.

John Paul II. "Pastores Dabo Vobis." *Acta Apostolicae Sedis* 84 (1992): 657–804.

John Paul II. "Ad eos qui plenario coetui Congregationis pro Clericis interfuerunt." *Acta Apostolicae Sedis* 88 (1996): 705–9.

Metzger, Marcel, ed. and trans. *Les Constitutions Apostoliques*, vol. 2. Sources Chrétiennes, vol. 329. Paris: Les Éditions du Cerf, 1986.

Mohlberg, Leo Cunibert, ed. *Sacramentarium Veronense.* 2nd ed. Rome: Herder, 1966.

Paul VI. "Sacrum Diaconatus Ordinem." *Acta Apostolicae Sedis* 59 (1967): 697–704.

Paul VI. "Ministeria Quaedam." *Acta Apostolicae Sedis* 64 (1972): 529–34.

Paul VI. "Ad Pascendum." *Acta Apostolicae Sedis* 64 (1972): 534–40.

Paul VI. "Sacrum Unctionem Infirmorum." *Acta Apostolicae Sedis* 65 (1973): 5–9.

Paul VI. "Evangelii Nuntiandi." *Acta Apostolicae Sedis* 68 (1976): 5–76.

Petrocchi, Giuseppe. "Sintesi della Commissione di Studio sul Diaconato Femminile." December 4, 2025. Vatican website. https://press.vatican.va/content/salastampa/it/bollettino/pubblico/2025/12/04/0950/01725.html.

Petrolino, Enzo, ed. *Enchiridion sul diaconato: Le fonte e i documenti ufficiali della chiesa*. Vatican City: Libreria Editrice Vaticana, 2009.

Pius XII. "Mystici Corporis Christi." *Acta Apostolicae Sedis* 35 (1943): 193–248.

Pius XII. "Mediator Dei." *Acta Apostolicae Sedis* 39 (1947): 521–95.

Pius XII. "Sacramentum Ordinis." *Acta Apostolicae Sedis* 40 (1948): 5–7.

Pontificale Romanum ex decreto sacrosancti oecumenici Concilii Vaticani II instauratum auctoritate Pauli PP. VI promulgatum: De ordinatione diaconi, presbyteri et episcopi. Vatican City: Libreria Editrice Vaticana, 1968.

Pontificale Romanum ex decreto sacrosancti oecumenici Concilii Vaticani II renovatum auctoritate Pauli PP. VI editum Ioannis Pauli PP. II cura recognitum: De ordinatione episcopi, presbyterorum et diaconorum. 2nd ed. 1990. Reprint, Vatican City: Libreria Editrice Vaticana, 2011.

Rahmani, Ignatius Ephraem II, ed. *Testamentum Domini Nostri Jesu Christi*. Mainz: Franz Kirchheim, 1899.

Sodi, Manlio, and Alessandro Toniolo, eds. *Pontificale Romanum: Editio Typica, 1961–1962*. Vatican City: Libreria Editrice Vaticana, 2008.

Synod of Bishops. "Coetus specialis pro regione amazonica documentum finale." *Acta Apostolicae Sedis* 111, no. 11 (November 2019): 1740–88.

XVI Ordinary General Assembly of the Synod of Bishops. *A Synodal Church in Mission: Synthesis Report*. October 28, 2023. Vatican website. https://www.synod.va/content/dam/synod/assembly/synthesis/english/2023.10.28-ENG-Synthesis-Report.pdf.

Tanner, Norman, P., ed. *Decrees of the Ecumenical Councils*. 2 vols. London: Sheed & Ward; Washington, DC: Georgetown University Press, 1990.

United States Conference of Catholic Bishops. *National Directory for the Formation, Ministry, and Life of Permanent Deacons in the United States*. Washington, DC: United States Conference of Catholic Bishops, 2005.

United States Conference of Catholic Bishops. *The National Directory for the Formation, Ministry, and Life of Permanent Deacons in the United States of America*. 2nd ed. Washington, DC: United States Conference of Catholic Bishops, 2021.

Other Primary Sources

Cicero, Marcus Tullius. *De Officiis*. Translated by Walter Miller. London: William Heinemann; New York: G. P. Putnam's Sons, 1928.

Corpus Christianorum, Series Latina. Turnhout: Brepols, 1953—.

Delp, Alfred. "Veni Sancte Spiritus." In Alfred Delp, *Gesammelte Schriften*, vol. 4, edited by Roman Bleistein, 263–305. Frankfurt am Main: Verlag Josef Knecht, 1984.

Funk, Franz Xaver, ed. *Patres Apostolici*. Vol. 1. Tübingen: Heinrich Laupp, 1901.

Heffernan, Thomas J. *The Passion of Perpetua and Felicity*. Oxford: Oxford University Press, 2012.

The New Oxford Annotated Bible: New Revised Standard Edition with The Apocrypha. 5th ed., rev. Edited by Michael D. Coogan, Marc Z. Brettler, Carol A. Newsom, and Pheme Perkins. Oxford: Oxford University Press, 2018.

Novum Testamentum Graece. 28th ed. Edited by Eberhard and Erwin Nestle, Barbara and Kurt Aland, Johannes Karavidopoulos, Carlo M. Martini, and Bruce M. Metzger. Stuttgart: Deutsche Bibelgesellschaft, 2012.

Thomas Aquinas. *Summa Theologiae*. Vol. 24, *The Gifts of the Spirit (Ia2ae. 68–70)*. Translated and edited by Edward D. O'Connor. 1974. Reprint, Cambridge: Cambridge University Press, 2006.

Secondary Sources

Ambrunster, Klemens, and Matthias Mühl. "Geweiht für was? – Die Weihe des Bischofs, der Priester und der Diakone. Ein Vergleich." In *Bereit wozu? Geweiht für was? Zur Diskussion um den ständigen Diakonat*, edited by Klemens Ambrunster and Matthias Mühl, 122–55. Freiburg im Breisgau: Herder, 2009.

Avis, Paul. "Introduction to Ecclesiology." In *The Oxford Handbook of Ecclesiology*, edited by Paul Avis, 1–30. Oxford: Oxford University Press, 2018.

Barnett, James Monroe. *The Diaconate: A Full and Equal Order*. Rev. ed. Valley Forge, PA: Trinity Press International, 1995.

Barratt, Anthony. "The Sacrament of Order and the Second Vatican Council: The Presbyter-Bishop Relationship Revisited." *International Journal for the Study of the Christian Church* 2, no. 2 (2002): 7–27.

Bernards, Matthäus. "Zur Lehre von der Kirche als Sakrament: Beobachtungen aus der Theologie des 19. und 20. Jahrhunderts." *Münchener Theologische Zeitschrift* 20 (1969): 29–54.

Beyer, Jean. "Nature et Position du Sacerdoce." *Nouvelle revue théologique* 76, no. 4 (1954): 356–73, 469–80.

Beyer, Jean. "De diaconatu animadversionses." *Periodoca de re morali, canonica, liturgica* 69, nos. 3–4 (1980): 441–60.

Beyer, Jean. "Il diaconato permanente nell'attuale vita ecclesiale." Translated by G. Sarzi Sartori. *Quaderni di diritto ecclesiale* 10 (1997): 134–42.

Boularand, Ephrem. "La consécration épiscoplae est-elle sacramentelle?" *Bulletin de littérature ecclésiastique* 54, no. 1 (January–March 1953): 3–36.

Borras, Alphonse, and Bernard Pottier. *La grâce du diaconat: Questions actuelles autour du diaconat latin*. Brussels: Éditions Lessius, 1998.

Borras, Alphonse. *Le diaconat au risque de sa nouveauté*. Brussels: Éditions Lessius, 2007.

Borras, Alphonse. "Les diacres d'après les nouveaux canons 1008 et 1009 §3." *Revue théologique de Louvain* 43, no. 1 (2012): 49–78.

Borras, Alphonse. "*Votum tantum consultivum:* les limites ecclésiologiques d'une formule canonique." *Didaskalia* 45, no. 1 (2015): 145–62.

Borras, Alphonse. "Le diaconat, cinquante ans après Vatican II." *Pistis & Praxis: Teologia e Pastoral* 7, no. 2 (2015): 309–20.

Borras, Alphonse. "Le diaconat permanent: questions et perspectives." *Nouvelle revue théologique* 138, no. 4 (2016): 568–84.

Borras, Alphonse. "The Diaconate after *Omnium in mentem* within the Context of the Shortage of Priests." In *Unlocking the Future: Women and the Diaconate*, edited by Hildegard Warnink, 91–106. Leuven: Peeters, 2020.

Botte, Bernard. "Le Rituel d'ordination des Statuta Ecclesiae antiqua." *Recherches de théologie ancienne et médiévale* 11 (July 1939): 223–41.

Botte, Bernard. "'Spiritus principalis' (formule de l'ordination épiscopale)." *Notitiae* 100 (December 1974): 410–11.

Bradshaw, Paul F. *Ordination Rites of the Ancient Churches of East and West*. New York: Pueblo Publishing Company, 1990.

Bradshaw, Paul F. *The Search for the Origins of Christian Worship: Sources and Methods for the Study of Early Liturgy*. 2nd ed. Oxford: Oxford University Press, 2002.

Bradshaw, Paul F. *Rites of Ordination: Their History and Theology*. Collegeville, MN: Liturgical Press, 2013.

Bradshaw, Paul F., Maxwell E. Johnson, and L. Edward Phillips. *The Apostolic Tradition: A Commentary*. Edited by Harold W. Attridge. Minneapolis: Fortress Press, 2002.

Brugnotto, Giuliano. "Alcune conseguenze pratiche per il diaconato permanente dal *motu proprio Omnium in mentem*." *Quaderni di diritto ecclesiale* 24, no. 2 (April 2011): 169–77.

Castellucci, Erio. "Il 'ministero della soglia.' Una lettura teologica del diaconato a partire dal Nuovo Testamento." *Seminarium* 48 (2008): 615–47.

Chavasse, Antoine. "L'onction des infirmes dans l'Église latine du IIIe siècle à la réforme carolingienne: les textes." *Revue des Sciences Religieuses* 20, nos. 1–2 (1940): 64–122; 20, nos. 3–4 (1940): 290–364.

Cnudde, Matthieu. "L'ordination des diacres." *La Maison-Dieu* 98 (1969): 73–94.

Codina, Víctor. *Creo en el Espíritu Santo: Pneumatología narrativa*. Santander: Editorial Sal Terrae, 1994.

Codina, Víctor. *El Espíritu sopla desde abajo*. Barcelona: Cristianisme i Justícia, 2023.

Collins, John N. *Diakonia: Re-interpreting the Ancient Sources*. New York: Oxford University Press, 1990.

Collins, John N. *Are All Christians Ministers?* Collegeville, MN: Liturgical Press, 1992.

Collins, John N. *Deacons and the Church: Making Connections between Old and New*. Leominster, Herefordshire: Gracewing; Harrisburg, PA: Morehouse Publishing, 2002.

Como, Giuseppe. "Der Diakon im Leben der Kirche: Die Erfahrung der Diözese Mailand." In *Der Diakonat: Geschichte und Theologie*, edited by Manfred Hauke and Helmut Hoping, 145–56. Regensburg: Verlag Friedrich Putest, 2019.

Congar, Yves. "Le diaconat dans la théologie des ministères." In *Le diacre dans l'Église et le monde d'aujourd'hui*, edited by Paul Winninger and Yves Congar, 121–41. Paris: Les Éditions du Cerf, 1966.

Congar, Yves. "Ministères et structuration de l'Église." In Congar, *Ministères et communion ecclésiale*, 31–49. Paris: Les Éditions du Cerf, 1971.

Congar, Yves. *La Parole et le Souffle*. Paris: Desclée, 1984.

Congar, Yves. "Le troisième article du Symbole: L'impact de la pneumatologie dans la vie de l'Église." In *Dieu, Église, Société*, edited by Joseph Doré, 287–303. Paris: Éditions du Centurion, 1985.

Coriden, James A. *The Parish in Catholic Tradition: History, Theology and Canon Law*. New York: Paulist Press, 1997.

Coronelli, Renato. "Il diaconato alla luce delle modifiche apportate al Codice dal *motu proprio Omnium in mentem*." *Quaderni di diritto ecclesiale* 24, no. 2 (April 2011): 142–68.

Costache, Doru. "Athanasius on Deacons and the Diaconate." In *Deacons and Diakonia in Late Antiquity*, edited by Bart J. Koet, Edwina Murphy, and Esko Ryökäs, 64–77. Tübingen: Mohr Siebeck, 2024.

Coyle, J. Kevin. "The Laying on of Hands as Conferral of the Spirit: Some Problems and a Possible Solution." *Studia Patristica* 18, no. 2 (1989): 339–53.

Daufratshofer, Matthias. "Did Pius XII Change a Dogma in 1947? The Apostolic Constitution *Sacramentum ordinis* and its Underestimated Potential." *Journal of Modern and Contemporary Christianity* 3, no. 1 (April 2024): 247–90.

De Clerck, Paul. "Note sur l'expression *non ad sacerdotium, sed ad ministerium (episcopi)*: De l'évolution du sens des mots et des choses." *La Maison-Dieu* 249 (2007): 53–70.

Deniau, Francis. "Le diaconat à la lumière des trois 'fonctions' du Christ et de l'Église, selon Vatican II." In *Diaconat, XXIe siècle: Actes du Colloque de Louvain-la-Neuve (13–15 septembre 1994)*, edited by André Haquin and Philippe Weber, 103–15. Brussels: Éditions Lumen Vitae, 1997.

Deniau, Francis. "Diacres et prêtres en France: des années 1970 aux transformations actuelles." In *Le diaconat permanent: Relecture et perspectives*, edited by Bruno Dumons and Daniel Moulinet, 291–303. Paris: Les Éditions du Cerf, 2007.

Desjonquères, Alain. *Être diacre permanent, pourquoi?* Paris: Éditions Salvator, 2019.

Didier, Jean-Charles. "Sur le ministre de l'Onction des Malades." *L'ami du clergé* 74, no. 31 (July 30, 1964): 488–92.

Dilschneider, Otto A. "Die Geistvergessenheit der Theologie: Epilog zur Diskussion über den historischen Jesus und kerygmatischen Christus." *Theologische Literaturzeitung* 86, no. 4 (April 1961): cols. 255–65.

Ditewig, William T. *The Emerging Diaconate: Servant Leaders in a Servant Church*. New York: Paulist Press, 2007.

Ditewig, William T. *The Deacon's Ministry of Charity and Justice*. Collegeville, MN: Liturgical Press, 2015.

Ditewig, William T. *Courageous Humility: Reflections on the Church, Diakonia, and Deacons*. New York: Paulist Press, 2022.

Ebertz, Michael N. "Diakon—ein Marginalberuf? Thesen, Anfragen, Zuspitzungen." In *Ständige Diakone—Stellvertreter der Armen? Projekt Pro Diakonia: Prozess—Positionen—Perspectiven*, edited by Klaus Kießling, 129–35. Berlin: LIT Verlag, 2006.

Eguiarte, Enrique A. "Liturgical Roles of the Deacon in Augustine: A Punic-Speaking Deacon is Needed (*Ep.* 84)." In *Deacons and Diakonia in Late Antiquity*, edited by Bart J. Koet, Edwina Murphy, and Esko Ryökäs, 287–98. Tübingen: Mohr Siebeck, 2024.

Ellacuría, Ignacio. *Freedom Made Flesh: The Mission of Christ and His Church*. Translated by John Drury. Maryknoll, NY: Orbis Books, 1976.

Ellacuría, Ignacio. "The Church of the Poor: Historical Sacrament of Liberation." Translated by Margaret D. Wilde. In Ignacio Ellacuría, *Essays on History, Liberation, and Salvation*, edited by Michael E. Lee, 228–53. Maryknoll, NY: Orbis Books, 2013.

Ellacuría, Ignacio. "The Crucified People: An Essay in Historical Soteriology." Translated by Phillip Berryman and Robert R. Barr. In Ignacio Ellacuría, *Essays on History, Liberation, and Salvation*, edited by Michael E. Lee, 195–224, Maryknoll, NY: Orbis Books, 2013.

Francis, Pope, with Carlo Musso. *Spera: L'autobiografia*. Milan: Mondadori, 2025.

Fuchs, Ottmar. "Wer ist der Diakon? Seine Berufung, seine lokalen, überregionalen und globalen Aufgaben." *Diaconia Christi* 35, nos. 3 and 4 (2000): 115–30.

Fuchs, Ottmar. "Das diakonale Amt als Sacrament der Kirche für die Welt." In *Ständige Diakone—Stellvertreter der Armen? Projekt Pro Diakonia: Prozess—Positionen—Perspectiven*, edited by Klaus Kießling, 67–91. Berlin: LIT Verlag, 2006.

Gaillardetz, Richard R. "Towards a Contemporary Theology of the Diaconate." *Worship* 79, no. 5 (September 2005): 419–38.

Ghirlanda, Gianfranco. *Il sacramento dell'ordine e la vita dei cherici (Cann. 1008-1054; 232 297)*. 2nd ed. Rome: Edizioni Studium, 2024.

Glover, Matthew A. "The Permanent Diaconate: A Holy Order in Search of (Canonical) Reality." *Proceedings of the Canon Law Society of America Convention* 81 (2019): 192–216.

Gonneaud, Didier. "Pour le quarantième anniversaire du rétablissement de l'ordo diaconal: réflexions autour d'une maxime doctrinale." *Nouvelle revue théologique* 126, no. 4 (2004): 555–66.

Gonneaud, Didier. "La sacramentalité du ministère diaconal." *Revue théologique de Louvain* 36 (2005): 3–20.

Gonneaud, Didier. "Diaconat et ministères." In *Le diaconat permanent: Relecture et perspectives*, edited by Bruno Dumons and Daniel Moulinet, 223–35. Paris: Les Éditions du Cerf, 2007.

Grau, Alain. "'Diaconie du Christ': De l'analogie pratique à la catégorie théologique." *Communio: revue catholique internationale* 26, no. 2 (March/April 2001): 29–51.

Greshake, Gisbert. *Priester sein in dieser Zeit: Theologie, Pastorale Praxis, Spiritualität*. [Würzburg:] Echter Verlag, 2005.

Grondelski, John M. "Lay Ministries? A Quarter Century of *Ministeria Quaedam*." *Irish Theological Quarterly* 63, no. 3 (September 1998): 272–82.

Hahn, Judith. "*Potestas incerta*: The Ambiguity of the Ecclesiastical Law on Power with Respect to Lay Leadership." *The Canonist* 13, no. 2 (2022): 177–95.

Hauke, Manfred. "Der Diakonat und das Handeln *in persona Christi capitis*: Randbemerkungen zum Motuproprio *Omnium in mentem*." *Forum Katholische Theologie* 26, no. 3 (2010): 191–205.

Hauke, Manfred. "Die spezifische Christusrepräsentation des Presbyters und des Diakons." In *Der Diakonat: Geschichte und Theologie*, edited by Manfred Hauke and Helmut Hoping, 341–60. Regensburg: Verlag Friedrich Pustet, 2019.

Hauke, Manfred. "Cristologia e diaconato." *Il diaconato in Italia* 52, nos. 224–25 (September/Decmeber 2020): 40–47.

Haunerland, Winfried. "Das Amt des Diakons nach den Zeugnissen der römischen Liturgie." In *Der Diakonat: Geschichte und Theologie*, edited by Manfred Hauke and Helmut Hoping, 85–100. Regensburg: Verlag Friedrich Pustet, 2019.

Hefele, Carl Joseph von. *Conciliengeschichte. Nach den Quellen bearbeitet*. Vol. 1, 2nd ed. Freiburg im Breisgau: Herder, 1873.

Heffernan, Thomas J. *The Passion of Perpetua and Felicity*. Oxford: Oxford University Press, 2012.

Hentschel, Anni. *Diakonia im Neuen Testament: Studien zur Semantik unter besonderer Berücksichtigung der Rolle von Frauen*. Tübingen: Mohr Siebeck, 2007.

Hentschel, Anni. *Die Fußwaschungserzählung im Johannesevangelium: Ein Beitrag zur johanneischen Ekklesiologie*. Tübingen: Mohr Siebeck, 2022.

Hilberath, Bernd Jochen. "Thesen zur Theologie des Diakonats." In *Ständige Diakone—Stellvertreter der Armen? Projekt Pro Diakonia: Prozess—Positionen—Perspectiven*, edited by Klaus Kießling, 92–104. Berlin: LIT Verlag, 2006.

Holder, Arthur G. "Bede and the New Testament." In *The Cambridge Companion to Bede*, edited by Scott Degregorio, 142–55. Cambridge: Cambridge University Press, 2010.

Hoping, Helmut. "Der dreifache Tischdienst des Diakons und die Einheit des Ordosakraments: Theologische Beobachtungen zur Liturgie der Diakonenweihe." In *Manifestatio Ecclesiae: Studien zu Pontifikale und bischöflicher Liturgie*, edited by Winfried Haunerland, Otto Mittermeier, Monika Selle, and Wolfgang Steck, 189–204. Regensburg: Verlag Friedrich Pustet, 2004.

Hoping, Helmut. "Die liturgische Verortung des Diakonats und seine Stellung innerhalb des sakramentalen Ordo: Ein Beitrag aus römisch-katholischer Sicht." *Internationale kirchliche Zeitschrift* 95, no. 4 (2005): 248–65.

Hoping, Helmut. "Das Priestertum des geistlichen Dienstamtes—Diakonat und Presbyterat." In *Der Diakonat: Geschichte und Theologie*, edited by Manfred Hauke and Helmut Hoping, 285–300. Regensburg: Verlag Friedrich Pustet, 2019.

Huels, John M. "Interpreting an Instruction Approved *in forma specifica*." *Studia Canonica* 32, no. 1 (1998): 5–46.

Hünermann, Peter. "Gutachten zur Bestellung des Diakons (der Diakonin) zum ordentlichen Spender der Krankensalbung." *Diaconia Christi* 9, no. 3 (August 1974): 25–28.

Hünermann, Peter. "Theologischer Kommentar zur dogmatischen Konstitution über die Kirche *Lumen gentium*." In *Herders Theologischer Kommentar zum Zweiten Vatikanischen Konzil*, vol. 2, edited by Peter Hünermann and Bernd Jochen Hilberath, 263–582. Freiburg im Breisgau: Herder, 2004.

Hürth, Franz. "Commentarius ad Const. Apostolicam." *Periodica de re morali, canonica, liturgica* 37, no. 1 (1948): 9–41.

Johnson, Elizabeth A. *Ask the Beasts: Darwin and the God of Love*. London: Bloomsbury Continuum, 2014.

Joncas, Jan Michael. "The Public Language of Ministry Revisited: *De Ordinatione Episcopi, Presbyterorum et Diaconorum* 1990." *Worship* 68, no. 5 (September 1994): 386–403.

Jounel, Pierre. "La nouvelle édition typique du rituel des ordinations." *La Maison-Dieu* 186 (1991): 7–22.

Kasper, Walter. "Kirche als Sakarament des Geistes." In *Kirche—Ort des Geistes*, edited by Walter Kasper and Gerhard Sauter, 13–55. Freiburg im Breisgau: Herder, 1976.

Kasper, Walter. "Der Diakon in ekklesiologischer Sicht angesichts der gegenwärtigen Herausforderungen in Kirche und Gesellschaft." In Kasper, *Theologie und Kirche*, vol. 2, 145–62. Mainz: Matthias-Grünewald-Verlag, 1999.

Kehl, Medard. "Kirche – Sakrament des Geistes." In *Gegenwart des Geistes: Aspekte der Pneumatologie*, edited by Walter Kasper, 155–80. Freiburg im Breisgau: Herder, 1979.

Kelly, Gerard, and Richard Lennan. "The Diaconate: Possibilities and Challenges." *Australian Catholic Record* 74, no. 2 (April 1997): 131–41.

Kirschner, Martin. "Amtlich in der Person Christi handeln – als Diakon?" *Diaconia Christi* 45, nos. 1 and 2 (2010): 231–43.

Kleinmeyer, Bruno. "Der Diakon im Lichte der römischen Weiheliturgie." In *Diaconia in Christo: Über die Erneuerung des Diakonates*, edited by Karl Rahner and Herbert Vorgrimler, 76–91. Freiburg im Breisgau: Herder, 1962.

Koet, Bart J. *The Go-Between: Augustine on Deacons*. Leiden: Brill, 2019.

Komonchak, Joseph A. "The Permanent Diaconate and the Variety of Ministries in the Church." *Diaconal Quarterly* 3, no. 3 (1977): 15–23; 3, no. 4 (1977): 29–40; 4, no. 1 (1978): 13–25.

Kohlschein, Franz. "'Sende auf sie herab den Heiligen Gest . . .': Zur Ordination der Diakone in der Kirche." *Liturgisches Jahrbuch* 46, no. 2 (1990): 80–89.

Lanzetta, Serafino. "Die Erneuerung des ständigen Diakonats auf dem Zweiten Vatikanum: Anliegen, Ergebnisse und Probleme." In *Der Diakonat: Geschichte und Theologie*, edited by Manfred Hauke and Helmut Hoping, 125–44. Regensburg: Verlag Friedrich Pustet, 2019.

Legrand, Hervé. "Le diaconat dans sa relation à la théologie de l'Église et des ministères: Réception et devenir du diaconat depuis Vatican II." In *Diaconat, XXIe siècle: Actes du Colloque de Louvain-la-Neuve (13–15 septembre 1994)*, edited by André Haquin and Philippe Weber, 13–41. Brussels: Éditions Lumen Vitae, 1997.

Lehmann, Karl. "Die Entwicklung des Ständigen Diakonats. Beobachtungen und Überlegungen aus der Sicht des bischöflichen Amtes." In *Ortsbestimmungen: Der Diakonat als kirchlicher*

Dienst, edited by Richard Hartmann, Franz Reger, and Stefan Sander, 11–31. Frankfurt am Main: Verlag Josef Knecht, 2009.

Longhitano, Adolfo. "Come leggere il *Motu proprio?*" *Il diaconato in Italia* 42, no. 161 (March/April 2010): 27–30.

Luciani, Rafael. *Synodality: A New Way of Proceeding in the Church*. Translated by Joseph Owens. New York: Paulist Press, 2022.

Marliangeas, Bernard Dominique. *Clés pour une théologie du ministère: In persona Christi, In persona Ecclesiae*. Paris: Éditions Beauchesne, 1978.

Marmion, Declan. "Karl Rahner, Vatican II, and the Shape of the Church." *Theological Studies* 78, no. 1 (March 2017): 25–48.

McKnight, W. Shawn. *Understanding the Diaconate: Historical, Theological, and Sociological Foundations*. Washington, DC: The Catholic University of America Press, 2018.

Miranda Vicente, Francisco. "Signification théologique de la Constitution *Sacramentum Ordinis.*" *La Maison-Dieu* 47–48 (1956): 197–208.

Müller, Andreas. "The Diaconate according to John Chrysostom." In *Deacons and Diakonia in Late Antiquity*, edited by Bart J. Koet, Edwina Murphy, and Esko Ryökäs, 112–21. Tübingen: Mohr Siebeck, 2024.

Müller, Gerhard Ludwig. "Theologische Überlegungen zur Weiterentwicklung des Diakonats." *Münchener Theologische Zeitschrift* 40, no. 2 (June 1989): 129–43.

Moons, Jos. "The Holy Spirit as the Protagonist of the Synod: Pope Francis's Creative Reception of the Second Vatican Council." *Theological Studies* 84, no. 1 (March 2023): 61–78.

Noceti, Serena. "*In persona Christi:* Limits and Potential of an *Espressione abusata*." *Studia Canonica* 56, no. 2 (2022): 441–70.

Noceti, Serena. *Reforming the Church: A Synodal Way of Proceeding*. Translated by Joseph Owens. New York: Paulist Press, 2023.

Nußbaum, Otto. "Theologie und Ritus der Diakonenweihe." In *Der Diakon: Wiederentdeckung und Erneuerung seines Dienstes*, edited by Josef G. Plöger and Herman Johann Weber, 122–46. Freiburg im Breisgau: Herder, 1980.

O'Donnell, Tim. *The Deacon: Icon of Christ the Servant, Minister of the Threshold*. New York: Paulist Press, 2020.

O'Laughlin, Thomas. "Equality as a Theological Principle within Roman Catholic Ecclesiology." *Ecclesiology* 18, no. 1 (2022): 35–56.

O'Meara, Thomas F. *Theology of Ministry*. Rev. ed. New York: Paulist Press, 1999.

Pabel, Hilmar M. "Karl Rahner's Theology of the Diaconate: A Reappraisal." *Journal for the History of Modern Theology* 31, no. 1 (May 2024): 43–72.

Petrolino, Enzo. *Il Concilio Vaticano II e il Diaconato: La Chiesa mistero di commune e di servizio*. Vatican City: Libreria Editrice Vaticana, 2013.

Rahner, Karl. "Der Einzelne in der Kirche." *Stimmen der Zeit* 139, no. 4 (January 1947): 260–76.

Rahner, Karl. "Friedliche Erwägungen über das Pfarrprinzip." *Zeitschrift für katholische Theologie* 70, no. 2 (1948): 169–98.

Rahner, Karl. "Dogmatische Vorbemerkungen für eine richtige Fragestellung über die Wiedererneuerung des Diakonats." In *Theologie in Geschichte und Gegenwart: Michael Schmaus zum sechzigsten Geburtstag*, edited by Johann Auer and Hermann Volk, 135–44. Munich: Karl Zink Verlag, 1957.

Rahner, Karl. "Die Freiheit in der Kirche." In Rahner, *Schriften zur Theologie*, vol. 2, 95–114. Einsiedeln: Benziger Verlag, 1958.

Rahner, Karl. *Das Dynamische in der Kirche*. Freiburg im Breisgau: Herder, 1959.

Rahner, Karl. *Kirche und Sakramente*. Freiburg im Breisgau: Herder, 1960.

Rahner, Karl. "Zur Theologie des Symbols." In Rahner, *Schriften zur Theologie*, vol. 4, 275–311. Einsiedeln: Benziger Verlag, 1960.

Rahner, Karl. "Die Theologie der Erenuerung des Diakonats." In *Diaconia in Christo: Über die Erneuerung des Diakonates*, edited by Karl Rahner and Herbert Vorgrimler, 285–324. Freiburg im Breisgau: Herder, 1962.

Rahner, Karl. "Diakonat und Diakon." In *Handbuch der Pastoraltheologie: Praktische Theologie der Kirche in ihrer Gegenwart*, vol. 1, edited by Franz Xaver Arnold, Karl Rahner, Viktor Schnurr, Leonhard M. Weber, 190–92. Freiburg im Breisgau: Herder, 1964.

Rahner, Karl. *Vom Sinn des kirchlichen Amtes*. Freiburg im Breisgau: Herder, 1966.

Rahner, Karl. "Die Lehre des Zweiten Vatikanischen Konzils über den Diakonat." In Rahner, *Schriften zur Theologie*, vol. 8, 541–52. Einsiedeln: Benziger Verlag, 1967.

Rahner, Karl. "Das Gebet des Einzelnen und die Liturgie der Kirche." In *Strukturen christlicher Existenz: Beiträge zur Erneuerung des geistlichen Lebens*, edited by H. Schlier, E. von Severus, J. Sudbrack, and A. Pereira, 189–98. Würzburg: Echter-Verlag, 1968.

Rahner, Karl. "Bemerkungen über das Charismatische in der Kirche." *Geist und Leben* 42, no. 4 (July-August 1969): 251–62.

Rahner, Karl. "Über den Diakonat." In Rahner, *Schriften zur Theologie*, vol. 9, 395–414. Einsiedeln: Benziger Verlag, 1970.

Rahner, Karl. "Zum Selbstverständnis des Amtspriesters." In Rahner, *Schriften zur Theologie*, vol. 10, 448–66. Zurich: Benziger Verlag, 1972.

Rahner, Karl. "Pastorale Dienste und Gemeindeleitung." *Stimmen der Zeit* 195, no. 11 (November 1977): 733–43.

Rahner, Karl. "Erwägungen über Inhalt und Aufbau eines Sammelwerkes über die zeitgemäße Erneuerung des Diakonates." In Rahner, *Sämtliche Werke*, vol. 16, *Kirchliche Erneuerung: Studien zur Pastoraltheologie und Struktur der Kirche*, edited by Albert Raffelt, 357–68. Freiburg im Breisgau: Herder, 2005.

Ratzinger, Joseph. "The Holy Spirit as Communio: Concerning the Relationship of Pneumatology and Spirituality in Augustine." Translated by Peter Casarella. *Communio* 25, no. 2 (Summer 1998): 324–37.

Remenyi, Matthias. "Die Autorität des Dienens. Der Diakonat als Paradigma des kirchlichen Amtes." In *Amt und Autorität: Kirche in der späten Moderne*, edited by Matthias Remenyi, 159–81. Paderborn: Ferdinand Schöningh, 2012.

Reynolds, Roger E. "The Portrait of the Ecclesiastical Officers in the Raganaldus Sacramentary and its Liturgico-Canonical Significance." *Speculum* 46, no. 3 (July 1971): 432–42.

Rouillard, Philippe. "Le ministre du sacrement des malades." *Nouvelle revue théologique* 101, no. 3 (1979): 395–402.

Sander, Stefan. *Das Amt des Diakons: Eine Handreichung*. Rev. ed. Freiburg im Breisgau: Herder, 2013.

Sander, Stefan. "Die Marginalisierten: Sorgenvolle Bestandsaufnahme des Diakonats." *Herder Korrespondenz* 74, no. 9 (September 2020): 32–36.

Sander, Stefan. "Die Marginalisierten: Sorgenvolle Bestandsaufnahme zur Entwicklung des Diakonats." In *Das Gesicht der Kirche im Alltag der Menshcen? Der Ort des Diakonischen Amtes in einer diakonischen Kirche*, edited by Klaus Kießling and

Verena Wodtke-Werner, 187–96. Mainz: Matthias Günewald Verlag, 2023.

Seewald, Michael. *Reform—Dieselbe Kirche anders denken*. Freiburg im Breisgau: Herder, 2018.

Seewald, Michael. "Wer stellt wen dar? Über drei Formen der Repräsentation und die Stellung des ordinierten Amtes in der katholischen Kirche." In *Christusrepräsentanz: Zur aktuellen Debatte um die Zulassung von Frauen zum priesterlichen Amt*, edited by Margit Eckholt and Johanna Rahner, 19–43. Freiburg im Breisgau: Herder, 2021.

Seewald, Michael. "Die Einwohnung des Heiligen Geistes. Spekulationen über die Pneumatologie von *Lumen gentium* 4." In *Gott ist Geist: Perspektiven der Pneumatologie*, edited by Michael Seewald, 195–221. Freiburg im Breisgau: Herder, 2023.

Seidl, Johann Nepomuk. *Der Diakonat in der katholischen Kirche, dessen hieratische Würde und geschichtliche Entwicklung: Eine kirchenrechts-geschichtliche Abhandlung*. Regensburg: Georg Joseph Manz, 1884.

Schmaus, Michael. "Gaben des Heiligen Geistes." In *Sacramentum Mundi: Theologisches Lexikon für die Praxis*, edited by Karl Rahner et al., vol. 2, cols. 151–55. Freiburg im Breisgau: Herder, 1968.

Sobrino, Jon. *The True Church and the Poor*. Translated by Matthew J. O'Connell. Maryknoll, NY: Orbis Books, 1984.

Stefanski, Jerzy. "Die römischen Ordinationsriten von 1968 and 1990: Eine geschichtlich-liturgische Studie." Translated by Sebastian Zgraja. In *Manifestatio Ecclesiae: Studien zu Pontifikale und bischöflicher Liturgie*, edited by Winfried Haunerland, Otto Mittermeier, Monika Selle, and Wolfgang Steck, 129–59. Regensburg: Verlag Friedrich Pustet, 2004.

Troupeau, Martin. "La question des diacres en *Lumen gentium* 41." *Nouvelle revue théologique* 143, no. 3 (2021): 393–409.

Vallee, Sherri L. "The Restoration of the Permanent Diaconate: A Blending of Roles." *Worship* 77, no. 6 (November 2003): 530–52.

Vitali, Dario. *Diaconi: che fare?* Milan: San Paolo, 2019.

Vorgrimler, Herbert. "Kommentar zum III. Kapitel, Artikel 29." In *Das Zweite Vatikanische Konzil: Konstitutionen, Dekrete und Erklärungen, Latein und Deutsch—Kommentare*, vol. 1, edited by Herbert Vorgrimler, 256–59. Freiburg im Breisgau: Herder, 1966.

Vorgrimler, Herbert. *Buße und Krankensalbung*. 2nd ed. Freiburg im Breisgau: Herder, 1978.

Vorgrimler, Herbert. *Understanding Karl Rahner: An Introduction to His Life and Thought*. Translated by John Bowden. New York: Crossroad, 1986.

Wackenheim, Charles. "Esquisse d'une théologie des ministères." *Revue des Sciences Religieuses* 47, no. 1 (1973): 3–26.

Weber, Hermman Johann. "Zur theologischen Ortsbestimmung des Diakonats im einen Weihesakrament." In *Der Diakon: Wiederentdeckung und Erneuerung seines Dienstes*, edited by Josef G. Plöger and Herman Johann Weber, 104–21. Freiburg im Breisgau: Herder, 1980.

Werckmeister, Jean. "Le motu proprio *Omnium in mentem* et le mariage des ex-catholiques." *Revue de droit canonique* 57, no. 1 (2010): 241–54.

Winninger, Paul. "Les ministères des diacres dans l'Église d'aujourd'hui." In *L'Église de Vatican II: Études autour de la Constitution conciliarie sur l'Église*, vol. 3, edited by Guilherme Baraúna and Y. M.-J. Congar, 994–1009. Paris: Les Éditions du Cerf, 1966.

Wodtke-Werner, Verena. "+Dr. Stefan Sander: Ein Go-Betweener." In *Das Gesicht der Kirche im Alltag der Menshcen? Der Ort des Diakonischen Amtes in einer diakonischen Kirche*, edited by Klaus Kießling and Verena Wodtke-Werner, 7–10. Mainz: Matthias Günewald Verlag, 2023.

Wong, Emily. "The Lord Is the Spirit (2 Cor 3,17a)." *Ephemerides Theologicae Lovaniensis* 61, no. 1 (April 1985): 48–72.

Wood, Susan K. *Sacramental Orders*. Collegeville, MN: Liturgical Press, 2000.

Wood, Susan K. "The Paschal Mystery: The Intersection of Ecclesiology and Sacramental Theology in the Care of the Sick." In *Recovering the Riches of Anointing: A Study of the Sacrament of the Sick*, edited by Genevieve Glen, 1–20. Collegeville, MN: Liturgical Press, 2002.

Zizioulas, John D. *Being as Communion: Studies in Personhood and the Church*. Crestwood, NY: St. Vladimir's Seminary Press, 1985.

Zollitisch, Robert. "Der Diakonat – ein modernes Amt." In *Bereit wozu? Geweiht für was? Zur Diskussion um den ständigen Diakonat*, edited by Klemens Ambrunster and Matthias Mühl, 372–80. Freiburg im Breisgau: Herder, 2009.

Zulehner, Paul M. *Dienende Männer – Anstifter zur Solidarität: Diakone in Westeuropa*. Ostfildern: Schwabenverlag, 2003.

Index

Apostolic Tradition, see under church orders
Aquinas, Thomas, 22, 41–42
Arles, Synod of, 167 n. 180
Augustine, St, 40–41

Barnett, James, 12–13, 57, 181–82
Barratt, Anthony, 91–92
Benedict XVI, Pope, *see also* Ratzinger, Joseph, 93–94, 96, 102, 133, 168–69
Beyer, Jean, 7, 23
Borras, Alphonse, 6, 29, 78, 79, 84–85, 100, 101–102, 110, 132, 137, 138–39, 140, 150, 180–81
Botte, Bernard, 37
Boulerand, Ephrem, 23
Bradshaw, Paul, 37 n. 78, 45

Catechism of the Catholic Church, 28–29, 66–67, 93, 96, 102–103, 106, 108
canon law, 48, 127, 145, 152, 154, 155, 156, 160
  Omnium in Mentem (cc. 1008–1009), 93–108, 114, 115–16
  proposed reforms of, 121–23, 172–73
Cerrato, Dominic, xiii
church councils
  Nicaea, xiv–xv
  Chalcedon, 112
  Florence, 22, 117, 152, 154
  Trent, 21–22, 24, 26, 65, 152, 153, 154, 168
  see also Second Vatican Council,
church orders
  Apostolic Tradition, 37, 44–45, 47, 58, 122, 166
  Constitutiones ecclesiae aegyptiacae, 47
  Statuta ecclesiae antiquae, xx, 45–46, 47, 48, 55
  Testamentum Domini, 17, 122
Cicero, 44 n. 101
Codina, Víctor, xxii, 2, 129, 173–74
Collins, John, 16
Congar, Yves, 3, 78, 110, 147, 157
Congregation for Bishops
  Directory for the Pastoral Ministry of Bishops, 72, 145, 149
Congregation for the Catholic Education

Basic Norms for the Formation of Permanent Deacons (1998) = *Ratio fundamentalis*, 29, 65, 86, 88–89, 97, 108–109, 146, 171, 178–79
Congregation for the Clergy
Directory for the Ministry and Life of Permanent Deacons (1998), 29–30, 72, 75–76, 82, 83, 84, 86, 88–89, 91, 92, 97, 100, 108–109, 146, 152–53
Congregation for the Doctrine of the Faith
Note on the Minister of the Sacrament of the Anointing of the Sick (2005), 154–55, 156–57, 158, 160, 161
Coyle, Kevin, 66
Creed, Apostles', 1
Čule, Petar, 25
cursus honorum, xx, 14
Cyprian of Carthage, 158 n. 143

deacons / diaconate
communion with bishops and priests, xvi, xvii, xviii, xx, xxi, xxii, 5, 6, 7, 8, 9–11, 14, 15, 17, 19, 23, 25, 28, 30, 35, 38, 39, 55, 60, 63, 67, 69–125, 128–29, 166, 174, 183, 185, 186
as *medius ordo* or intermediate order, 131, 140, 141–43, 146, 162
as ministers of the Holy Spirit, 63–65
and ministry of justice, 177–80
ordination not to priesthood but to ministry, xvi, 33, 43–58, 60, 165, 166
and ordination of women, 14–15, 59, 128, 182
and representation of Christ, 10, 60, 62–63, 77, 79, 81, 92–119, 157, 160
sacramentality of, xvii, 7, 9, 15, 17, 21–30, 42, 50, 58, 60, 61, 63, 89, 86, 106, 108, 170, 186
and the sacrament of the anointing of the sick, xii, 99, 150–62
and supply or substitutional ministry (*suppléance*) as a characteristic of subordinate or auxiliary status, 10, 70, 71, 73, 76, 77–78, 84, 119, 183
and the threefold office of Christ, 10, 55, 63, 77, 85, 87–92, 95, 96, 98, 146, 169–70, 183
and threshold ministry, 10, 13, 147–51, 159, 161–64, 167–68, 170–73, 175
Delp, Alfred, 39
Deniau, Francis, 3–4, 81, 82, 144
Desjonquères, Alain, xvii, xxi, 13
Didier, Jean-Charles, 153–54
Dilschneider, Otto, 1, 11
diocesan pastoral council, 122–23

Ditewig, William, 13, 55–6, 63, 80, 158, 181–83
Dix, Gregory, 44
Döpfner, Julius, 26–27

Ellacuría, Ignacio, 124, 179–80
Episcopal conference
  Australia, 97–98, 170
  Canada, 98–99
  France, 69–71
  Germany, 74–75, 96–97
  Italy, 61–62, 65, 88
  Quebec, 116
  United States of America, 86–87, 92, 99, 177–79, 181

Fares, Armando, 26
Francis, Pope, xii, 4, 8, 129, 133–34, 136–37, 140, 155, 162, 174
Fuchs, Ottmar, 120, 123–24

Geistvergessenheit, *see under* Holy Spirit
Ghirlanda, Gianfranco, 50–51
Glover, Matthew, 79, 119–20, 121
Gonneaud, Didier, 60, 90–92
Grau, Alain, 110, 112–13
Greshake, Gisbert, 157–58

Hauke, Manfred, 107–108
Haunerland, Winfried, 35
Hefele, Carl Joseph von, 167 n. 180
Helmsing, Charles Herman, 28
Hentschel, Anni, 17
Hervás y Benet, Juan, 25
Hilberath, Bernd Jochen, 123
Holy Spirit
  and communion, 38, 40–41, 42, 172
  diakonia of, 63
  and evangelization, 85–86
  Geistvergessenheit, 1–2, 9, 11, 30, 182
  and the poor, 174
  sacrament of, as expression of the church, 134, 135–36, 137, 139
  self-gift of in the sacrament of order, 4, 8, 9, 17, 30, 31, 43, 50, 56, 71, 77, 82, 140, 144, 159, 170, 183, 186
  sevenfold grace or gift of, 4, 36, 39–40, 43, 64
Hoping, Helmut, 36, 53

International Theological Commission
  From the Diakonia of Christ to the Diakonia of the Apostles (2002), 52–53, 76, 113–14, 147
  Synodality in the Life and Mission of the Church (2018), 8–9, 104, 137, 138, 185
  Jesus Christ, Son of God, Saviour (2025), 124 n. 204

John Paul II, Pope, 32, 88, 89, 92, 96, 97, 110, 111, 144–45
  Pastores Dabo Vobis (1992), 110–11, 144–45, 146
Johnson, Elizabeth, 129
Jubany Arnau, Narciso, 25

Kasper, Walter, 2, 58–59, 60, 82–83, 134, 135, 163
Kehl, Medard, 134, 136
Kelly, Gerard, 180
Kohlschein, Franz, 65
Komonchak, Joseph, 38

Lanzetta, Serafino, 50
Legrand, Hervé, 6, 183
Lennan, Richard, 180
Leo XIV, Pope, 14
Longhitano, Adolofo, 106–107
Lubac, Henri de, 134
Luciani, Rafael, xxii, 137–38

Maurer, Josef Clemens, 25
McKnight, W. Shawn, 142–43, 145–46, 147, 165–66
Miranda Vincente, Francisco, 23
Müller, Gerhard, 113

Nkongolo, Joseph, 27–28
Noceti, Serena, xxii, 118–19, 143–44

O'Donnell, Tim, 77, 109, 115, 148–49
O'Meara, Thomas, 127–28, 140

Paul VI, Pope
  Sacrum Diaconatus Ordinem (1967), xi–xii, 25, 97
  Ministeria Quaedam (1972), 131–33
  Ad Pascendum (1972), 62, 86 n. 74, 131–33
  Sacrum Unctionem Infirmorum (1972), 158–59
  Evangelii Nuntiandi (1975), 85–86
Petrocchi, Giuseppe, 14, 15
Petrolino, Enzo, 50
Pius XII, Pope
  Mystici Corporis Christi (1943), 130, 130 n. 15, 168, 169, 170
  Mediator Dei (1947), 115, 117
  Sacramentum Ordinis (1947), 21–23, 37, 117
poor and marginalized
  Christ's love for, 19, 115, 125, 174
  church of and with, 18, 174
  as evangelizers of the church, 174, 175
  ministry or mission to, xii, xvii, 10, 16, 17, 34–35, 42–43, 44, 58, 69, 81–82, 120, 133, 138, 140, 142–43, 145, 150, 173, 175, 177, 178, 184, 186
presbyteral council, 121, 122

Rahner, Karl, xvi, xvii, 11–12, 21, 26, 27, 28, 31, 38, 62 n. 181, 63–64, 65, 73–74, 80–81, 129–30, 134, 135, 160–61, 163–64, 166–67, 170–71
Ratzinger, Joseph *see also* Benedict XVI, Pope, 41, 154–55
Remenyi, Matthias, 8
Roman Pontifical, 18 n. 68, 32–34, 37, 40, 55, 100
Rouillard, Philippe, 157

sacraments
  anointing of the sick, xiii, 99, 150–62, 179 n. 7
  Eucharist, xv, 4, 5, 46, 48, 50, 57, 76, 78, 82, 83, 88, 90, 100, 107, 108, 115, 118, 124, 147, 148, 149, 152, 163–64, 167, 168, 169, 170, 171, 172, 177, 178
  order, xi, xvii, 4, 7, 8, 11, 17, 21–67, 70, 72, 77, 82, 83, 84, 85, 86, 87, 88, 90–91, 92, 102, 105–106, 107, 108, 109, 110, 113, 116, 117–18, 120, 122, 128, 138, 140, 141, 148, 153–54, 159, 163, 165, 166, 168–70, 173, 182, 183, 186
  penance / reconciliation, 50, 100, 157, 158, 158 n. 143, 164–65, 167, 168, 172
Sander, Stefan, xiii–xiv, 49, 73
Schillebeeckx, Edward, 134
Second Vatican Council
  debate on the diaconate, 24–28, 141–42
  Doctrinal Commission, 21–24, 28, 47–48
  Apostolicam Actuositatem, 149
  Christus Dominus, 28, 81, 83
  Dei Verbum, 4, 19
  Gaudium et Spes, 8, 118, 130, 137
  Lumen Gentium, xvi, xviii, xxii, 5–7, 8, 9, 18, 21, 23–24, 25, 28, 33, 47–50, 51, 52–55, 56, 67, 73, 79, 80, 81, 83, 87–88, 96, 101, 102, 107, 115, 120, 125, 130–31, 135, 136, 149, 150, 151, 165, 166, 168, 172, 174, 186, 187
  Presbyterorum Ordinis, 29–30, 82, 83, 116, 118, 121, 144
  Unitatis Redintegratio, 172
Seewald, Michael, 3, 13, 101, 117
Semmelroth, Otto, 134
Sobrino, Jon, 174
Synod on Synodality, xiii, 9–10, 14, 15, 104–105, 122, 167, 182, 185, 186, 187

Troupeau, Martin, 53–54

Valee, Sherri, xi, 79
Vatican II, *see* Second Vatican Council
Verona Sacramentary, 18 n. 68, 34, 44 n. 101
Vitali, Dario, 58, 77
Vorgrimler, Herbert, xvi, xviii

Winninger, Paul, 165
women
  in leadership roles or ministries in the church, 10, 125, 133, 159
  and ordination to the diaconate, 14–15, 59, 128, 182
  relation to men in the church, 15–16, 144
Wood, Susan, 34, 57–58, 158

Zizioulas, John, 38
Zulehner, Paul, 15, 179

www.ingramcontent.com/pod-product-compliance
Ingram Content Group UK Ltd.
Pitfield, Milton Keynes, MK11 3LW, UK
UKHW051022010926
474892UK00002B/89